Fifth Edition

Practice Exercises in News Writing

George A. Hough 3rd

Professor Emeritus
The University of Georgia

HOUGHTON MIFFLIN COMPANY   BOSTON   TORONTO
Geneva, Illinois   Palo Alto   Princeton, New Jersey

400-20

Sponsoring Editor: Margaret H. Seawell
Editorial Assistant: Jeanne Herring
Production Coordinator: LuAnn Belmonte Paladino
Senior Manufacturing Coordinator: Marie Barnes

Acknowledgments

Pages 219–220: "Spending a Life in the Law," by James Vorenberg, from The New York Times, September 16, 1985. Copyright © 1985 by The New York Times Company. Reprinted by permission of The New York Times and the author.

Pages 221–222: "College Is Big Business," by Edward T. Foote, from The New York Times, November 13, 1984. Copyright © 1984 by The New York Times Company. Reprinted by permission of The New York Times and the author.

Pages 223–224: "Why Women Opt to Go It Alone," by John B. Parrish, from The New York Times, February 9, 1986. Copyright © 1986 by The New York Times Company. Reprinted by permission of The New York Times and the author.

Pages 224–226: Excerpt from speech given by Gilbert C. Fite at a Founders' Day Dinner in Athens, Georgia, on January 26, 1982, and reprinted in the Georgia Alumni Record, Spring, 1982. Copyright © 1982. Used by permission.

Page 229: Excerpt from "Our Country Relies on the Quality of Its Ideas," by John Chancellor, from The Chronicle of Higher Education, November 26, 1986. Copyright © 1986. Used by permission.

Page 230: "A Case for Controls," by Derrick Z. Jackson, The Boston Globe, February 22, 1994. Reprinted courtesy of The Boston Globe.

Pages 232–233: "A Note from the President: It Is Time for Editors to Stand Up for Newspapers," by Seymour Topping, from The ASNE Bulletin, May/June 1992. Reprinted with permission of the ASNE Bulletin and the author.

Printed in the U.S.A.

ISBN: 0-395-70878-8

123456789-VG-98 97 96 95 94

Contents

Preface

This fifth edition of "Practice Exercises in News Writing" has been reorganized, revised and updated. New material has been added, and earlier exercises have been updated and improved. It is still, however, a very basic workbook intended for a first course in news writing or reporting.

"Practice Exercises" asks students to assume that they are reporters and news writers for a mid-size daily newspaper, The Morning Record, in a mid-size city called Carolton, in which a mid-size college, Northwest College, is located. In this setting, the student has the opportunity of writing realistic news stories, working with a believable cast of characters — from the Record's city editor to college faculty and students to public officials and residents of Carolton. In their work as reporters, students will write local news stories presented variously as notes, telephone conversations or assignments to cover speeches. They will learn to localize wire stories and to rewrite other stories to update or improve them. A city directory, a college directory and maps of Carolton and vicinity will enable them to check names and addresses and the location of streets, public buildings and places.

Organization

"Practice Exercises" is divided into 12 sections. Each section introduces one or more news writing skills, starting with the preparation of news copy, then news leads, the inverted-pyramid story and so on. At the beginning of each section, students are given specific references to chapters and pages in "News Writing" where they will find background and discussion of the relevant writing skills.

Changes in This Edition

There has been some shifting of material from one section to another in this revised edition of "Practice Exercises," and two sections have been added.

Section 3, "Style," consisting entirely of style exercises, has been restored in this edition.

Section 11, consisting of stories that require students to work with numbers, has been added. Some of the exercises were included under "Hard News" in previous editions, but much of the material is new and is based on new material in "News Writing."

Carolton, like the rest of the country, has changed since 1988, when the fourth edition of "Practice Exercises" was published. The city has grown, and the problems of today's society are reflected in new exercises that recognize the realities of AIDS, drugs, guns and changing attitudes among young and old.

What's Not New

"Practice Exercises" in this revised edition continues to provide realistic exercises in news writing problems. Those who have used "Practice Exercises" in the past will find organization and exercises familiar. Many familiar exercises have been retained. Some have been revised, however, to make them more contemporary.

Every effort has been made to see that this edition of "Practice Exercises" continues to be useful to both instructor and student.

Reporting Skills

While "Practice Exercises" is primarily a primer in news writing skills, it also introduces a number of important reporting skills. First of all, every exercise in "Practice Exercises" is based on a real event and a news story published in a daily or weekly newspaper. Students can learn about news values through classroom discussion of each story and its relevance to real newspaper readers and to real newspapers.

Exercises can also teach the student the need for careful handling of facts, for verification of names, addresses and other details, and for care in spelling difficult words and in making clear the meaning of technical terms. The exercises also suggest the value of direct quotation and demonstrate the kind of facts a reporter needs to gather in order to write a story that will satisfy a reader. A number of writing exercises raise questions about libel, privacy and good taste.

Many of the exercises require the student to seek additional information: the name of a college from The World Almanac or biographical information from Who's Who, for example. A number of exercises will require students to visit the library and verify information in an unabridged dictionary or a reference on quotations. All good reporters know how to use a library.

Practice exercises taken from even a realistic workbook can't teach reporting. But they can pave the way. Instructors can supplement workbook exercises with out-of-class reporting assignments. Students who learn to write stories about coming events in the classroom can, for example, be asked to look around campus and bring in a story on some lecture, speech or program to show that they know how to handle that particular type of story. The "Instructor's Manual" includes suggestions for this sort of supplementary work.

Language and Spelling

Each section in "Practice Exercises" includes a spelling list consisting of words that present various spelling difficulties and a usage list of words whose meanings are commonly misunderstood.

The spelling lists have been accumulated over the years. The original list came from an editor who had compiled a list of 100 words he found younger reporters having trouble with. Additions have come from various sources, including the classroom.

Much of the usage is cited in the AP Stylebook.

Language drills are included at the end of each section, and suggested spelling quizzes are included in the "Instructor's Manual."

Style

Style exercises are based on the "Basic Guide to News Style" in "News Writing." That style guide conforms in all basic matters to the AP Stylebook.

The introductory matter and end matter for each exercise follow news style, but the raw notes and other information on which the student will base a news story deliberately do not follow the stylebook. Students must learn at the outset that what they hear or read probably won't follow style. They must learn that the news writer, not his sources, is responsible for style.

A Complete Package

In this new edition, "Practice Exercises" is closely coordinated with the fifth edition of my text, "News Writing," although it may easily be used alone. Both "Practice Exercises" and "News Writing" have been revised and reorganized around a number of basic news writing skills or competencies. A list of these competencies, accompanied by carefully worded instructional objectives, is included in the "Instructor's Manual" that accompanies "Practice Exercises."

The "Instructor's Manual" also includes a model story or key for every exercise or drill. Suggestions for expanding on or following up a story or for tying it to material in the text are included with many of the models.

Acknowledgments

I developed the first version of this workbook more than 30 years ago. Since then, it has been shaped and improved in a number of ways. I owe a great deal to the thousands of students who wrote and rewrote the exercises in the introductory news writing course at Michigan State University, where I taught for 22 years, and to the many students who later used this workbook at The University of Georgia. Their reactions to the exercises have suggested many changes, refinements and improvements. Much has been contributed, too, by the graduate teaching assistants who have worked with me in my news writing courses.

I also owe a great deal to colleagues who have reviewed this and earlier editions of "Practice Exercises." Their suggestions have been most useful. I am especially grateful for the suggestions of the reviewers of this edition: Lawrence Beery, Grand Valley State University; Frederick Fico, Michigan State University; and Jack Lule, Lehigh University.

George A. Hough 3rd
West Tisbury, Mass.
August 1994

How to Use
This Book

This workbook of news writing exercises supplements the fifth edition of my text, "News Writing."

The text and workbook are closely coordinated. At the beginning of each section in "Practice Exercises," you will find notes on the writing skills to be practiced and references to the chapters and pages in the text where these are explained.

It is essential that you read and understand the relevant chapters and pages in "News Writing" before you undertake any exercise in "Practice Exercises."

The Exercises

The practice exercises are presented in a consistent fashion throughout the workbook. They include, first, instructions that explain the assignment and, second, the information — the facts — you will need in writing a story. In some instances, additional notes or suggestions follow the facts provided for the story.

The facts you are given to work with are raw, unedited material — the type of material news writers have to deal with every day. Whatever the form of the facts — a press release, notes given you by another reporter, a wire service story, a memo from an editor or your own notes — they may contain inconsistencies. You may find, for example, ambiguities in reference that will require you to verify names, addresses or identities in the directories in the appendix to "Practice Exercises" or from some outside source.

In addition, the raw information is presented in most exercises in a deliberately disorganized manner — much as it is in real life—so that you will be forced to think through the story and to make an independent decision about the lead and the structure. Many exercises contain more facts than you need to write the story. Some may include irrelevant material. You will have to learn what to include and what to leave out.

There will be inconsistencies in style in most exercises. You will be expected to learn style and follow the rules in the "Basic Guide to News Style" in "News Writing."

Before attempting to write, read the assignment carefully and ask yourself: "What is the point of the story? What news values are involved here? What am I being asked to do?" In most news writing assignments there is one obvious requirement — for example, to demonstrate the ability to write a summary lead, to make use of direct quotation or to recognize the need to localize the story.

There are no tricks in the exercises, but you are working with raw material. You will have to give the facts shape, form and emphasis. In every assignment you will find the everyday traps that every news writer must avoid: style errors, incomplete names, incorrect or missing addresses, ambiguities, irrelevancies, too much or too little material to work with, even errors in fact. Some exercises will include material that raises questions about libel, privacy or good taste.

In short, the writing exercises are realistic. Each is based on an actual news story published in a daily or weekly newspaper. They are the raw material of today's news. Lessons learned in dealing with the exercises here will be useful later on when you are working on your college newspaper or at a general circulation newspaper as an intern or beginning reporter.

The Setting

"Practice Exercises" asks you to assume that you have a new job. You are a reporter and news writer on a medium-sized daily newspaper in a medium-sized city. You may very well get your first job on such a newspaper. The city and the newspaper are not real, but they have counterparts in real life.

The Morning Record is a fairly representative daily newspaper. It is published seven days a week for distribution in the early morning. The first edition deadline is 5:50 p.m., and the final edition goes to press at 10:45 p.m. The Record is delivered by carrier to homes in Carolton and is delivered on motor routes outside the city. Carolton has grown in the last few years, and the Record's circulation is now 48,238 in the city zone and retail trade zone. This is a market penetration of about 64 percent. This means that the Record is delivered daily to 64 percent of the households in its circulation area — excellent these days, and a reflection of the thorough news coverage provided by the Record's news staff.

The Record is respected in the community and among faculty and students at the college. It gives thorough coverage to college affairs and to the college's athletic programs.

The Record has a superior editorial staff. The executive editor is Marilyn Carter. She has been at the Record for 26 years, first as assistant city editor, then as city editor, managing editor and now executive editor. She is a highly competent reporter, writer and editor, and holds the Record staff to exacting standards.

The Record's city editor — the editor you work for — is Linda Miller. She is a former United Press International reporter who worked for several years for UPI in the state capital bureau. She is a graduate of Northwest College, where she had a double major: journalism and political science. She is 48 years old and a little hard to work for. She is impatient of delay and intolerant of anyone who turns in a story containing errors. She dislikes bad leads, misspelled words and sloppy writing. She is, however, infinitely patient and helpful with beginners who try. She is fiercely loyal to the Record and to the best standards of journalism. You can learn a lot from an editor like this.

The Record has a small staff — 22 reporters and editors, about half of them women. There are four African-American reporters and two Hispanic reporters. You will work general assignment much of the time, but you may be asked to work in the newsroom occasionally. On those days, you will take stories over the phone from other staffers, do some rewriting and editing, and generally help out the assistant editors. Most of the staff work days, but you may be asked to work nights once in a while. On the day shift you will start at 7 a.m. and work until 4 p.m. Most of those on the night shift work from 2 p.m. to 11 p.m. You work five days a week, but days off rotate, so that sometimes you will work Saturday and Sunday and have weekdays off.

The Record is not listed in the Editor & Publisher International Year Book, but if it were, you would learn these additional facts about it:

Carolton
Washington County
The Morning Record
(m-mon-sat; S)

Morning Record Publishing Co.,
    312 E. Main St., Carolton;
Circulation: 48,238; ABC Sept. 30,
    1994;
Population, 112,352; ABC City Zone
    and Trade Area, 235,783
ABC Households City Zone and
    Trade Area: 75,220
Advertising: (flat line rate) 94 cents
National Advertising Representa-
    tives: Shannon & Cullen, Inc.,
    New York, N.Y.
Independent: AP; Est. 1920; offset
No editions published Christmas
    Day, New Year's Day, July 4, Labor
    Day, Thanksgiving Day.
Special editions: Progress
    (January); Welcome Week
    (September)
ROP Color — Full Color. Minimum
    1,000 lines.

Publisher	Fred Courtwright III
Executive Editor	Marilyn Carter
Managing Editor	William H. Irving
City Editor	Linda Miller
Assistant City Editor	Kellie Ellenburg
Assistant City Editor	Esmeralda Santos
Graphics/Design Editor	Anna Tosi
Editorial Page Editor	Greg Kelly
Sunday Editor	Frank Cuomo
Sports Editor	Mark McCallum
Controller	Ralph Boggs
Production Mgr.	Donald E. Peters
Advertising Mgr.	Henry B. Quirk
Circulation Mgr.	Arthur E. Madeiros
Promotion Mgr.	Deborah Williams

Carolton is a hypothetical city in a hypothetical state somewhere east of the West Coast and somewhere north of the Gulf of Mexico. Carolton could be your hometown or the city in which you are attending college. Its residents are much like the people you know at home and much like those in your college or university city.

The things that happen in this city and on the college campus here are, I hope, familiar, for they are the ordinary and everyday events that occur everywhere. Some of the stories you will be asked to write may seem trivial or dull or boring, but keep in mind that everything that is published in a newspaper like The Morning Record is of interest to someone. No one reader reads everything, but every story has readers, some of them passionately interested in that particular story.

So, in suggesting that you act as a reporter for The Morning Record in the hypothetical city of Carolton, I expect that you will find yourself in familiar surroundings.

To add to the sense of reality, maps of the city and its neighborhood and of the campus have been created and will be found in the back of "Practice Exercises." And people, buildings, clubs and organizations named in the practice exercises are listed in the directories. The reverse directory will enable you to use street addresses to identify people, organizations and businesses.

Real-Life Assignments

Every news story assignment in "Practice Exercises" is based on something that actually happened and on a story published in a newspaper. The writing exercises provide a real and lifelike series of assignments that simulate the kind of news writing experience you would get during a summer's work on a newspaper almost anywhere. Approach your work, your job as a reporter on The Morning Record, with this in mind.

The Goal

The text, "News Writing," and "Practice Exercises" were written primarily for the student who intends to make a career of newspaper journalism. Many of you who will use the text and workbook will, however, be looking toward other careers — in public relations, advertising, magazine work, broadcast journalism or other journalistic fields. If you are one of those students, keep this in mind: The real purpose of this workbook is to help you learn to write better. This is not an idle promise. Many hundreds of students who have taken courses in news writing have found that "News Writing" and "Practice Exercises" have indeed helped them learn to write better. No matter what your career plans, the mastery of news writing skills will be instrumental, first, in finding an internship or summer job somewhere in journalism; second, in securing and doing well on your first job; and, finally, in moving up the professional ladder.

News writing is basic throughout journalism and mass communications.

1 News Copy

Spelling

accessible, conquer, fiend, knowledgeable, adviser,* nemesis, repetitious, surveillance, colossal, mischievous, likable, exaggerate, employee,* receive

Usage

affect/effect, allude/refer, allusion/illusion, anecdote/antidote, among/between, rights/rites, fewer/less, principle/principal

Newsroom Vocabulary

copy, copy editor, copy-editing marks, proofreader's marks, slug, more, end mark, thirty, stet, hard copy, typo

1

Spelling

The spelling words on the section pages in this workbook present various difficulties. Many are trick words. Learn to spell them now, and you will save yourself a lot of difficulty later on.

An asterisk after a spelling word, for example, the word *adviser* on page 1, indicates that spelling follows AP style. That is, the spelling given is the spelling preferred by the Associated Press Stylebook, and preferred also by The Morning Record, the newspaper you are writing for.

See "News Writing," "Basic Guide to News Style," Appendix C, pages 451 to 458.

Usage

The usage list on the section pages in this workbook is a list of words and phrases whose meanings and use cause trouble for writers and editors. As a news writer, a person who works with words, you must use words precisely and accurately. Learn the meanings and uses of the words and phrases in the usage lists.

Newsroom Vocabulary

The newsroom vocabulary on the section pages in this workbook includes words necessary and useful to the news writer. Most will be readily learned by reading "News Writing" and by discussion and practice work in the classroom. They are all defined in the glossary in "News Writing."

Preparation of News Copy

1. If you are using a typewriter

   a. Type your copy on 8½-by-11-inch copy paper.

   b. Double-space all copy unless, as is the case with some typewriters, spacing is not adequate, in which case triple-space.

   c. Set margins on the typewriter so as to leave a one-inch or one-and-one-quarter-inch margin at left and a one-inch margin at right.

   d. Set the tab so as to indent six or eight spaces for paragraphs.

2. If you are using a computer terminal, set margins, line spacing and paragraph margins as required by your instructor.

3. Identifying copy

   a. If you are using a typewriter, identify each page of copy. Your name and a slug line for the story you are writing should be on each page of copy. On the second and later pages, include a page number. See models on pages 6 and 7.

   b. If you are using a computer, you need only put your name and a slug line at the top of the first page since most computer systems automatically number the pages. If the system you are using does not automatically number pages, then add a page number to your slug line. See models on pages 6 and 7.

4. Clean copy

   a. Dirty copy is unprofessional. Strive for copy that is typed neatly and clearly. Typewritten copy should be edited using standard editing marks. If you are using a computer terminal, go over your copy carefully and make changes and corrections before printing it out.

5. Typographical effects

   a. Type all your copy with normal margins and normal spacing between lines. Special typographical effects such as indenting, boldfacing and so on are matters of typography and are decided by the copy desk, not by the news writer.

   b. Type all copy upper- and lowercase. Only in rare instances, when you wish to emphasize a single word, should you type it in capital letters.

   c. Never underline in news copy.

   d. Do not divide words at the end of a line. That is, do not hyphenate words at the end of a line, and do not divide a hyphenated word at the end of a line. You should be able to turn off any automatic hyphenation in your software to avoid this. Ask your instructor.

6. Meeting deadlines

    a. Edit and correct your copy carefully before turning it in. The writer is responsible for making all corrections in fact, spelling, typing and so on.

    b. You may turn in copy ahead of a deadline, but never after one. Get your copy in on time.

7. Revising copy

    a. If your copy is not publishable, that is, cannot be brought up to publishable quality with minor changes, you may be asked to rewrite.

    b. Copy that needs rewriting should be revised and returned to your instructor or editor promptly. If you are given another deadline, honor it.

8. Typing tricks

    a. Distinguish between a hyphen and a dash in typing. A hyphen will be found on the keyboard; a dash will not.

        1. The hyphen is a linking punctuation mark commonly used in compound words, thus:

```
ready-made

self-employed
```

        2. The dash is a separating punctuation mark, made by striking the hyphen key twice. Make your dash obvious by leaving one space on either side of the dash. The dash is commonly used in place of a semicolon or in place of paired commas:

```
He was an able person -- a very able
person -- but highly unreliable.

He was an able person -- still, he was
sometimes unreliable.
```

4

Editing Marks

Paragraph this

Capitalize carolton

Make this Lowercase

Abbreviate (street)

Spell out (st.)

Make (twelve) an Arabic figure

Spell out (9,) thus: nine

Transpose words two

Delete extra extra words

Delete an extra letter or figure

Delete the "quote marks"

Delete an unnecessary, punctuation mark

Join words, thus: week end

Separate words, thus: trial run

Insert a mising letter, thus

Insert a single word or phrase

Insert a period

Insert a comma in text thus:

Insert a semicolon in text;

Insert a colon in text, thus:

Insert opening "quote marks

Insert closing quote marks"

Insert a hyphen in H bomb

Insert a dash thus in text

Insert an apostrophe in word boys

Leave altered news copy as it is (STET)

There is more of this (more)

End of copy #

Copy-Editing Models

The models on pages 6 and 7 will guide you in editing hard copy. They show newsroom usage of standard copy-editing marks. A model of the first page of a news story is shown on page 6, and the second page of a different story is shown on page 7.

Copy-editing marks, as you can see, enable you to make corrections and add or delete matter from your copy without redoing the entire page. For example, you can change capitalization, delete a letter or a word or correct spelling or mistakes in style, grammar or usage.

hough
news writing

damage suit

 Local (twenty) of the institutional and Public Works
Employees Union has filed a ~~$2,500,000~~ *$2.5million* damage suit against
the city of Car/olton for violating work rules for union
employees at the /city jail.

 The suit was filed in (United States) district court
here ~~yesterday~~ \Monday./

 The suit ~~xlxxxx~~ alleges that the city has radically
changed working hours for employees at the jail. Other
~~xxxxxxx~~ contract violations, the suit charges, include
failing to hold meetings with the union once a month,
failing to establish a safety committee at the jail and
failing to discuss quarterly employee evaluations with
employees.

 Jose Garcia, business agent for the union, said
\Monday/ ~~yesterday~~ that the suit was ~~xxxxxx~~ filed only after the
/city had refused to discuss problems at the jail with the
union.

(more)

The Federal Deposit Insurance Corp. is the agency ~~that~~ that insures bank deposits up to $100,000 for some 15,000 ~~nationally~~ member commercial and savings ~~banks~~ banks.

In this state, two banks, both owned by Capital City Bankcorp, were declared ~~bankxbxoke~~ insolvent last week. ~~Wxxxxxxxxxx~~ The Westminster Savings Bank, with assets of $29.1 million, and the Polk County ~~xxxxxxxxxxxxxxxxxxxxxxx~~

~~xxxxxxxxxxxxxxxxxxxxxxxxxxxxxxxxxxxxxxxxxxxxxxxxxxxxxxxxxxxxxx~~

National Bank, with assets of $37.2 million, were closed on Monday and reopened on Tuesday as branches of BankOne Corp. of Capital City.

The closing of these two banks by the state increased the year's total of bank failures to 115. Last year 120 banks failed, a post-depression ~~banking~~ record.

The closings, according to Harold Williams are a reflection of ~~kakyxx~~ growing ~~new~~ problems in some sectors of the economy, particularly agriculture, energy and real estate.

"We're not out of the woods yet," Williams said. "We look for more bank problems."

FDIC officials have predicted that as many as 150 banks could fail or need government ~~xxxxxxxx~~ assistance before ~~xxxx~~ the end of the year.

-30-

EXERCISE 1-1

Using the standard copy-editing marks, make the changes asked for in the examples that follow.

1. Indicate a paragraph at the beginning of the second sentence:

   The quick brown fox jumped over the lazy dog. The quick
   brown fox jumped over the lazy dog.

2. Capitalize the word *midwest:*

   The midwest is an industrial and agricultural region.

3. Do not capitalize the word *Democratic:*

   Both speakers extolled the Democratic system.

4. Abbreviate the word *August:*

   They asked for a roll call vote August 1 because . . .

5. Write out the word *August:*

   They want to meet before Aug. in order to . . .

6. Transpose the words *only won:*

   He only won the first relay before leaving the field.

7. Delete the second occurrence of the word *time:*

   No man may tether time time nor tide.

8. Close up the space in *an other* so that it reads *another:*

   He gave an other man his seat in the train.

9. Change the Arabic figures to words:

   He left 2 books, a bicycle, 4 bottles and 3 boxes.

Student _____

EXERCISE 1-2

Using the standard copy-editing marks, make the changes asked for in the examples that follow.

1. Separate the words *another* and *man:*

   He gave anotherman his seat in the train.

2. Insert the word *the* after *all:*

   Where have all flowers gone?

3. Insert a period after the words *waste time:*

   Don't waste time Time is what life is made of.

4. Insert a comma after the word *party:*

   He owed a lot to his party his state and his country.

5. Insert quote marks around the phrase *special interests:*

   He said his opponent was a tool of special interests.

6. Delete the quote marks around the word *maverick:*

   He called his opponent a "maverick."

7. Insert the missing letter in the word *illustrated:*

   The tattooed man was ilustrated all over.

8. Delete the extra letter in *inoculated:*

   He was innoculated for diphtheria.

9. Indicate that the Arabic figure 9 should be written out:

   Spell out numbers one through 9 in news copy.

Student _____

11

EXERCISE 1-3

Using the standard copy-editing marks, make the changes asked for in the examples that follow.

1. Insert a colon after the word *said:*

   The speaker said "My fellow Americans, listen to me."

2. Indicate that the word *ten* should be an Arabic figure:

   Use Arabic figures for numbers ten, 11, 12 and so on.

3. Insert a semicolon in this list after the word *president:*

   Jane Doe, president John Q. Public, vice president;

   and Martha Washington, treasurer.

4. Insert a hyphen in *civic minded:*

   Some words, like civic minded, require a hyphen.

5. Insert a dash after the words *right way:*

   There's a right way and the Navy way.

6. Insert an apostrophe in the word *shes:*

   Shes very ambitious, but the others are not.

7. Indicate that the words *and women* are to remain in the copy:

   Now is the time for all good men ~~and women~~ to come to

   the aid of the party.

8. Put a *more* mark at the end of the copy:

   A strong performance by General Motors also increased

   investor confidence. The market closed at the highest

   level since last August.

Student _____

EXERCISE 1-4

Using the standard copy-editing marks, make the changes asked for in the examples that follow.

1. Delete the unnecessary letter in the word occurred:

   The accident occurrred at Broad and Main streets.

2. Insert the missing word or figure:

   The Declaration of Independence was signed on July, 1776,

   in Philadelphia.

3. Put an *end* mark at the end of the copy:

   It works out to $2.08 a share of common stock, compared

   with 41 cents a share in the first quarter.

4. Delete the unnecessary comma after the word *shortstop:*

   He played first base, shortstop, and center field equally

   well.

5. Insert space between the words incorrectly run together:

   Hesaid the treaty negotiations were as usual a

   completedisaster.

6. Insert a hyphen in *A bombs* and *H bombs:*

   The committee expressed concern about the usefulness of

   A bombs and H bombs.

7. Correct the improper spacing:

   He acted un interested but actually was verymuch concerned.

8. Correct capitalization:

   They lived in Albany, N.y. Later they moved to baltimore,

   Md., where they lived in an Exclusive Suburb.

Student _____

Instructions for Exercise 1-5

Make the following changes in Exercise 1-5. Use standard editing marks. Mark all paragraphs as you go along.

line 01	Make *fire fighters* one word.
line 02	The words *circuit court* should be capitalized.
line 04	Spell out *depts.*
line 05	Capitalize *civil service.*
line 06	Insert the word *of* after *21.*
line 07	Insert the courtesy title *Miss* before *Choate.*
line 08	Insert a hyphen in *parttime.*
	Capitalize *college.*
line 09	*Carolton* is spelled with one r. Delete the extra letter.
line 10	Draw a couple of lines through the deleted word and bridge it.
	Abbreviate *Nevada.*
line 13	Make *Electrical Engineering* lowercase.
line 14	Delete the periods in *F.B.I.*
	Abbreviate *Pennsylvania.*
line 15	Make *Police Chief* lowercase.
	Spell out *West* in *W. Palm Beach.*
line 16	Make *Supervisor* lowercase.
line 17	Abbreviate *Company.*
line 18	Make *Court's* lowercase.
lines 19/20	Make *Legal Adviser* lowercase.
line 21	Make *City* lowercase.
	Spell out *4.*
line 22	Make *thirty* an Arabic figure.

Place an end mark at the end of the copy.

Instructions for Exercise 1-6

Make the following changes in Exercise 1-6. Use standard editing marks. Mark all paragraphs as you go along.

line 01	Insert a comma in *3000.*
	Correct spelling: word is *sodium.*
line 02	Make *Electrical Condensers* lowercase.
line 03	Capitalize *river.*
line 04	Delete *yesterday* and insert the day of the week.
line 05	*Employe* needs another *e.*
	Insert *Co.* after name of utility.
line 06	Capitalize *hospital.*
line 07	Capitalize *general.*
line 09	Word should be *threat.* Correct it.
line 10	*Carolton* is spelled with one *r.*
line 11	Capitalize the word *agency.*
	Delete *last* and insert the day of the week.
line 13	Spell out *DNR.* Don't circle. Write out the full name above the line.
line 14	Is it *disipates* or *dissipates*?
line 16	Spelling: it should be *occurred.*
line 18	Delete *Midstate* and insert *utility's.*

line 19   Make *Plant* lowercase.

line 20   Delete apostrophe in *1960's*.

               Insert a comma in *1100*.

line 21   Insert a hyphen in *oil fired*.

line 22   Make *two hundred* an Arabic figure.

               Delete *yesterday* and insert the day of the week.

Place an end mark at the end of the copy.

EXERCISE 1-5

01   The first of the new fire fighters the city of

02   Carolton must hire as a result of a circuit court

03   decision will begin work next week. The court has

04   ordered all city depts. to hire from a statewide

05   civil service list.

06   William A. Hughes, 21, Lynn, Mass., and Anna May

07   Choate, 24, of New Orleans, have been hired. Choate is

08   a parttime student at Northwest college.

09   Hughes is a newcomer to Carrolton. He has been

10   working in ᴿᴱᴺᴺᴼ Reno, Nevada, and finds that the move

11   to this area has not been an easy transition.

12   Miss Choate is a graduate of Purdue, where she

13   majored in math and Electrical Engineering. Her father

14   is an F.B.I. agent in Bethlehem, Pennsylvania. Her

15   mother is a lawyer. A brother is Police Chief in W. Palm

16   Beach, Fla. A sister is Supervisor with the General

17   Telephone Company in Carolton.

18   The city had expected to appeal the Court's

19   decision, but last week Marion Orr, the city's Legal

20   Adviser, and members of the City Council decided

21   against appeal. Mrs. Orr said the City will hire 4

22   more firefighters within the next thirty days.

Student _____

19

EXERCISE 1-6

01   About 3000 gallons of sodiam hypochlorite, a

02   chemical used to keep Electrical Condensers clean,

03   spilled from a storage tank on the Indian river

04   yesterday.

05   Six employes of Midstate Gas and Electric were

06   taken to Carolton General hospital. Two firefighters

07   were also treated at Carolton general. All were released

08   afer examinations revealed no injuries.

09   The spill poses no treat to public health, James

10   L. Moore, Carrolton area representative of the

11   Environmental Protection agency, said last night.

12   Most of the liquid went into the Indian River.

13   Herbert Cooper of the DNR office in Carolton said

14   sodium hypochlorite disipates quickly in water. Any

15   environmental damage that might result, would have

16   occured by now, he said.

17   The cause of the spill was a break in a pipe

18   connected to the Midstate storage tank.

19   The Midstate Plant was built in two stages in the

20   1960's and the 70s. The plant is a 1100-megawatt

21   oil fired generating facility. The plant employs about

22   two hundred workers, Midstate said yesterday.

Student _____

2 News Leads

Spelling

vernacular, satellite, resistible, supersede, temblor, reconnaissance, privilege, nitpicking, liaison, hemorrhage, occur/occurred/occurring/occurrence

Usage

consul/council/counsel, apposite/opposite, character/reputation, cite/site/sight, title/entitle, a number of/the number of

Newsroom Vocabulary

Five W's, lead, summary, summary lead, body/development, news peg, play up, byline, deadline, no-news lead, newsprint

News Leads

The following topics are discussed in detail in George A. Hough 3rd, "News Writing," fifth edition.

News Leads
Chapter 3, "Writing the Lead," pages 48 through 51, for a discussion of summary leads.

Chapter 3, "Writing the Lead," pages 57 through 59, for a discussion of blind leads.

Chapter 3, "Writing the Lead," page 61, Figure 3.3, for a model of a summary lead and a blind lead.

EXERCISE 2-1

A good lead requires precise use of language. Once you have determined the subject of a lead, you must find a verb that is directly related to the subject, a verb that will create the right picture in the mind of the reader.

In the spaces below, supply the appropriate verb for the nouns on the left. Item 1 shows the appropriate verbs for a story about a fire.

1. fire	destroys	damages	injures
2. robbery			
3. holdup			
4. theft			
5. accident			
6. appointment			
7. promotion			
8. grant			
9. arraignment			
10. taxes			
11. sentence		(as to prison, to jail)	
12. fine		(a legal penalty)	
13. reception			
14. inauguration			
15. conference			
16. temperatures			
17. authors			
18. chairmen			
19. voters			
20. warrant			

Student _____

EXERCISE 2-2

Write a one-sentence summary lead based on these facts:

Fact 1   The Washington county chapter of Habitat for Humanity has acquired a site for a single-family house it plans to build for a low-income family.

Fact 2   The 10,000 square foot lot is on West State road west of Western avenue.

Fact 3   The house will cost approximately $40,000 to build.

Fact 4   The house will be awarded to a family eligible for affordable housing.

Fact 5   Applicants must have a stable income and be able to afford a mortgage payment of $450 a month.

EXERCISE 2-3

Write a one-sentence summary lead based on these facts:

Fact 1   Women's golf team from Northwest college is taking part in an invitational tournament at Guadalajara, Mexico.

Fact 2   The college's team score yesterday was 304. The team finished in 4th place.

Fact 3   Maryanne Sims, a senior at the college, had lowest score for the college team. She shot a 72.

Fact 4   Yesterday Florida finished first, Oklahoma second, Southern Methodist third and Northwest 4th.

EXERCISE 2-4

Write a one-sentence summary lead based on these facts:

Fact 1   The Franklin library is expanding its programs.

Fact 2   One new program is called "Book Buddies."

Fact 3   In this program, adults read children's books to patients in the pediatrics wards at local hospitals.

Fact 4   The library is also trying to find volunteers who speak Spanish to help with other library programs.

Fact 5   The library wants to add Spanish-language stories to the English-language stories now available on tape and needs volunteers to record the stories.

27

Practice Exercises in News Writing

EXERCISE 2-5

Write a one-sentence summary lead based on these facts:

Fact 1   Northwest college is planning to build a new residence hall.

Fact 2   The college has raised $4 million toward the projected cost of eight million dollars and earlier this year asked the federal government for additional funds.

Fact 3   Yesterday, at a meeting of the college's board of trustees, you learned that the federal government has given the college the money it needs.

Fact 4   The federal grant is for $4 million.

Fact 5   Construction will start early next year.

Fact 6   Architect for the college is the Carolton firm of McKim, Oglethorpe and Dodge.

Fact 7   The new residence hall will be built near the Chartwell residence hall.

Fact 8   The building will accommodate 400 students.

EXERCISE 2-6

Write a one-sentence summary lead based on these facts:

Fact 1   Carolton applied for and has been awarded a state youth employment grant.

Fact 2   Grant comes from the state Human Resources Commission.

Fact 3   Purpose of the grant: to provide part-time summer jobs for low income students ages 16 to 21.

Fact 4   The $45,000 grant will permit hiring between 60 and 70 students.

Fact 5   They will work 25 hours a week for ten weeks at the minimum wage.

Fact 6   Work will consist of general cleanup and maintenance around city hall and other public buildings.

Fact 7   Applications for summer work and selection of those who will be employed will be handled by the Carolton public schools.

Question: Will your readers know what the minimum wage is?

EXERCISE 2-7

Write a one-sentence summary lead based on these facts:

Fact 1   The state vocational rehabilitation services office in Carolton has been looking for a new director.

Fact 2   A new director was named yesterday.

Fact 3   Her name is Janice Sanders.

Fact 4   She has been assistant director of the Massachusetts vocational rehab services office in Taunton, Massachusetts, for the past three years.

Fact 5   Her salary will be $50,508 a year.

Fact 6   The director's position has been vacant since the first of the year, when the former director, Herbert Krug, resigned.

Fact 7   The vocational rehab office here serves residents of Washington County and three adjacent counties.

EXERCISE 2-8

Write a one-sentence summary lead based on these facts:

Fact 1   The city clerk has been given the ok to buy a new computer system.

Fact 2   The clerk's office uses the system for budgeting and accounting for all city departments.

Fact 3   The city's present system, purchased in 1991, is no longer able to handle the work.

Fact 4   Purchase of a new system was approved by city council last night at its regular weekly meeting. There were no dissenting votes.

Fact 5   City Council allocated $225,000 for the purchase.

Fact 6   Donna Williams, the city clerk, told you after the meeting that she will ask for bids for the new system as soon as possible.

EXERCISE 2-9

Write a one-sentence summary lead based on these facts:

Fact 1   The Presbyterian Home, a retirement facility on East State road, is building an addition to its infirmary.

Fact 2   The addition will cost $4,000,000 and will add 12 beds. The infirmary now has only 8 beds.

Fact 3   Construction will start Monday. There will be a ground-breaking ceremony Sunday at 4 in the afternoon.

Fact 4   The Presbyterian Home has 112 residents living in 65 two- and three-room apartments.

EXERCISE 2-10

Write a one-sentence summary lead based on these facts:

Fact 1   New programs for elderly residents of Carolton will be available soon.

Fact 2   Programs will include recreational activities, social events and craft sessions.

Fact 3   Residents sixty years of age and older are invited to take part.

Fact 4   Programs will be at the Carolton-Washington Adult center at 412 East Main. This is a new city facility.

Fact 5   The center will open for the first time on Monday.

Fact 6   Plans call for the center to be open weekdays from 9 in the morning until 5 in the afternoon.

Fact 7   The center will be operated by the Washington county department of public health.

Fact 8   Funding for the center is coming from a state grant and from funds provided by the city and county.

EXERCISE 2-11

Write a one-sentence summary lead based on these facts:

Fact 1   Temperatures yesterday at the airport: high 91, low 68.

Fact 2   Rainfall: none.

Fact 3   Yesterday's high temperature set a record. Previous record for this date was set here in 1941, when temperature reached 89.

Fact 4   Yesterday was 17th consecutive day with a temperature over 80.

Fact 5   Yesterday was 22nd consecutive day without precipitation. This part of state is extremely dry. Average rainfall to date is 26 inches. Up to yesterday, total for year is 18 inches.

Fact 6   Weather service gives you this forecast: No change expected in next four or five days. Continued hot and dry.

EXERCISE 2-12

Write a one-sentence summary lead based on these facts:

Fact 1   Children starting kindergarten in Carolton schools will need a birth certificate and a certificate of immunization.

Fact 2   School district staff will be at elementary schools tomorrow and Monday from 8 in the morning until five so parents can register their children.

Fact 3   Kindergarten classes meet half days only.

EXERCISE 2-13

Write a one-sentence summary lead based on these facts:

Fact 1   The Women's Studies Center on the Northwest College campus had a reception this noon.

Fact 2   Guest of honor was Carol Ellis, director of Women's Opportunities for the American Association of Community and Junior Colleges.

Fact 3   She is a 1982 graduate of Northwest college.

Fact 4   She is in Carolton to visit Northwest College and to study its women's program.

Fact 5   About 200 faculty, students and Carolton residents attended the reception.

Fact 6   The reception was held in the student union building on campus.

EXERCISE 2-14

Write a one-sentence summary lead based on these facts:

Fact 1   The Eric Griswold Prizes for this year were announced yesterday.

Fact 2   Two Northwest College faculty members won the awards.

Fact 3   Each will be presented a gold medal and $1000 in cash.

Fact 4   Prizes are for quote original research contributing to the welfare of humanity unquote.

Fact 5   The prizes are given by the Griswold Foundation. Nominations for the prizes are submitted by colleges and universities in this and other countries.

Fact 6   Winners are Professors Julia Trosko and Charles Tsui.

Fact 7   They have been experimenting with new varieties of plants that have potential as sources of food in semi-arid areas of the world.

Fact 8   The prizes will be presented Saturday at a faculty convocation in the LaFollette auditorium.

EXERCISE 2-15

Write a one-sentence summary lead based on these facts:

Fact 1   Washington County Public Relations Club held its annual "Awards Celebration" last night.

Fact 2   Program was held at the Commerce Club.

Fact 3   The PR club made two major awards.

Fact 4   One award was given to Alfred Carew. He is superintendent of the Carolton public schools.

Fact 5   He was given the club's "distinguished public relations award."

Fact 6   A second award went to W. H. Handy III, vice president for community relations of the First National Bank.

Fact 7   Carew's award is for "improving the image of the Carolton school system."

Fact 8   The award was given to Handy for his continuing contributions to the PR club.

EXERCISE 2-16

Write a one-sentence summary lead based on these facts:

Fact 1   The board of education has been working on a teacher's guide on AIDS education.

Fact 2   The board had expected to have the guide in use in classrooms by now.

Fact 3   Community groups have asked for a delay in introducing the guide into the curriculum to permit more public input.

Fact 4   The board has agreed to put off use of the guide until the end of next month.

Fact 5   The individuals and groups asking for delay included parents, teachers, church groups and physicians.

Fact 6   The board believes it is important to promote sexual abstinence as the key to fighting AIDS.

Fact 7   Critics of the proposed guide say it does not give children enough information about AIDS.

EXERCISE 2-17

Verbs have been called the muscle of good writing. These sentences need a little more muscle. Review Exercise 2-1. Then rewrite and use a strong, vigorous verb. For example:

Weak   The stabbing of a 31-year-old man occurred Friday morning in front of the First National Bank.

Better   A 31-year-old Carolton man was stabbed Friday morning in front of the First National Bank.

1. Three teen-agers charged in connection with the random shooting of vehicles that left one man wounded have been arrested and turned over to County Family Court.

2. The state Highway Patrol is investigating two accidents that resulted in injuries Friday.

3. A Carolton man has been arrested in connection with the March 12 burglary of the County Line Liquor Store.

4. Washington County police received calls from people reporting nearly a dozen burglaries.

5. A traffic accident on Highway 30 yesterday left a 27-year-old Carolton man in serious condition.

6. A winter storm that battered the midstate area yesterday left hundreds of motorists stranded on highways and in emergency shelters.

7. A Carolton man and two juveniles have been arrested in connection with two school burglaries here last month.

8. Twenty-six establishments have received renewals of their liquor licenses.

Student _____

EXERCISE 2-18

Verbs have been called the muscle of good writing. These sentences need a little more muscle. Review Exercise 2-1. Then rewrite and use a strong, vigorous verb. For example:

Weak   A collision between a car and a Carolton police unit resulted in the death of a Florida man Tuesday night.

Better   A Florida man was killed Tuesday night when his car collided with a Carolton police car.

1. Carolton police are investigating a two-car wreck Monday on California Avenue in which both drivers were injured.

2. A police shoot-out in the City Hall parking lot Saturday left two local men injured and in police custody.

3. The Washington County Sheriff's Department has asked for an armed robbery warrant against a Carolton teenager.

4. Carolton police reported that a thief entered an automobile belonging to James Wang of 504 E. Utah Ave. Monday while the vehicle was parked at Wang's home and stole a stereo.

5. A 13-year-old Carolton boy ran into the path of a car near the high school Monday and was hospitalized.

6. Judge John Rowland Friday gave suspended sentences and $300 fines to the four men convicted of trespassing.

7. The Athenian Grille on East Main Street was the victim of vandals Tuesday night.

8. It was only a short ride to the emergency room for two Carolton women involved in a two-car accident in the Receiving Hospital parking lot.

Student _____

EXERCISE 2-19

A lead should be brief, concise and make one point. The following lead is long and involved:

> The 4-year-old son of a Carolton police officer was seriously wounded early Monday when he accidentally shot himself in the head with his father's service revolver only moments after the father had stepped out of the room in their West Side home, police said.

This could be tightened up. Details could be omitted. There is no need for attribution. It could be revised to read:

> The 4-year-old son of a Carolton police officer accidentally shot himself in the head Monday with his father's service revolver.

Now, revise the following leads. Remember, you are writing a lead. Summarize for your reader. Details and explanation can be left to the body of the story.

1. Five people were injured Monday when a Carolton Police Bomb Squad unit was involved in an accident with a Morning Record delivery truck while traveling to the scene of a reported pipe bomb on Western Avenue that later turned out to be a harmless device.

2. The State Legislature ended its session Monday in a swirl of broken agreements, and without enacting many of its major initiatives. The state body's unfinished business included bills on gambling casinos, radioactive waste disposal, state employee pensions and, most prominently, crime.

3. Brush fires in nearby states have burned over more than 79,000 acres, and officials are asking the Federal Government to declare a state of emergency. In this state, grass fires burned out of control Monday and caused more than $2 million in damage to buildings on the campus of South Central Community College in Davenport.

4. A Carolton man abducted his girlfriend's 1- and 3-year-old daughters at knifepoint Monday, fled with them, and led police on a high-speed chase on Interstate 210 while dangling one of the children outside his car window. The chase ended after 25 minutes when police blockaded the highway and stopped the car.

Student _____

3 News Style

Spelling

judgment, flaccid, aerial, sheriff, tariff, bailiff, plaintiff, restaurateur, temperament, rendezvous, prejudice, accidentally, dissertation

Usage

continual/continuous, eminent/imminent, empathy/apathy, expatiate/expiate, parameter/perimeter, media/medium, noon/midnight

Newsroom Vocabulary

style, stylebook, uppercase, lowercase, down style, up style, journalism/journalist, broadsheet, tabloid, point, pica

News Style

News style is discussed in George A. Hough 3rd, "News Writing," fifth edition, Chapter 4, "Style and the Stylebook," pages 65 through 77.

The "Basic Guide to News Style" is in "News Writing," Appendix C, pages 426 through 461.

EXERCISE 3-1

Fill in the blanks in this news story, using the key at the bottom of the page. The key tells you what words or numbers go in the blanks, and the numbers in parentheses refer you to the appropriate sections of the "Basic Guide to News Style" in "News Writing."

01   A Canadian poet will lecture on her work _____

02   on the Northwest _____ campus.

03   Carol Greenwood, author of _____ volumes of poetry,

04   will speak on _____.

05   The lecture will be in the LaFollette Auditorium at

06   _____. Tickets are _____.

07   Miss Greenwood's only novel __ "Singing Women __" is an

08   _____ utopian story set in the future in what was once

09   the _____.

10   The lecture is one in a series scheduled during

11   _____ and November by the department of English.

12   The next lecture will be on _____.

line 01   tomorrow (see 6.3)
     02   college (see 2.1)
     03   twenty (see 3.1)
     04   The Poet's Voice (see 4.7)
     06   eight o'clock at night (see 3.6, 6.1 and 6.4)
           four dollars (see 3.7 and 3.12)
     07   paired commas (see "News Writing," pages 420 through 423)
     08   anti (see 4.4)
     09   U.S. or United States? (see 1.13)
     11   October (see 1.12)
     12   November first (see 1.12, 3.13, and 6.7)

Student _____

EXERCISE 3-2

Fill in the blanks in this news story, using the key at the bottom of the page. The key tells you what words or numbers go in the blanks, and the numbers in parentheses refer you to the appropriate sections of the "Basic Guide to News Style" in "News Writing."

```
01          _____ of the Carolton Community Mental

02   Health _____ have a new _____ contract.

03       Wage provisions of the contract will be renegotiated

04   after _____ year.

05       Board members approved the contract _____.

06   ____ Mary McLeod, _____, said

07   the contract will be signed _____.

08       The _____ professional, _____ clerical and six

09   other workers at the clinic are represented by

10   _____.

11       The union's previous contract expired _____.
```

line 01 Employes or employees? (see Section 1 spelling list in this workbook)
    02 clinic (see 2.1)
       two-year (see 3.1 and 4.4)
    04 one (see 3.1)
    05 last night (see 1.14 and 6.3)
    06 Miss McLeod is a medical doctor (see 5.7)
       director of the clinic (see 5.13 and paired commas)
    07 next Monday — day or date? (see 6.5)
    08 one hundred and ten; nine (see 3.1)
    10 AFSCME, the American Federation of State, County and Municipal Employees (see 1.1, 1.2 and 1.3)
    11 the 30th of last month (see 1.12, 6.5 and 6.7)

Student _____

EXERCISE 3-3

Edit this news story. Correct errors in style. Use standard editing marks and practices. Do *not* rewrite or revise. There may be errors in spelling, usage or punctuation.

01   A Carolton service station owner was seriously injured

02   yesterday in a two car accident in front of his service

03   station on Territorial Rd.

04   Don E. Waldron, 115 E. Main St., and Mrs. Helen Vogel,

05   504 West Vermont Avenue, were taken to Carolton General

06   hospital.

07   Police said the accident attracted an unruly crowd.

08   Fifteen persons, including 7 juveniles, were arrested

09   for loitering.

10   Both cars were badly damaged. Waldron said it would

11   cost him $2000 to repair his car.

12   Police said Mrs. Vogel's car was heading north on

13   Territorial Road at 5 P.M. Waldron was driving south.

14   Mrs. Vogel, a retired teacher, is a volunteer at a

15   24 hour crisis center at Carolton General Hospital.

Number Correct _____

Student _____

EXERCISE 3-4

Edit this news story. Correct errors in style. Use standard editing marks and practices. Do *not* rewrite or revise. There may be errors in spelling, usage or punctuation.

01   Two Carolton Central High school seniors won awards

02   yesterday at the Washington County Youth Science Fair.

03   They are Harold Baker, 17, son of William and Mary

04   Baker, 84 Oak Street, and Nancy Williams, 16, daughter of

05   Henry and Samantha Williams, 710 East Main St.

06   Baker and Williams will share a $2,000 cash award and

07   are eligible for a freshman scholarship at Northwest

08   college.

09   Central High administrators were pleased with the

10   award won by the two student team.

11   James Hardy, head of of the high school physics

12   department called the two seniors knowledgeable, bright,

13   and ambitious at an "honors day" program yesterday.

14   The two worked together on a study of the affect of

15   marigolds on nematode infestations in commercial tomato

16   crops.

17   More than two hundred high school students from Carolton

18   and Washington county entered projects.

19   The Science Fair opened Monday at 9 a.m. and will

20   close Saturday at 12 p.m.

Number Correct _____

Student _____

EXERCISE 3-5

Edit this news story. Correct errors in style. Use standard editing marks and practices. Do *not* rewrite or revise. There may be errors in spelling, usage or punctuation.

01   The Reverend Angus Glencannon, assoc. rector of St.

02 John's Church, Baltimore, Maryland, will be the new rector of

03 All Saint's Episcopal Church here.

04   Mr. Glencannon is expected to arrive here November 20.

05   He has worked as a high school teacher and principal and

06 has a Bachelor of Arts degree from Wheaton College, Wheaton,

07 Illinois. He has a Doctor of Divinity degree from General

08 Theological Seminary, New York.

09   His doctoral dissertation is titled New Insights Into

10 the Origins of the Nicene Creed.

11   He and his wife, Amy, have 2 daughters, Carrie, 15, and

12 Katherine, 9.

        Mr. Glencannon told the Morning Record yesterday that he

13 is very pleased to be named rector of All Saints.

14   "I hope to become an active participant in community

15 affairs in Carrolton," he said.

16   All Saints is the oldest church building in Carolton. It

17 was built in the late 18th Century and extensively renovated

18 in the 1920's. It was built on what was once the cite of an

19 aboriginal village.

Number Correct _____

Student _____

EXERCISE 3-6

Edit this news story. Correct errors in style. Use standard editing marks and practices. Do *not* rewrite or revise. There may be errors in spelling, usage or punctuation.

01   Michael Hempstead, son of Judge and Mrs. Arthur B.

02   Hempstead, Jr., 657 North Sheridan St., is among two hundred

03   students studying at the Armand Hammer United World College

04   of the American West at Montezuma, New Mexico.

05   Mr. Hempstead, a graduate of Carolton Central High

06   school, is one of thirty entering students from the United

07   States at the international college.

08   Undergraduates at the college come from more than 70

09   countries, including Canada, Venezuela, and Swaziland.

10   The college expects all students to devote at least ten

11   hours a week to community service.

12   A bachelor of arts degree is awarded at the end of the

13   four year program of study.

14   Hempstead spent the past summer in Carolton, where he

15   worked for The Morning Record as a copy clerk. He worked

16   most of the summer on the 4 p.m. to 12 midnight shift.

17   He left for college yesterday. The fall semester begins

18   October 15.

Number Correct _____

Student _____

EXERCISE 3-7

Edit this news story. Correct errors in style. Use standard editing marks and practices. Do *not* rewrite or revise. There may be errors in spelling, usage or punctuation.

01   A convention of Licensed Practical Nurses will be held

02   next week at the conference center on the Northwest

03   college campus.

04   The Mid-State Licensed Practical Nurses Assn. has

05   planned the program. Opening ceremonies will be held Friday

06   morning at 10 A.M.

07   A banquet is scheduled for 8:00 P.M. Saturday night.

08   Miss Ellen Marks, a registered nurse will conduct a

09   workshop on health problems of the elderly.

10   About 1000 licensed practical nurses belong to the

11   association. Membership is based on a three-tier concept of

12   local, state, and national enrollment.

13   Dr. Hubert Shanks, Director of Health Services at

14   Northwest College, will be the keynote speaker. He will

15   address a plenary session of the assn. Friday. Shanks is host

16   of the popular PBS program Ask the Doctor.

17   He is optimistic about health care.

18   "I think we can look forward to the day when the U.S.

19   population is 100% healthy," he said yesterday in a talk at

20   a meeting of the Washington County Council on Aging.

Number Correct _____

Student _____

EXERCISE 3-8

Edit this news story. Correct errors in style. Use standard editing marks and practices. Do *not* rewrite or revise. There may be errors in spelling, usage or punctuation.

01   Tornados touched down in Washington, Lake, and Beaufort

02   Counties yesterday.

03   At least 20 people were injured when high winds ripped

04   through Western sections of Washington county and Carolton

05   suburbs north and west of Airport and Perimeter Roads.

06   The storm struck at 5:00 P.M. at the height of the rush

07   hour when traffic on Western Ave. was especially heavy.

08   At the Washington County Airport, the weather service

09   said, two inches of rain fell in thirty minutes. Robert

10   Brown, Professor of Physics at Northwest College

11   reported that only 3/4 of an inch fell on the campus.

12   Winds gusted to nearly a hundred miles an hour at the

13   airport, the weather service said.

14   At the Delta Mall on Airport Rd., rain flooded parking

15   lots and many stores were inaccessible. Sheriff's

16   officers reported the underpass at Airport Rd. and U.S. 210

17   was flooded. Ten people were rescued from stalled cars.

18   Mrs. Horace A. Gilmore, 335 West Oregon Avenue, was taken

19   to Carolton General Hospital. She was treated for

20   lacerations and contusions and released.

Number Correct _____

Student _____

EXERCISE 3-9

Edit this news story. Correct errors in style. Use standard editing marks and practices. Do *not* rewrite or revise. There may be errors in spelling, usage or punctuation.

01   The League of Women Voters (LWV) has began an intensive

02   drive to turn out the vote for the coming election.

03   The effort will include a voter registration drive, a

04   voter education campaign, and an election day program to get

05   voters to the polls.

06   Mrs. Virginia Main, league President, said yesterday that

07   voter registration is too low.

08   "No more than 45 per cent of eligible voters are

09   registered," she said.

10   City Clerk Donna Williams said yesterday that eligible

11   Carolton residents may register daily from 9 A.M. to 5 P.M.

12   at the Municipal building, 210 East Main Street.

13   "You can also register at the Administration Building on

14   N. Campus Drive on the campus," she said.

15   Albert H. Sawyer, Jr., Professor of History is heading

16   the Northwest College voter registration drive.

17   Senator Ernest F. Higginbotom is helping with the

18   registration drive. He will speak on campus tomorrow. His

19   talk is titled The Bandwagon Affect in Local Elections.

20   He will speak at 8:00 p.m.

Number Correct _____

Student _____

EXERCISE 3-10

Edit this news story. Correct errors in style. Use standard editing marks and practices. Do *not* rewrite or revise. There may be errors in spelling, usage or punctuation.

01   The Washington county Council on Aging is sponsoring a

02   two day program on health quackery.

03   The program will be at the Carolton-Washington County

04   Adult Center, 412 East Main St., from 1:30 P.M. to 5 P.M.

05   Lucille Good, a representative of the state Health

06   Department, will speak on Health Quackery: Fact or Fraud?

07   Miss Good, a registered nurse is a graduate of Northwest

08   College and Boston College. She has experience in

09   community health, long-term care, and psychiatric health

10   care work.

11   Dr. Alpha E. Bates, director of the Community Mental

12   Health clinic, will discuss over-the-counter drugs.

13   Dr. Bates said Monday that the public does not fully

14   understand the safe use of over-the-counter and prescription

15   drugs.

16   "Older people especially need education about drugs," he

17   said.

18   Bates is president of the Carolton chapter of the

19   American Association of Retired Persons and a captain in

20   the United States Naval Reserve.

Number Correct _____

Student _____

EXERCISE 3-11

Edit these sentences so that hyphenation conforms to rules given in "News Writing," pages 414 through 415 and 440 through 442. You may also want to consult Webster's New World Dictionary. Use standard editing marks to insert or delete punctuation. Some of the sentences may be correct as written.

1. The city-county reporter blamed the rainy weather on the H-bomb his father-in-law built in his newly renovated garage.

2. No one can jump higher than the 7 foot, 6-inch center on the Northwest College award winning basketball team.

3. The pilots climbed into the two man craft and plied their six foot long oars.

4. The coach said the players were second rate performers.

5. Most French Canadian nationals speak English, but not all Mexican American citizens speak Spanish.

6. He had a know it all attitude and had always been filled with self pity.

7. The transAtlantic voyage was an anti-climax to the tour.

8. "Turn to the next chapter," the instructor said, "and study the three- to four-year contracts."

9. The team scored a first quarter touchdown but trailed at the end of the third quarter.

10. Tom Thumb was a little man, but he was not little-known.

Number Correct _____

Student _____

EXERCISE 3-12

Informal written American English, the language of newspapers, requires that pronouns and their antecedants agree in number and case. Subjects and verbs must also agree, that is, singular subjects require singular verbs. Revise any of the following sentences that are not acceptable grammar.

1. When the class ended, everybody picked up their books.

2. Neither of his written excuses were accepted.

3. The City Council will meet Monday to review their bylaws.

4. Each student picked up his books and quietly left the room.

5. A number of voters were waiting in line to cast their ballots.

6. Everybody in the class was expected to do their own work.

7. The trustees will meet tomorrow to elect their new chairman.

8. Not one of the students considered that they might fail.

9. Neither of them was willing to give up their seat.

10. The Bill of Rights deal with fundamental American liberties.

11. Ten tons are too much for a wheelbarrow to carry.

12. Neither the reporters nor the editor were on time.

13. The student judiciary handed down their verdict.

14. The number of possible errors is immense.

15. Neither the mayor nor his opponent were pleased at the vote.

16. Two weeks are not long enough for a real vacation.

17. The housing authority has a plan for the vacant land and will
    discuss their proposal at next week's meeting.

18. Everyone has to pull their own weight around here.

19. Judges may order a person to surrender their firearms license.

20. The court is making their decisions available by fax.

Number Correct _____

Student _____

4 Writing the Story I

Spelling

hypocrisy, inseparable, misspelled, parishioner, dietitian, relevant/irrelevant, subtle/subtleties, siege, chauffeur, limousine, innuendo, consistent

Usage

flout/flaunt, healthful/healthy, historical/historic, illusive/elusive, persuade/convince, half-mast/half-staff

Newsroom Vocabulary

story, attribution, brief, hole, news hole, paragraph, identification, inverted pyramid, stick/stickful, dateline, First Amendment

Writing the Story I

These topics are covered in George A. Hough 3rd, "News Writing," fifth edition.

Inverted Pyramid/Single-Incident Stories
Chapter 5, "Writing the Story," pages 79 through 82.

Identification
Chapter 5, "Writing the Story," pages 85 through 91.

Attribution
Chapter 5, "Writing the Story," pages 82 through 85.

Time Elements
Chapter 5, "Writing the Story," pages 91 through 96.

Paired Commas
Appendix B, "Newspaper Grammar and Punctuation," pages 420 through 423.

Style
Appendix C, "Basic Guide to News Style," pages 426 through 461.

Errors in News Copy

Errors in news stories are serious matters. At the very least, they annoy readers who know better, undermine confidence in the reliability of the newspaper and may even provide grounds for a libel suit against the newspaper.

You must make every effort in writing news stories to avoid errors in fact or interpretation. The byword of the professional journalist is "accuracy always."

The news writing exercises in every section of "Practice Exercises" may include errors deliberately placed there to test your journalistic reliability — the care with which you check and verify facts that you use as the basis for a story.

First, the exercises probably will not follow news style as it is set forth in the "Basic Guide to News Style" in the appendix of "News Writing." You will have to know the style rules and follow them.

Second, you will find discrepancies in names and addresses in the exercises. You will be expected to check every name and every address against the model directories in the appendix. The directory is correct. The exercise may omit a middle initial, misspell a name or give an incorrect address.

When you have completed a news story assignment, read your copy over carefully. Check your story against the assignment and verify the accuracy of names and addresses. Check your copy against the style guide.

When — and only when — you are sure that all names, addresses and facts in your story are correct, write "all names verified" at the top of your copy.

You will be penalized for errors in news story assignments. First, you will have to revise and correct your story. Your instructor will lower your grade. And, finally, you may be asked to write a correction.

Most newspapers publish correction notices as soon as errors are discovered. These are sometimes published under standing heads like "For the Record" or "Getting It Straight." Sometimes they are simply labeled "Correction." Slug your correction stories *correction*.

Your correction story, following in general form the model in Figure 6.3 in Chapter 6, will begin:

```
A story in (day)'s Morning Record incorrectly
reported that . . .
```

Then set the record straight by explaining what the facts were.

If something was left out of the story that should have been included, your correction story might begin:

```
A story in (day)'s Morning Record omitted the
(name of) (fact that) (date of) . . .
```

Develop the habit of careful workmanship. Check, check and check again. Don't let errors creep into your copy.

EXERCISE 4-1

This morning your city editor handed you a press release from Northwest College. "Here," she said, "write something on this."

The press release said that the National Institute of Education has decided to provide funds for a research project to study how ninth graders solve algebra problems.

The Institute has allocated $37,300 for this study.

The study will be conducted by Dr. Shirley Wagner. Dr. Wagner is on the faculty of the School of Education at Northwest College. She is an assistant professor.

Her grant is one of three being made by the Institute. The grants continue the Institute's funding for studies of learning disabilities.

Dr. Wagner's grant is the only NIE grant awarded in this state.

Dr. Wagner is nationally known for her research in early childhood educaton.

EXERCISE 4-2

While you were on campus this morning, you stopped in at the college bookstore. During a conversation with the manager, he asked you if you had the story on Charlie Applegate. He told you that Applegate had been elected president of the booksellers association. He gave you these facts:

The Mid-State Booksellers Association held its annual meeting in New Orleans Thursday and Friday of last week. Mr. Applegate has been active in the association for the past 10 years. This past year he was vice president.

The association has about 2000 members in 50 states. At this year's meeting, Applegate was elected president. He will serve until the next annual meeting.

Applegate, the manager reminds you, is owner of the bookstore on New York avenue.

The association holds an annual trade show and meeting. It also watches legislation that may affect book publishers and booksellers.

About a thousand bookstore owners and managers were at the convention.

Applegate is on the city council and is chairman of the county Democratic committee.

EXERCISE 4-3

You are working the early shift today. When you came in at 6:45 a.m., the assistant city editor asked you to do a story on last night's storm. You made a few phone calls and picked up enough information for a story.

From the weather service office at the airport:

```
When the storm struck, temperature dropped from 70 to 55
degrees in less than an hour. Rainfall in 24 hours ending at
midnight was 1.1 inches. Weather service at airport clocked
wind gusts at 45 miles an hour.
```

From the power company:

```
There were several outages during the evening. Lightning
struck a transformer on Old Meetinghouse Road about 8
o'clock, and about 1500 homes and businesses on the east side
of Territorial road were without power for from one to three
hours. Power company crews worked until four this morning
repairing the transformer and wires knocked down by falling
limbs. Worst hit was West Wisconsin Avenue, where several big
trees fell across power lines.
```

From police:

```
Traffic was a problem for a while on West Wisconsin Avenue.
Cars had to be diverted for a couple of hours until trees
were removed and power lines repaired. The problem was in the
300 block. There were no serious auto accidents. Just a few
fenderbenders.
```

From the fire department:

```
One call, to 503 East Vermont, about 11:30, house fire.
Damage about $7,500. Lightning struck the house.
```

From department of public works:

```
City crews worked from 9 last night till after 4 this morning
clearing fallen limbs and assisting power company crews.
```

From a reader who calls as you are getting ready to write:

```
East of Old Meetinghouse road where he lives there was a lot
of wind. Some trees down, fallen tree limbs. He lost some
shingles off his roof. Several other houses in his
neighborhood were also damaged by the high winds.
```

FYI: The storm blew up too late last night for the night staff to get a story into the final edition of today's paper.

EXERCISE 4-4

While you were in the office this morning, your city editor asked you to take a call. You spoke with Maureen Kelly, HIV coordinator for the county Visiting Nurses Association, who gave you the following:

The Carolton HIV/AIDS Community Partnership met last night.

The partnership is making an appeal to the community for volunteers to help with HIV and AIDS patients.

Volunteers will:

> take patients to and from medical appointments —
>
> help with errands and shopping —
>
> help with homemaking tasks —
>
> provide respite periods for primary caregivers —

Volunteers will not be involved in nursing or personal care of HIV or AIDS patients.

The partnership will provide 14 hours of training on four evenings this month and next.

Training will cover:

> basic information about HIV/AIDS —
>
> the psychosocial impact of AIDS on patients and their families —
>
> importance of sensitivity to those with HIV and AIDS —
>
> the need for confidentiality —
>
> practical skills useful in working AIDS patients —

Anyone who wants to volunteer can get an application from the nursing assn. or from the county human services office.

EXERCISE 4-5

The public relations office at the college called this story in this morning. Write it for tomorrow's paper.

An award to Joan Lawrence — presented Saturday at Iowa City, Iowa. She is a senior at Northwest College majoring in speech. Her home is in Austin, Tex. She is a member of the Northwest College forensics team.

The award was made by the Central States Forensics Assoc.

Joan was in Iowa City with the forensics team for a meet at the University of Iowa. The meet was sponsored by the Central States Forensics Assoc.

Joan won first place in expository speaking.

Teams from 76 colleges and universities took part in the meet on Friday and Saturday. Northwest sent a team of six. The Northwest team placed 34th in the meet.

EXERCISE 4-6

Joyce McLaren, director of public relations for the Tri-State Educational Association, called just now with a story. Write it for tomorrow's paper:

The Tri-State Educational assn. has had an acting director for the past six months. He is Bernard Palmer. Palmer was principal of Carolton high school until he retired last year. Yesterday the association named a new director.

The new director has been executive director of United Charities in Paoli, Pennsylvania. He will start his new job here July 1st.

His name is Anthony L. Rhodes. He is 42, a native of Lancaster, Pennsylvania, and a graduate of Teacher's College at Columbia university.

Rhodes has a wife and two children. Mrs. Rhodes name is Amy. The children are Frank, eight, and Sara, five.

Tri-State has about 2500 members in four states. Its headquarters is in Carolton at 255 Washington Road.

You ask, but Miss McLaren will not tell you what Rhodes' salary will be.

EXERCISE 4-7

While you were in the office this morning, a subscriber called with a story she would like to have in the Record. She told you:

Her daughter, Cheryl Ann, is a 1992 graduate of the high school here. She enlisted in the Air Force a couple of months ago. Now she has finished her basic training at Lackland Air Force Base. She is an airman.

After her leave, she is going to Rickenbacker Air Force Base, where she will be attached to the 310th Combat Support Group. She's home now on a 10-day leave.

Lackland is in Texas. Rickenbacker is in Ohio. Mother is Mrs. Virginia Main.

EXERCISE 4-8

Your city editor has handed you a press release that came in the mail this morning and asked you to write a story based on it. You read it and learn:

The University of Texas has awarded a number of fellowships for the study of foreign languages. Among the recipients is a graduate of the local high school.

Linda Anne Vogel is a graduate student at Ohio Wesleyan University. She is studying Romance languages.

The fellowship will enable her to spend next summer traveling and studying in Portugal.

Her parents' names are in the press release, so you call her mother, Mrs. Helen Vogel, and verify the facts in the release. She tells you that Linda graduated from high school here in 1988. She got her BA at Wesleyan in June 1992.

Write a story for tomorrow's paper. Some of your readers may not know where Ohio Wesleyan is, so include that in your story. If you don't know where Ohio Wesleyan is located, look it up. There are reference books in your newspaper library.

EXERCISE 4-9

The Record's city hall reporter called just now with a story. You took the call and learned:

The city and Northwest college have signed a memorandum of understanding establishing a payment of a million dollars by the college to the city.

Mayor and President McKay signed this morning in mayor's office.

College considers this a gift. Money is to cover costs to city of providing city services to the college — basically police and fire services.

Northwest as a state institution pays no taxes to the town.

Money will be applied to city budget over next 10 years.

McKay said the payment represents college's fair share of cost of local government.

Mayor said that the payment will help meet escalating tax burden on property owners. Says payment is more than a token gesture.

EXERCISE 4-10

Write a news story based on the information given to you today by the publicity chairman of the Women's Club. Verify all names.

The Carolton Professional Women's Club offers scholarships each year to teachers in the Carolton and Washington county school system.

The names of the teachers who are being given scholarships this year were announced yesterday at a meeting of the club.

Scholarships are $500.

Susan Christo teaches at O'Higgins junior high. Alice Short teaches at Central high.

The scholarships may be used toward a graduate degree, enrichment courses or continuing education courses.

EXERCISE 4-11

While you were having coffee this morning in the Hotel Lenox coffee shop, you chatted with Ralph Turner, secretary of the Franklin library board. Turner tells you that the board has finally found a head librarian. He says:

The board has picked Richard Tassinari for the job. He is a 1985 graduate of the school of library science at the University of Michigan. Since then he has been a branch librarian in Ann Arbor.

He will start work here at the end of next month.

You check the newspaper library files on the library and learn that the head librarian position has been vacant since August, when Mrs. Helen Kirby, who had been head librarian for 10 years, retired. Library has had a search committee looking for a new library head.

You can write this for tomorrow's paper. Where necessary, attribute to Turner.

EXERCISE 4-12

Heather Duglay, secretary of the Carolton chapter of NOW, called you this morning with a story. She tells you:

The chapter has had an affiliate on campus, a student group, which has worked with the Carolton chapter.

Now the campus group has been organized as an independent chapter of the national organization.

The campus NOW chapter is a registered student organization.

She says that campus chapter will offer students more access to activities of the national organization.

The campus group, she tells you, is not just a women's organization. It welcomes the participation of men students.

EXERCISE 4-13

The Record reporter who covers the campus called in with this story. Write it for tomorrow's paper.

Ardath Rodale was on campus yesterday. She was here to give the Luther Burbank lecture, an annual lecture sponsored by the college. Her title was The World Food Crisis.

She also accepted the college's Founder's Medal on behalf of Organic Gardening magazine for quote distinguished contributions to horticulture unquote.

She is chairman of the board of Rodale Press, Emmaus, Pennsylvania, which publishes "Organic Gardening."

The lecture was in LaFollette auditorium. About 300 faculty and students attended. She was introduced by William Donnelly, head of the school of agriculture.

EXERCISE 4-14

A local woman, Mrs. James McGregor, called you this morning to tell you that both her sons have made the dean's list at college. She thinks it's worth a story. She told you:

Michael on fall semester list at Babson College. He is June graduate of Central high. Majoring in computer science. He's a freshman.

James Jr. on fall semester list at University of Wisconsin at Madison. He is a journalism major. He was graduated from Central high three years ago. He is a junior.

Where is Babson College? It should be properly identified.

EXERCISE 4-15

You got a call this morning from a real estate dealer who gave you these facts. Write a story for tomorrow's paper.

Local real estate agent — elected to board of national real estate association — nation's largest trade association — she is Lorraine M. Worthington — she's with Higginbotham Sons — will be one of nine directors of the National Association of Realtors.

EXERCISE 4-16

Earl May called you this morning with a story. May is director of the Washington County Extended Care Facility. He told you:

The federal government has agreed to loan the facility nine million dollars to build an apartment complex for elderly people with low or moderate incomes.

The loan is coming from the Department of Housing and Urban Development.

The facility has 16 acres of land on Washington road, adjacent to the existing facility building just east of Old Meetinghouse road. May says the facility has plans for a three-story complex consisting of studio and one-bedroom apartments. There will be 160 units in the complex.

Construction will start early next year.

HUD has also agreed to provide two million dollars annually to subsidize rents for occupants of the complex.

You ask May about zoning. He tells you that the land is outside the city and suggests you check with the county. You call Henry Dickens, the county manager, and he tells you:

The land the center plans to build on is in a single-family residential area. Zoning will have to be changed to multifamily residential. That will require approval by the county plan commission and the board of county commissioners. Dickens expects no problem getting approval.

A check of the files in the Record's reference library refreshes your memory about the facility. It is operated by the county and is managed by a board appointed by the county commissioners.

EXERCISE 4-17

While you were on campus this morning, you picked up this story:

```
Beverly Gibbs — professor — business administration — also
assistant chairman of the school of business.

Governor named her to state banking commission yesterday.
Commission has four members. She will fill a vacancy on the
commission. The appointment is for three years.

She is a Democrat. She lives on West Florida.
```

You ask the college public relations office for a biographical sketch, but there isn't much to add. She is 42, has been on the faculty for 10 years and has written a book on bank regulation. She teaches, among other things, a course on money and banking.

EXERCISE 4-18

Write a news story for tomorrow's paper based on these facts, gleaned from a press release from the Marine Corps Development and Education Command at Quantico, Va.

```
The Corps maintains a basic school for newly commissioned
officers. They spend 26 weeks at the school, after which they
are assigned to a duty station.

Among recent graduates of the basic school is George D. Main
of Carolton.

He has been assigned to Fleet Marine Force as a rifle platoon
commander — he will be stationed at Norfolk, Virginia.

Main is a graduate of high school here — and a graduate of
the U.S. Naval Academy — earned a Bachelor of Science degree
at the academy.
```

You want a little more information, so you call his mother. You find out from her that he completed the course at Quantico last month and has been home on leave since then. His leave is up next week. Mrs. Main tells you it was just a coincidence, but his sister, who is in the Air Force, has also been at home on leave. All this makes a nice little human interest story.

EXERCISE 4-19

You were in the office this morning when the public information officer of the local National Guard unit called with a story. Write it for tomorrow's paper.

Local woman, Rebecca Sylvester, honored by National Guard during the unit's annual two weeks of active duty at Camp Edwards at Bourne, Massachusetts.

She was named the national guard's "soldier of the year."

She was interviewed by a board of senior non-commissioned officers who questioned her on nuclear, biological and chemical warfare, weapons, drill and ceremonies and land navigation.

She is a specialist first class and a clerk-typist with her unit, Battery D.

She took basic training and advanced individual training at Fort Jackson, South Carolina. She has been drilling with Battery D since 1989.

She is a gradute of Carolton high. She is a heavy equipment operator with Kelly Construction.

EXERCISE 4-20

You covered city council last night and among other things accomplished, the council enacted an ordinance banning cigarette machines throughout the city. Your notes:

Carolton is the fourth city in the state to ban the machines.

Ban includes all city buildings and all public places — including stores, restaurants and so on.

Vote was unanimous.

The ban is the result of a petition submitted to the council last month by a group of junior high school girls — leader of the group is Betsy Tsui, age 16. Girls pointed out health hazards in smoking and said it was too easy for young people — including children — to obtain cigarettes.

Ban becomes effective the first of the month.

———————————

Strengthen identification by including Miss Tsui's parents' names in the story. And parents like to get credit for their children's accomplishments.

EXERCISE 4-21

While you were in the office this morning, you took a call from the Record's police reporter. She told you:

Police have raided an illegal drug lab and arrested two men. They will be charged with violation of state controlled substance laws.

Lab hadn't actually produced any drugs, but was set up and ready to go. Lab was to produce methamphetamine.

Could have produced up to 25 pounds a week.

Bill Malcolm, head of the police drug enforcement unit, says the drug has been a relatively serious problem in the Carolton area. It has a street value of $25,000 a pound.

In police cells are:

      John Ricketts, age thirty five, 622 West Lexington.

      Bert Shanker, age thirty one, same address.

Lab was in a barn behind the Ricketts home.

_____

You can attribute to Malcolm.

EXERCISE 4-22

While you were at the Delta Mall today, you noticed an interesting exhibit at the Children's Museum. Your notes:

Title: Visit With the Indians Who Met the Pilgrims — on display through first of month —

Exhibit on loan from Boston Children's Museum — shows village life of Wampanoag Indian child in the 1600s —

Museum staff says exhibit developed to give children a sense of native American culture and family experiences —

_____

Write something for tomorrow's paper.

EXERCISE 4-23

In news writing, it is necessary to be as clear and as definite as possible. Vague words and general descriptions don't inform the reader adequately. Be specific. For example:

vague   several students   *specific*   six students

1. local school   Harvey O'Higgins Junior High

2. middle-aged man   _____

3. tall high school senior   _____

4. member of the faculty   _____

5. a local resident   _____

6. a college senior   _____

7. for many years   _____

8. store owner   _____

9. state official   _____

10. prominent businessman   _____

11. small foreign car   _____

12. unmarked currency   _____

13. public transit system   _____

14. car crash   _____

15. senior citizen   _____

16. taught school here   _____

17. earned a master's degree   _____

18. a young girl   _____

19. several months ago   _____

20. missing for several days   _____

Number Correct _____

Student _____

EXERCISE 4-24

These leads are cluttered with details and could be improved by judicious trimming and rearrangement. See what you can do. For example:

Weak   Carolton police are trying to identify a man killed last night after he was hit by a train on the Territory and Western tracks about five miles north of the city.

Better   An unidentified man was struck and killed by a train Monday night about five miles north of Carolton.

1. A federal judge sentenced a Carolton woman charged with embezzling $340,000 from the Washington County Chemical Co. where she was a bookkeeper to three years in prison yesterday.

2. Police arrested two men and a woman in connection with burglaries last month in the Cedar Village and Colonial Village Apartments, Detective Thomas Worth said.

3. A Washington County couple convicted of using counterfeit credit cards to bilk banks out of more than $91,000 were sentenced yesterday by a judge who said they should both spend some time in prison.

4. Arthur Becker made a lot of green over the years watching grass grow. His small grass business has sprouted into one of the largest suppliers of grass seed in the state.

5. A jump in layoffs of adult men sent unemployment climbing in January from 6.5 percent to 7.3 percent, the highest rate in 18 months and a possible sign of an approaching recession.

6. A 91-year-old woman yesterday became the victim of a street robbery. Two young men knocked her down and fled with her purse. It held all of $5.

EXERCISE 4-25

Edit this news story. Correct errors in style. Use standard editing marks and practices. Do *not* rewrite or revise. There may be errors in spelling, usage or punctuation.

```
01    An earthquake rocked Carrolton and Washington county
02    at 4:33 p.m. yesterday afternoon.
03    The National Weather Service (ok) said the tremblor
04    measured 4.5 on the Richter (ok) scale.
05    John V. Dobbins, weather service senior meteorologist,
06    said the quake was the first recorded here in ten years.
07    Donna Williams, city clerk, said the Municipal building
08    shivered and shook during the 30 second shock.
09    The quake occured during a city council meeting at which
10    council members were considering the appointment of James J.
11    Jeffries of Athens, Georgia, as city manager.
12    Yesterday's quake was not the 1st in Carolton. Older
13    residents will recall the earthquake of 1960, more than
14    thirty years ago, that damaged many downtown buildings.
15    Details of that quake are no longer accessable. Records
16    kept at the Municipal Building and at "The Morning Record"
17    were destroyed in a collossal fire fifteen years ago.
18    The 1960 quake killed ten Carolton residents and injured
19    more than five hundred. Damage was estimated at $100,000,000.
20    Every bridge in Washington county collapsed.
```

Number Correct _____

Student _____

EXERCISE 4-26

Edit this news story. Correct errors in style. Use standard editing marks and practices. Do *not* rewrite or revise. There may be errors in spelling, usage or punctuation.

01   The Washington county Senior Writers Group will meet in

02   the Carolton-Washington Adult Center, 412 East Main Street,

03   tomorrow at 10 A.M. for a magazine writing workshop.

04   The workshop will be followed at 12 p.m. by a lunch in

05   the Center cafeteria after which Anne Dickens will discuss

06   her new book, Art and the Power of Imagination.

07   Miss Dickens earned a B.A. degree at Wellesley College

08   and a doctorate in English at Emory university.

09   She is a free-lance writer. She is on the board of the

10   Washington County Heritage Foundation. She lives at 27 Maple

11   Street.

12   The writing group will meet again Saturday from 10

13   a.m. to 12 noon.

14   Speaker at that meeting will be a Carolton native,

15   Howard James, editor and publisher of the Troy, New York,

16   "Evening Standard." He will discuss John Hay and John

17   Nicolay and their 6 volume biography of Abraham Lincoln.

18   Next month the writers will hear Everett Hale, professor

19   of Irish literature at Northwest college, who will discuss

20   the work of John Boyle O'Reilly, the Irish American poet

21   and patriot.

Number Correct _____

Student _____

5 Writing the Story II

Spelling

discernible, compatible, seize/seizure, soluble/dissolve, weird, peninsula, serendipity, irreligious, defendant, veteran, veterinarian/veterinary

Usage

imply/infer, ingenious/ingenuous, nauseous/nauseated, odious/odorous, damage/damages, loath/loathe, all right, censor/censure

Newsroom Vocabulary

localize, print, publish, issue, edition, media/print media, publisher, editor, to edit, editorial matter

Writing the Story II

These topics are treated in detail in George A. Hough 3rd, "News Writing," fifth edition.

Coming Events
Chapter 7, "Writing the Story II," pages 115 through 119.

Lists
Chapter 7, "Writing the Story II," pages 119 and 120.

Localizing
Chapter 7, "Writing the Story II," pages 120 through 125.

EXERCISE 5-1

This exercise introduces the news writer's trick of using commas and semicolons to organize lists of names or other items into a concise or readable form. For example:

```
John Smith, 127 Wisconsin Ave., treasurer; Jane
Jones, 11 E. Nevada Ave.;
```

Assume that you have already written the lead on a story about an election of officers and now need only to list the names. Write a paragraph giving the names and begin it:

```
The new officers are
```

Here are the names of the new officers and their offices. You will find their addresses in the city directory.

president	Marshall Reeves
vice president	Maurice Henderson
secretary	Stewart MacDonald
treasurer	Mrs. George Howe
trustee	Harrison L. Nightingale

Follow the model in Figure 7.2 on page 121 in "News Writing." Don't forget about style for names, courtesy titles and addresses.

EXERCISE 5-2

The school district's public relations officer, Marlene Brackett, has mailed you a press release. You learn:

```
Central High school seniors have been earning college credits
by taking advance college credit exams administered by the
College Entrance Examination Board. The credits are for
advanced work done in high school courses. The credits can
be used at any college. The college determines the amount of
credit it will allow.
```

```
Advance college credits have been earned by these students:
```

Dave Brewster	French
Kim Clark	history
John Coolidge	English
Robert Franklin	English
Luis Gomes	history
Ng, Anna	French
Mary Jones	history
Lorie Twardsynski	mathematics
Debra Green	biology

You don't need addresses or other identification in this story. Make your list as concise as possible. You can combine names of students who have earned credit in the same subject.

93

EXERCISE 5-3

Your city editor has asked you to write a story based on this press release. It came in the mail today from the state Department of Education. If you list the names of the students who do not live in Carolton, omit their street addresses.

CAPITAL CITY (today's date) — Fourteen state college students are among 550 students nationwide who have been awarded National Science Foundation Graduate Fellowships, the state Board of Education announced today.

The fellowships are awarded for outstanding ability in the sciences, mathematics and engineering. They provide an annual stipend of $6,000 for three years of graduate study, the state board said.

State winners, listed by hometown, are:

Dalton: James M. Offer, 337 Third St.; Craig Archer, 417 Lyons Ave.; Rebecca Rountree, 530 Linwood Blvd.

Southfield: Robert Morris, 205 S. Seventh St.

Williamstown: Peter L. Tobias, 551 Foster Road.

East Point: James L. Pye, 1601 Chelsea St.

Livonia: Kenneth J. Brady, 35 Wood St.

Carolton: Helen E. Rivera, 87 S. Meade; Mark H. Stahl, 650 W. Florida; Raymond L. Miskell, 415 E. Maryland.

Washington: John L. Sullivan, 52 Goldcrest Drive.

Mount Pleasant: Michael E. Nathanson, 1011 Deptford Drive.

Eastville: Martha L. Rizzo, 1701 N. Beech St.

Plymouth: Susan Short, 610 W. Lakeshore Drive.

You make a few phone calls, and learn that Miss Rivera is a senior at Vassar, Stahl a senior at Fairleigh Dickinson and Miskell a first-year graduate student at Purdue. Verify spellings for these institutions. Are they colleges or universities? Where are they? Use full names and locations in your story. Include names of parents.

EXERCISE 5-4

Your city editor handed you this story, with instructions to rewrite it for tomorrow's paper. "Check the name," she said. "It doesn't sound quite right."

```
     WASHINGTON — The National Advisory Child Health and Human
Development Council has invited four distinguished American
scholars to join its board.
     They are Hobart Ransom, Williams College, Williamstown,
Mass.; Eugenia Watson, Vassar College, Poughkeepsie, N.Y.;
Jane E. Phelps, University of Minnesota, Minneapolis; and
Robert Leavitt, Northwest College, Carolton.
```

EXERCISE 5-5

While you were on rewrite this morning, your friend George Robinson called you with a story about his service club's monthly meeting. You can write it for tomorrow's paper.

Friend: Will you get this in tomorrow's paper? The Challenge club will be meeting Monday. Jim Wilson will speak.

You: Wilson? What's his full name?

Friend: James L. And the meeting is at the Eagle restaurant as usual. At seven.

You: What's Wilson going to talk about?

Friend: Just a second. Got it right here. Okay. Legislative Trends in Mental Health.

You: He an expert or something?

Friend: Oh, he'll be okay. He's the community health representative of the county mental health department.

You: Okay, he's an expert. What's the correct name of this club of yours?

Friend: Carolton Chapter of the National Challenge Club. By the way, if you want to come, we'd be glad to have you.

You: Well, perhaps, but I may have to work. Do you want your name on this?

Friend: No, that's not necessary. And don't forget the time. Seven.

You: Okay, thanks, got it.

95

EXERCISE 5-6

While you were on campus this morning, you picked up a story on what sounds like an interesting program. Your notes:

```
Program sponsor: The Native American Cultural Society

Where:   Student Union/campus

Time: Day after tomorrow at 6 o'clock

Speaker:  Elmer Running Deer/a Lakota Sioux elder

Subject:  Reclaiming our Roots

Occasion: Society's annual fund-raising dinner
```

EXERCISE 5-7

You were in the office this morning when your city editor handed you the latest copy of a newspaper trade publication. She pointed out a story about the Newspaper Advertising Bureau in which she had circled the name of John L. Wallington. "Write a story about this," she told you. "Wallington is a graduate of Northwest College and worked for the Record while he was a student. A lot of people here know him."

Here's the story:

```
    The Newspaper Advertising Bureau elected officers Monday
and added five new members to its board of directors.
    New directors are Marguerite Brown, Tacoma News; Ralph
Giddings, Houston Telegraph; Robert Mackie, Wausau (Wis.)
Observer; Christine Fowler, Rock City (Maine) Blade; and John
Secord, Port Royal (Fla.) Sun-Times.
    Officers re-elected for one-year terms:
    John L. Wallington, publisher, San Jose Morning Post,
chairman.
    Frank Doolittle, publisher, Virginia Beach (Va.) Times and
Record, vice chairman.
    Darlene E. Pickett, president and publisher, Lawson
(Okla.) Evening Standard, treasurer.
    Howard S. Wood, publisher, Fairhaven (Mass.) Daily Camera,
secretary.
    The Ad Bureau board met in New York in conjunction with
the annual meeting of the Newspaper Association of America.
```

You check with the Northwest College Alumni Office and learn that Wallington was graduated in 1970 with a B.A. in journalism. Your city editor recalls that he worked for the Record from the fall of 1968 through the spring quarter of 1970 as a general assignment reporter. Rewrite and trim the story. Use a blind lead.

EXERCISE 5-8

While you were on rewrite this morning, the publicity chairman of the Washington County Democratic Women's Organization called in a story about a meeting. She told you:

Meeting at county Democratic headquarters. Open meeting.

Program: panel discussion on proposal to establish a quote women's commission unquote here.

Meeting time: eight o'clock Thursday night.

Panelists: Mrs. Christine Harris (chairman of the county Democratic Committee)

Mrs. H. C. Smith (chairman, Carolton Women's Caucus)

Francis Norton (member state Democratic committee)

Sue Ellen Dendramis (state representative from Carolton)

The Women's commission proposal will be on the ballot in next county election.

EXERCISE 5-9

This morning you got a call from Helen Olejnik at the Women's Crisis Center with a story about a program the center is sponsoring. Write it for tomorrow's paper.

The speech will be in the student union on Friday afternoon. Time: 3:30.

Speaker is Alison Hooper. She is author of a guide for teen-agers titled Be Streetwise, Be Safe.

She will discuss her new book, a critical analysis of the press.

Title of the book is How the Press Covers Sex Crimes.

A review in a national publication said her book "brilliantly analyzes the many ways the press perpetuates myths and stereotypes about rape."

Tickets are twelve dollars. Proceeds go to the crisis center, where counseling and legal advocacy are provided for victims of all kinds of abusive treatment.

EXERCISE 5-10

This morning your city editor called over to you: "Hey, take this call, will you? On two." You picked up the phone and found yourself talking to Bill Morrissey at the news bureau on campus.

Morrissey: Say, I thought you'd want to get something in tomorrow's paper on the commencement speaker.

You: Sure. Who is it?

Morrissey: Derek Bok. We were lucky to get him.

You: Tell me about him.

Morrissey: I don't have much. He's the former president of Harvard. I'll have a bio sketch for you the first of the week.

You: Okay. When's commencement?

Morrissey: It will be on (date). In LaFollette auditorium as usual.

You: What time?

Morrissey: Eight in the evening. Same as last time.

You thank Morrissey and start to write the story. Then you realize you need a little background on Bok. You can check Who's Who in the newspaper library. Ask your instructor to provide day and date for commencement.

EXERCISE 5-11

As you may know, a city election is scheduled for next month. In preparation, the city clerk is conducting a voter registration drive. The city clerk today gave you a schedule for registration. Write a story for tomorrow's paper.

Dates and places where voters may register:

    Franklin library/10th
    Central Fire Station/12th
    First Baptist church/14th
    National Guard armory/17th
    Trinity A.M.E. church/19th
    Central high/21st

FYI: The election will be on the first Tuesday after the first Monday of the month.

Include street addresses in your story.

EXERCISE 5-12

Your city editor handed you this story and asked you to rewrite it. "Use a blind lead," she said, "and just list the runners-up."

```
    Brian Kane, a senior at Carolton Central High School,
Monday won first place in the Northwest College school of
engineering's annual design competition.
    He will receive a four-year, full-tuition scholarship to
Northwest College worth $20,500.
    Roberta Wilson, a senior at Lincoln High School, Hastings,
won second place in the competition and will receive a
four-year, half-tuition scholarship worth $16,000.
    Two students tied for third place in the contest and will
each receive a $4,000 four-year scholarship. They are Debra
King of Meigs High School, Meigs, and John Edwards, Eaton
High School, Eaton Rapids.
    The students were asked to design a small city bank that
wanted to attract new customers and provide both walk-in and
drive-in services.
```

FYI: Hastings, Meigs and Eaton Rapids are cities in your state.

EXERCISE 5-13

Write a news story based on this information:

```
There will be an interesting lecture next week. A poet and
author from South Africa will speak. His lecture will be in
French.

Title of his lecture is: Cultural Rights and the Rights of
Man. Lecture will be at 8 o'clock Tuesday at the Maison
Francaise, 575 Newton Road.

Speaker is Breyten Breytenbach, the author of The True
Confessions of an Albino Terrorist. He spent seven years in
prison in South Africa because of his opposition to
apartheid.

His lecture is sponsored by the Department of Romance
Languages at Northwest College.
```

Breytenbach is an internationally known writer. You could add something to this and make a larger story. Try The New York Times Index. He has been in the news recently.

EXERCISE 5-14

This press release came in today's mail. Your city editor handed it to you with instructions to rewrite it for tomorrow's paper.

The press release:

Westinghouse Electric Corporation has announced state winners in its 54th annual science talent search, the nation's oldest science contest.

The winners were chosen from 15 finalists out of 350 entrants from schools throughout the state.

The Westinghouse is designed to encourage the nation's most promising high school scientists to pursue careers in scientific disciplines.

Winners of $5,000 scholarships are William Alan Schwartz, 18, son of Mr. and Mrs. Peter B. Schwartz, Lake City; Joel S. Fajane Jr., 17, son of Mr. and Mrs. Joel S. Fajane, Monroe; Scott D. Smith, 18, son of Mrs. Annette W. Smith, Union City; Karen B. Brickhouse, 17, daughter of Mr. and Mrs. Sigmund Brickhouse, Owosso; and Diane Rivera, 18, daughter of Mr. and Mrs. Carlos Rivera, Carolton.

The scholarships were awarded for original research submitted to the panel of Westinghouse judges. The winners are all high school seniors.

Schwartz' entry was a study of the chemical nature of the transport of substances into the cells of bacteria; Fajane studied a number theory introduced by the Pythagoreans, who developed some of the basic principles of mathematics and astronomy; Smith designed and built a computer for use in his school; Brickhouse experimented with a chemical capable of changing the patterns of genetic inheritance in green algae; and Rivera studied the regenerative ability of a type of earthworm.

The 10 finalists who did not win scholarships were each awarded a cash prize of $250.

There are local names here. Include names of parents of local students.

EXERCISE 5-15

Your city editor tossed you this story. "Rewrite it," she said. Follow her suggestion. Rewrite to conform to the STOP formula.

"Carnivorous Plants and Their Insect Associates" is the title of a lecture scheduled for Wednesday afternoon by the entomology department.

Dr. Genevieve LaFrance, distinguished professor of entomology and zoology, will speak at 4 in room 125 of the biological sciences building.

EXERCISE 5-16

You are working today on general assignment. This morning you picked up these facts from the public relations office on the Northwest College campus. Write a story for tomorrow's paper.

```
Conference here Friday and Saturday — at Northwest College
conference center — governor will be keynote speaker — will
open conference with his address Friday morning at 10 —

For owners of small businesses and of minority businesses —
sponsor is the school of business at Northwest college —

Program consists of panels and speeches — names of speakers
and participants below —

Issues to be examined: employment, incorporation, licensing,
taxes, hazardous waste, economic development, minority
employment and agribusiness —

(on the program besides the governor)

        George Murray — state department of trade and
        industry (director)

        Maurice Cleveland — secretary of state (state, not
        U.S.)

        Mark Crimmins — director, state department of
        revenue

        Theodore DuPont — cooperative extension service
        (director)

        John Timmins — state labor department
        (commissioner)

        Marilyn Breed — state department of industry and
        trade (commissioner)
```

The handout from the college public relations staff says that small and minority businesses accounted for more than two-thirds of the new jobs created in the state last year.

You check the governor's name in the state government directory: Walker L. Robertson.

You call Bill Crane, the governor's press secretary, and ask what the governor will talk about. Crane tells you his topic is "Rebuilding the State's Industrial Base."

EXERCISE 5-17

Your city editor handed you this press release. It came in today's mail from the state Board of Education in Capital City, the state capital. "Fix this up for tomorrow's paper," she said.

CAPITAL CITY — Six colleges and universities in the state have been awarded more than $95,000 by the National Science Foundation to help underwrite research projects that will involve undergraduate students, the State Board of Education announced today.

The participating students, usually juniors and seniors, will be selected on the basis of their work in college-level courses, the state board said.

Following is a list of the institutions receiving the NSF grants, the amount of the grant and the name of the department and science project director:

Wilson College, Oil City, $16,490, Ronald O. Knapp, biology.

Lenox Institute of Technology, Lenox, $7,260, James W. Sleeper, physics, and $15,200, Donald K. Abood, chemistry.

Northwest College, Carolton, $16,500, Charles Huang, physics.

Oakbrook College, Oakbrook, $8,700, Richard L. Tomboulian, biology.

Southern Baptist College, Riverside, $12,000, Lester Huzar, chemistry.

Holy Cross College, Doraville, $19,000, Henry Hunziker, psychology.

You call Professor Huang, and he tells you:

He will select six seniors to work on a project in the college's new cyclotron laboratory. He will be assisted in supervising the project by another faculty member, Julia Feldpausch.

EXERCISE 5-18

The secretary of the local chapter of Mothers Against Drunk Driving has given you a story about the installation of the organization's new officers. Write the story. Include street addresses.

President:	Bette Yaffee
1st vice president:	Catherine Tombs
2nd vice president:	Jane Bell
Secretary:	Harriet Howe
Treasurer:	Diana Robbins

The officers were installed Friday at the organization's regular monthly meeting at the Student union on campus.

EXERCISE 5-19

You were working in the office today, and your editor asked you to write a news story based on these facts:

Lecture this coming week on campus — Wednesday 8 in the evening in the auditorium at the law school.

Title: Nuclear Winter.

Tickets available on campus at the student union and at the Paragon newsstand.

Speaker is Dr. Carl Sagan. He is a professor of astronomy at Cornell university, Ithaca, New York.

Sagan is the author of Cosmos, a book on science that has been a best seller and was the basis for the television series of the same name.

Sagan and other scientists have become concerned about the effect a nuclear war might have on the environment. Soot and dust from a nuclear burst, they believe, might produce a severe, widespread and long-term cooling of the earth's surface.

They have termed this climatic catastrophe a "nuclear winter" and believe that even a brief period of cold and dark would have serious effects on world food supplies.

EXERCISE 5-20

Your city editor handed you this wire story with instructions to fix it up for tomorrow's paper:

CAPITAL CITY — The State Bar Association today released the names of 17 people who passed the bar examination given last month.

They are Mary Martin, Tyler; John Gooch, Monroe; Willis Sims, Haslett; Robert Kemp, Rogers City; Harry L. Richardson, Eastville; Larry Walker, Roseville; Rosa E. Morales, Saginaw; Ernest Beech, New Salem; Lawrence P. O'Donnell, Monroe; Ralph Haroldson, Jackson; Marilyn E. Rauch, Portage; Marcia Williams, Carolton; Harrison Hewins, Stevensville; Ervin Sinclair, Plymouth; Don Myers, Dodgeville; Edna Anderson, Williamstown; Larry Lee Smith, South Haven.

You call Marcia Williams, and she tells you that she got her law degree in June at Northwest College. She intends to practice tax law.

EXERCISE 5-21

Write a story based on these facts, given to you by the Northwest College news bureau:

Keynote Speaker:	Art Buchwald.
Topic:	Humor: The Only Way to Cure People.
Organization:	The Northwest College School of Journalism.
Place:	Memorial Hall.
Day/hour:	Saturday at 10 in the morning.
The occasion:	The school's annual "high school newspaper day." Buchwald is the keynote speaker.

The program will start with Buchwald's speech and will end after the last workshop at 3 p.m.

The school expects about 500 high school newspaper editors and about 50 of their advisers. Usually about 60 high schools are represented.

Buchwald is a nationally syndicated columnist. He has written some 30 books, including two children's books and two guides to Paris. His reminiscences of his early years, "Leaving Home," was published recently. He won a Pulitzer Prize in 1986 for political commentary. Buchwald lives in Washington, D.C., and summers on Martha's Vineyard.

You might verify Buchwald's background by checking Who's Who.

EXERCISE 5-22

You were routinely checking records today at the courthouse and found that tax liens have been filed against several local people by the Internal Revenue Service. The record shows:

Date Filed	Name	Tax	Amount Owed
7	Miller, Robert L.	individual income	$1,043.50
8	Lund, Aaron O.	individual income	2,783.00
9	Barth, Julius	unemployment	7,783.80
10	Teacher, Walker E.	individual income	1,060.00
17	Hawkins, Emma	unemployment	840.73
21	Funderburke, J.L.	individual income	604.28

You will need to identify these people by their addresses. You don't need to include the date the lien was filed.

Write the story for tomorrow's paper.

EXERCISE 5-23

This morning your city editor handed you this story, a wire story passed along by the news editor. Rewrite it for tomorrow's paper.

> LAKE CITY — Dwight McDonald of West Newton was elected president of the state Fraternal Order of Eagles yesterday at the organization's 88th annual convention.
>
> About 300 delegates are attending the convention here.
>
> Other officers elected are Oscar Jones, Cement City, vice president; William Hazelton, Carolton, treasurer; Robert Waldron, Becket, chaplain; and Ronald Shelton, Huron Bay, conductor.

EXERCISE 5-24

The Northwest College news bureau has given you a story about a conference that will be held here Saturday. Write it for tomorrow's paper.

What:	A multicultural festival — "Discovering Connections."
Speakers:	Amelia G. Bingham, a Wampanoag clan mother, Mashpee, Mass.
	Elias Fine, rabbi of the Carolton Jewish Congregation.
	Arturo Spinoza, Society of the Holy Ghost, Carolton.
	James Ong, Asian Student Organization, Northwest College.
	Caroline Gallina, Carolton Hispanic Alliance.
Sponsor:	Carolton Council of Churches.
Purpose:	To celebrate the diverse populations in the Carolton/Washington county region. The festival represents the council's continuing efforts to counteract violence in our society.
Program:	Activities showing diversity, such as ethnic song and dance performances, ethnic food booths, craft booths, demonstrations and exhibits prepared by school and community groups.
	Remarks by speakers.
Place:	Memorial Hall and softball field behind Memorial Hall.

EXERCISE 5-25

While you were in the office this morning, your city editor handed you a story that had just come in on the wire. She asked you to rewrite it for tomorrow's paper. You can do it in about three paragraphs.

CAPITAL CITY - (today's date) - The National Labor Relations Board today authorized elections at various state firms to determine what union representation, if any, is desired by employees in their dealings with management.

The firms, locations, number voting in the election, the union or unions seeking representation and the date of the election are as follows:

Willow Run Rubber and Lining Co., Farmington, 33 voting, United Mine Workers, (month) 10th.

Bugent Sand and Gravel Co., Eastville, 20 voting, Teamsters, (month) 12th.

Empire Hotel Co., Dalton, 16 voting, Hotel and Restaurant Employees union, (month) 15th.

Radio West Newton, Inc., West Newton, 16 voting, American Federation of Television and Radio Artists, (month) 18th.

Kelly Construction Co., Carolton, 28 voting, International Brotherhood of Electrical Workers, (month) 20th.

Canteen Service Co., Mount Pleasant, 10 voting, Teamsters, (month), 28th.

You really don't need expert knowledge to rewrite this story. Ask your instructor for the month.

EXERCISE 5-26

Here is a story that came over the state wire this morning. Your editor would like it rewritten for tomorrow's paper.

MONROE — Westphalia, Beaver Falls and Carolton artists won top honors in the State Fair art show, which opened here today.

More than 200 works are entered in three divisions. They will be on display in the Community Arts Building throughout the fair.

Prize winners in the oil painting division were:

Barbara Moore, Westphalia, first; Henry Love, Carolton, second; and Walter E. Shook, Madison, third.

Prize winners in the watercolor division were:

Charles Gifford, Beaver Falls, first; Jane Roberts, Clare, second; and Helen Lutz, Carolton, third.

Prize winners in the prints division were:

Horace N. Gilmore, Carolton, first; Dorothy Bond, Monroe, second; and Laurence Peters, West Allis, third.

EXERCISE 5-27

Your editor handed you this wire story. "Rewrite this for tomorrow's paper," she said.

HILLSDALE — Roger Wells, 28, of Carolton, was killed today when his car went off the road near Hillsdale. Wells was driving home from his job on the night shift at the Hillsdale Iron and Steel Co.

The accident occurred about 4 a.m. on U.S. 210 about 15 miles east of Carolton.

Dodge County sheriff's officers said Wells apparently fell asleep at the wheel of his car. The car left the road, traveled 150 feet into a field and turned over.

Wells was dead when he was found by a sheriff's highway patrol officer.

You have no time to get more on this story, but do verify the name before writing. Use a blind lead, please.

EXERCISE 5-28

Here's another story that needs a list of names. You have learned from the secretary of the Rose Society:

The Rose society's annual show was held Saturday and Sunday in the National Guard armory. It was the 35th annual show. Among the 147 awards presented:

best rose in show	Howard Baker
best hybrid tea	Gerald Ferguson
best arrangement	Mrs. William Miskell

These are Carolton residents, best identified here by their street addresses.

EXERCISE 5-29

The local American Legion Auxiliary installed officers Tuesday night, and the publicity officer has brought in the list of names. Write a story for tomorrow's paper.

President	Anna Turnbull
1st vice president	Wanda Murphy
2nd vice president	Myra Hall
Secretary	Helen Gillette
Treasurer	Mahalia MacComber
Chaplain	Evelyn Spaulding
Sergeant-at-Arms	Vivian Blake
Executive Board	Mildred Newhouse
	Gladys Powers
	Ella Jackson

EXERCISE 5-30

Edit these sentences to improve punctuation. Use standard editing marks to insert or delete punctuation. Do *not* rewrite.

1. James L. Wilson will address the Challenge Club, at the Eagle Restaurant, Monday, at 7 p.m.

2. Wilson, a community health representative with the state Health department will discuss recent health legislation.

3. Syndicated columnist, Art Buchwald will be the keynote speaker.

4. The speakers will be: William Tell, author of the new book "The Liberated Man", Marjorie Campbell, a medical student; and Anthony Lewis, New York Times columnist and author of "Gideon's Trumpet."

5. The meeting will be Monday, at 8 p.m., at the County Building.

6. William Cleveland, 34, of 539 S. Grant St. is at Carolton General Hospital. He is in fair condition according to the hospital.

7. Police arrested Jack Tumanis, a Sandusky, Ohio senior, for jaywalking.

8. The cars collided at 2 p.m. on Jan. 11, 1978 in Wichita, Kans., where Smith was living at the time police reported.

9. Commencement will be June 11, in the LaFollette Auditorium at 10 a.m.

10. Anthony Lewis, the New York Times columnist will address the graduating class the Northwest College News Bureau has announced.

Number Correct _____

Student _____

EXERCISE 5-31

Eliminate the *redundancies* in these items. Draw a line through the unnecessary
words or write or type a revision in the space at the right. Some of the items may
not be redundant.

1. still remains   _____

2. at the hour of noon   _____

3. spoke on the subject of sin   _____

4. an actual fact   _____

5. in real life he was   _____

6. present incumbent   _____

7. made out of iron   _____

8. took a walk   _____

9. for a period of 10 days   _____

10. was engaged in studying   _____

11. work has already begun   _____

12. strangled to death   _____

13. set a new record   _____

14. gave birth to a baby boy   _____

15. every single day   _____

16. at the intersection of   _____

17. at 10 p.m. tonight   _____

18. during the summer months   _____

19. in the event that   _____

20. for the purpose of   _____

Number Correct _____

Student _____

EXERCISE 5-32

Edit this news story. Correct errors in style. Use standard editing marks and practices. Do *not* rewrite or revise. There may be errors in spelling, usage or punctuation.

01   A Carolton woman was killed last night during an

02   exchange of gunfire between a Carolton police officer and

03   three men suspected of importing drugs into Washington

04   county.

05   Madeline Boomershine, 27, of 386 West Nevada Avenue

06   was killed in the crossfire.

07   Police said Boomershine was crossing the street when

08   detective Sgt. Bert Block exchanged shots with three men

09   in a late-model car with Fla. license plates.

10   She was given last rights by Rev. Sean O'Connor,

11   assistant pastor of St. Thomas Roman Catholic Church.

12   She was dead on arrival at Carolton General hospital.

13   Two of the men fled after the shooting, but the driver

14   of the car, Carl E. Manners, 40, of Sarasota, Florida,

15   was taken into custody.

16   Manners is at Carolton General Hospital with multiple

17   gunshot wounds in the abdomen and chest.

18   Police found a ten pound package of cocaine in the

19   trunk of the Florida car. Estimated street value is

20    $2,000,000, according to police Lieutenant Thomas

21   (Pinky) Maher.

Number Correct _____

Student _____

EXERCISE 5-33

Edit this news story. Correct errors in style. Use standard editing marks and practices. Do *not* rewrite or revise. There may be errors in spelling, grammar, usage or punctuation.

```
01      Verdicts are expected tomorrow in the lawsuit filed

02   by Carolton families whose homes have been damaged by

03   subsiding land in a former swamp.

04      Walter Nesbitt, attorney for the homeowners is

05   unusually optimistic about the outcome.

06      Nesbit said yesterday that he thinks the jury will

07   award his clients at least 400 thousand dollars.

08      Nesbitt is an experienced trial lawyer. He recently

09   defended a libel suit against "The Morning Record." The

10   Record lost the case, but the jury awarded the plaintifs,

11   an Albany, New York, couple, only five cents in damages.

12      He is a flamboyant figure who keeps a thermos of

13   coffee in his briefcase and once threw a coke bottle at

14   a bailif. He is a graduate of the University of

15   Michigan Law School and earned a Master of Arts in public

16   administration at Harvard.

17      He was expelled from college after he rode a unicycle

18   across the platform during a Memorial day program and

19   refused to stand when the band played The Stars and

20   Stripes Forever.

21      His clients have great faith in his judgement, however,

22   and he charges collossal fees.
```

Number Correct _____

Student _____

# 6 Quotation

Spelling

cigarette,* allegiance, uncontrollable, cemetery, leisure, implausible, changeable, inoculate, deterrent, strict/strictly, resuscitate, existence, ballistics

Usage

ordinance/ordnance, perspective/prospective, populous/populace, prostrate/prostitute, alumnus/alumni, alumna/alumnae, vulgar/profane/obscene

Newsroom Vocabulary

direct quote, indirect quote, partial quote, speech tag, libel, assignment, beat, press/working press, set/overset, ombudsman, art/graphics

117

Quotation

This topic is treated in detail in George A. Hough 3rd, "News Writing," fifth edition:

Quotation
Chapter 9, "Quotation," pages 157 through 179.

Models

Direct and indirect quotation fall into three categories, which for convenience can be referred to as Type 1, Type 2 and Type 3.

In Type 1, the speech tag comes first and the direct or indirect quote follows:

```
Smith said, "I am in this race to win."

Smith said he is in this race to win.
```

In Type 2, the order of quote and speech tag is reversed so that the quote comes first and the speech tag follows:

```
"I am in this race to win," Smith said.

He is in this race to win, Smith said.
```

In Type 3, the speech tag is inserted at some natural break in the quote:

```
"It's not likely," Smith said, "that I would do
that."

It's not likely, Smith said, that he would do that.
```

Type 1 quotes are used most often for indirect quotation. Type 2 quotes are preferred for direct quotation. Type 3 quotes provide a useful alternative to Type 1 and Type 2 quotes.

EXERCISE 6-1

Indicate by writing the appropriate number in the space at right whether the sentence is a Type 1, Type 2 or Type 3 quote:

1. "I'm on my way to Dublin Bay," she said.   _____

2. They chimed in, "Of course you'll take the train."   _____

3. "Pack my box," she ordered, "with a dozen roses."   _____

4. "Now is the time to pack your suitcase," he said.   _____

5. He ordered: "Pack my box with two dozen roses."   _____

6. She told him she would stay two or three weeks.   _____

7. "Congress must be more cooperative," he said.   _____

8. The country expects more of the Congress, he said.   _____

9. The country, he said, expects more of the Congress.   _____

10. "Help," she cried, "and please hurry!"   _____

11. "Help, help, and please hurry!" she cried.   _____

12. The instructor said he wanted the work done at once.   _____

13. "Turn this assignment in right now," he ordered.   _____

14. She said, "Develop the idea along these lines."   _____

15. "This way to the egress," the sign read.   _____

16. They cried in unison, "Don't go out that door!"   _____

17. "There's a fool born every minute," he said.   _____

18. She said, "No, no, a thousand times no!"   _____

19. "Keep moving, keep moving," the traffic officer said.   _____

20. The speaker said that he had one more question.   _____

Number Correct _____

Student _____

EXERCISE 6-2

(A) Revise these Type 1 quotes and convert them to Type 2 quotes.

1. He said, "The council has no authority for such an act."

2. Mayor Harold Orleans said: "I can't go along on this one."

3. Councilman Mary Hawks said, "I resent the mayor's attitude."

4. Another councilman said, "That's negative thinking."

5. City Clerk Donna Williams said, "I hate these arguments."

(B) Revise these Type 1 quotes and convert them to Type 3 quotes.

6. Smith said, "Nevertheless, I think the mayor will win out."

7. He added, "The mayor seems to be on top of the situation."

8. The mayor said, "Just like the council, always bickering."

9. He said, "They can never agree, but they'll never admit it."

10. Councilman Lambert said, "We'll take our stand right here."

Student _____

EXERCISE 6-3

(A) Revise these Type 2 direct quotes and convert them to Type 1 indirect quotes.

1. "I won't go along with the council this time," Jones said.

2. "I resent the mayor's attitude," Councilman Lambert said.

3. "The mayor seems to be on top of the situation," Smith said.

4. "I may have to vote against the mayor," Boyle said.

5. "I need the money to pay off a bad check," the man said.

(B) Revise these Type 1 indirect quotes and convert them to Type 2 direct quotes.

6. He said his men would just have to search for the money.

7. The sheriff said that nobody knew the trouble he'd seen.

8. The mayor said he'd just have to wait until next year.

9. The candidate said that he was all right on that question.

10. The city clerk said that it was just a matter of dirty politics.

Student _____

EXERCISE 6-4

Your city editor looked over the story you wrote about the new librarian (Exercise 4-11) and suggested that you call Tassinari and see what he has to say. You did, and this conversation took place:

You: Mr. Tassinari, I understand that you are going to be the new librarian at the Franklin library.

He: Yes, that's right. I just heard from the board. It was decided last night.

You: Very good. Congratulations. You're starting the first of the month?

He: Yes, but I'll be in Carolton before then, of course.

You: Have you any plans for changes in the library?

He: Not at the moment. I think the Franklin is a fine library. I'll have to look things over carefully before I make any changes.

You: What's your special field of interest in library work?

He: Well, I'm especially interested in children's literature. I have done a lot, too, with early reading programs here in Ann Arbor. I want to do everything I can to help children develop a love of reading.

You: Great! That sounds good. Thanks very much. I'll look forward to talking with you again when you get settled at the library.

He: Fine. Thanks. Goodbye.

Now go over your notes and select two one-sentence quotes. Use the first as a Type 1 indirect quote and the second as a Type 2 direct quote. The indirect quote must (1) identify the speaker and (2) tell the reader what he is talking about. The direct quote, which will follow in the next paragraph, will give the speaker's views in his own words. Insert these quotes, the second immediately following the first, into your earlier story. Follow the model on page 177 of "News Writing."

EXERCISE 6-5

Your editor suggested that you could improve your story on the college faculty member's appointment to the banking commission (Exercise 4-17) if you talked with her and got a couple of quotes. You called her, and she told you:

```
I am very pleased, of course, to have been appointed to the
banking commission.

I expect to be a working commissioner, and I hope I can do
a good job.
```

Both these statements are direct quotations. Put the first in the form of a Type 1 indirect quote. Put the second in the form of a Type 2 direct quotation. Insert the two quotes, the second immediately following the first, into your story. Your story on the new librarian will serve as a model.

EXERCISE 6-6

While you were in the office this morning, your city editor asked you to take a call. You found yourself talking with Ray Vanderpol, superintendent of the railroad. He told you about the grade crossing work the railroad has started and referred you to the county superintendent of roads for further information. Between the two, you have enough for a story. Be sure to use a direct quote in your story.

Vanderpol:

```
The railroad has started a program of rebuilding and
improving grade crossings here. Several crossings north of
the city need work.

First grade crossing to be improved will be the one on
Western avenue. This crossing will be closed to traffic for
two weeks beginning next Monday.

Quote we're going to rebuild the whole thing unquote.

Cost of the grade crossing program will be more than
$3,000,000. Rebuilding the Western Ave. crossing will cost
$225,000.
```

Wilson:

```
The county will not be involved in this work. It will be
strictly a railroad effort.
```

EXERCISE 6-7

At city hall today, the mayor's administrative assistant gave you a story about an award to the city. You also talk to the mayor and get some additional information from the police accident bureau. Your story should be written for tomorrow's paper.

From Mitchell:

```
The National Automobile Safety Association makes 2 national
awards each year for traffic safety. One is for large cities
— more than 150,000. The other is for cities with less than
150,000 population.

Carolton won this year in the small city category. Seattle
won in the large city category.

The awards will be announced today. The award will be
presented formally next week by someone from the Carolton
Safety Association office.

Carolton won for quote outstanding efforts to prevent
pedestrian traffic accidents unquote.
```

From Smith:

```
This is great. We're very pleased with the award. We owe it
all to the fine work done by the police traffic safety
division.
```

From the Accident Prevention Bureau:

```
In the past year (12 months ending 30th of last month), city
had only 27 traffic accidents in which pedestrians were
injured. Year previous: 51 injury accidents involving
pedestrians.
```

You know the population of Carolton [See "Practice Exercises," page xi]. What is the population of Seattle? You'll want to put both figures in your story.

EXERCISE 6-8

While you were at the high school this morning, you were told about the Special Olympics program that will be held this weekend. You talk with Ken Miller, the school district phys ed director, and get the details. It's worth a story. Write it for tomorrow's paper.

Special Olympics — program for handicapped children — sponsors — public schools and civic organizations — program open to the public — at the high school field

for ages 5 through 13 — includes track events — softball tournament

about 250 kids expected to participate — Saturday — 9 to 3 — kids have been practicing for weeks

quote — we've got a great program — the kids are as excited as any kids would be before a big athletic event — they're great — every one of them wants to go out there and win unquote

Review the use of *extended quotation* before you write.

EXERCISE 6-9

In today's mail you got a press release from the state Department of Transportation that has some local as well as statewide interest. Write a story based on these facts, excerpted from the press release:

The state DOT has organized a quote minority advisory committee unquote as a subcommittee of its Disadvantaged Business Enterprise Committee.

A number of prominent people statewide are on the committee. One is a local man, Gerald A. Cook. He is on the Northwest faculty.

The press release says Cook will be chairman of this committee and quotes T.C. Moore, state DOT commissioner, as saying:

I'm happy to say that we have an outstanding advisory board. I'm delighted that Dr. Cook has agreed to help us. I'm looking forward to working with Dr. Cook and with the committee.

The press release says that the advisory committee will quote advise the department in its administration of the DBE program and assist the department in identifying methods to increase minority participation on highway department projects unquote.

Use a blind lead. Quote Moore.

EXERCISE 6-10

This morning at city hall you noticed a change in the art exhibit. This month the artist is a city employee.

Donna Williams, the city clerk, tells you that the artist is Emma Daggett, an illustrator and cartographer who works for the city planning commission. And this is a first for the city hall art gallery — the first time the artist has been a city employee.

You talk with the artist, and she tells you she has worked for the city for three years. She does maps and illustrates city publications. She has an MFA degree from Northwest college.

Her last exhibit was at the art club.

Also from the artist: quote I'm pleased to have the recognition of the city hall exhibit . . . at first I was a bit concerned about the reaction to some of my abstracts. . . . I've had a lot of compliments, though . . . people seem to like them unquote.

There are about a dozen paintings in the exhibit, mostly oils, a mixture of abstracts, still life and landscapes. There are several watercolors.

You realize that you are not much of an art critic, so you call an acquaintance, a local artist, and ask him about Emma Daggett. Horace Gilmore tells you: quote she's really very good. She's probably at her best with abstracts, but she does some lovely still life. She's done some excellent portraits, too unquote.

The Record runs a story every month about the current exhibit at city hall. Attribute carefully and use the quotes.

EXERCISE 6-11

Rewrite this news story to conform to the STOP formula:

"Political Funny Business" is the title of John B. Cook's talk for the Carolton Professional Women's Club on Tuesday at the Franklin Library.
  Senator Cook of Brewster represents Washington County in the General Assembly.

EXERCISE 6-12

The Record's police reporter was off today, and you filled in on her beat. At Carolton General Hospital you learned that a state health department doctor had been in to look at a Carolton man who has been in the hospital for a week with an illness that the hospital had not been able to diagnose immediately. Now the state health people say the man has bubonic plague. The patient is William Cleveland, age 34. You talk to his family doctor, Dr. Bates, and to a doctor on the staff of the state health department's communicable disease division.

From Dr. Alpha Bates:

He has been quite ill. He's better now that we know what his illness is and are able to treat it. He'll go home in a day or so.

We think he contracted the plague from an infected rabbit. He was hunting upstate. He cut his finger on a bone while cleaning a rabbit he shot.

From Dr. Foster Seruda:

He had two rabbits in his freezer, and we sent these to the lab at Fort Collins for examination. They found evidence of plague immediately.

Quote There's no reason to panic . . . There is almost no chance of an epidemic unquote.

Hunters, though, should wear gloves while cleaning rabbits and not handle them at all if they have any break in the skin that might facilitate the entry of disease-causing organisms.

This is the fourth case of plague in the state since 1990. One man died in 1991. There were two cases last year.

_____

The Fort Collins lab the doctor referred to is the U.S. Centers (correct) for Disease Control lab. If you're not sure what bubonic plague is, your readers may not know either. Do a little research and include a brief explanation of bubonic plague in your story. Quote and attribute carefully. This is a somewhat technical story.

EXERCISE 6-13

While you were on campus today, you talked with Dr. Shanks at the Student Health Center. He told you:

The health center has completed a study that was begun last year in an effort to find ways in which the center could do more to educate students about alcohol-related health problems.

Shanks says quote 15 percent of students graduate with an alcohol problem and go on to develop more serious problems in later life unquote.

Many students don't realize the role alcohol has come to play in their lives.

Shanks says 87 percent of Northwest college students use alcohol.

Most students think they don't drink more than anyone else, yet some drink every night of the week.

Students who would like to take a closer look at alcohol and how it fits into their lifestyles can, if they wish, complete a questionnaire prepared by the center. Those who express further interest will be referred to health center staff members who have expertise in dealing with alcohol-related problems.

Shanks says quote we think we can be helpful unquote.

He also says quote what some students consider normal consumption of alcohol is considered overuse in the real world unquote.

Shanks' 15 percent figure is a national figure. Overindulgence in alcohol may not be as serious a problem at Northwest. Nevertheless, there is a growing awareness of the dangers of heavy drinking. There's a story here — with some good quotes.

EXERCISE 6-14

While you were in the office today, your city editor gave you a handout. "Write this for tomorrow's paper," she told you.

The handout tells you:

```
Program Monday at the Adult Center — 4 o'clock — planned
parenthood assn. — speaker — Luz Cordoba — PP community
coordinator —

Subject — safe sex — communication between partners about
sexually transmitted diseases —

Program will probably last an hour —
```

You think this could be pepped up a bit with quotes, so you call Ms. Cordoba, and she tells you:

```
We think this is an important subject — We plan several
workshops on this in the next several weeks — We are working
with the school board to take the message into the high
school — Later next week we are holding a workshop for senior
citizens — We don't expect anyone, especially young people,
to abstain — but we do want everyone to practice safe sex.
```

Your story should include both direct and indirect quotes. Be selective.

EXERCISE 6-15

You got a phone call this morning from Councilman John Clark who wants you to write a story about his idea for a state-wide initiative. Your notes:

```
initiative would go on ballot as referendum question in next
election — Clark will ask city council Monday to adopt a
resolution urging his proposal —

wants state to be able to revoke — for 5 years — driver's
license of anyone under 21 caught with a handgun —

quote teenagers covet a driving license — their passage to
freedom — taking away a driver's license sends a clear
message that we mean business about guns — unquote —

Clark plans to send 50,000 letters to county residents asking
them to join in his campaign against gun violence —

Clark says city and county have a growing problem with
teenage violence and quote criminal use of handguns unquote —
```

EXERCISE 6-16

While you were on campus this morning, you spoke with Joe Ng, director of the college's computer services, who tells you about a problem they are having with the system: a virus is affecting software all over the campus. You get what you can from him and then walk over to the Journalism Building where you talk with Ray Butler who manages the journalism system:

From Ng:

```
Virus has affected MacIntosh labs all over campus — and
nationwide —

Virus called WDEF — doesn't always destroy data — but on two
occasions it does seem to have — mainly causes glitches that
annoy users and slows work —

Quote — virus first appeared last month — we have programs
to detect and remove virus unquote
```

From Butler:

```
We started having problems last month, but virus has been in
system longer than that —

quote it's more of a nuisance than anything — frustrating
thing is — it takes only one infected disk to start the cycle
over unquote

Journalism uses a program called DISINFECT to detect and
destroy virus —
```

From Ng:

```
Library installed a "gatekeeper" program — to detect and
destroy virus — early last month — but virus was already in
library software —
```

You gather that the virus problem is not serious this time, but viruses can destroy software and valuable work stored in computer systems. Next time could be serious and expensive. You suggest to your city editor that the Record ought to safeguard its system.

EXERCISE 6-17

You covered the board of education meeting last night and took careful notes on the discussion about a proposed revision of the school district's sexual harassment policy.

Discussion centered on the word *unwelcome,* which was added to the policy during revision.

The board finally decided to postpone a vote on adopting the policy as revised. Your notes included:

Fred Roberts (board member):

```
     I don't like the word unwelcome when it defines sexual
harassment as quote unwelcome sexual advances, requests for
sexual favors, and other verbal or physical conduct of a
sexual nature unquote. I think that's too subjective.
     When you have an undefined word like this, you have
uncertainty in the application of the policy.
     The word doesn't appear in the state Fair Practices Act.
```

Alfred Carew (superintendent of schools):

```
     Unwelcome is the most important word in interpreting
conduct. It is very important to the recipient of the
behavior. If both perceive that the activity is welcome it
would not reach the stage of a complaint.
```

Octavio Gomes (school district personnel director):

```
     Any question of uncertainty will be addressed during the
processing of a complaint.
     The word unwelcome is important. It needs to be defined
for people who use the policy.
```

Richard Warren (board member):

```
     I supported the revisions at our last meeting, but now I'm
a little uncomfortable about it. I don't think it ought to
be approved tonight.
     It's going to open up a whole can of worms. Where do we
draw a line? Where does it stop?
```

Carew:

```
     The policy is a document that will guide development of
follow-through procedures and training programs. The policy
is already in place. We are only making minor revisions here.
```

You know that the policy has been in place for some time, but had applied only to teachers and staff. Not discussed at last night's meeting was the fact that the revised policy will apply also to students.

EXERCISE 6-18

You talked with Nancy Johnson, president of the Chamber of Commerce, about the new state law on sexual harassment. She reminds you of terms of the law and tells you:

The law:

— Requires employers to educate their workers about sexual harassment.

— Employers with six or more employees must hold training sessions about sexual harassment and explain procedures for filing complaints.

— Employers must post a notice with the definition of sexual harassment and showing examples.

Miss Johnson:

Our members will comply with the law.

Sexual harassment is still as strong as ever. It is used as a control technique.

Sexual harassment is not just a women's problem — it's a human problem.

We want every workplace in Carolton and Washington County to be free of harassment and a comfortable place for both men and women.

The Chamber has more than 300 members, and Miss Johnson tells you that two-thirds of them have at least six employees.

EXERCISE 6-19

Revise these paragraphs to bring the quotations within guidelines suggested in Chapter 9 of "News Writing."

1. Jacobson said he believes that fundamentalists are "never the mainstay of believers in any religious philosophy . . . The vast majority of Christians are entirely comfortable with science, and particularly with biology."

2. Jones said that in the second incident, Smith "was threatening us when we were outside the house. But when I had enough of it, I took after him. I met him on the stairs. He threatened me (with a knife), and when I took off after him, he took off and ran . . . jumped out the window and the officers below took him . . ."

3. If Johnson had run with the president in 1988 or 1992, he "would have won a convincing victory," Smith said. But "we would have lost anyway in 1984," he said.

4. Frazier also said: "We need to be very aggressive marketers (of American agricultural products). We need to be very aggressive salesmen. We have not been."

5. With Patrick Leahy (D-Vt.) as his Senate counterpart instead of Jesse Helms (R-N.C.), "the Democratic philosophy for agriculture will be given a higher priority," Anderson predicted.

6. He said that philosophy advocates funding "the necessary tools" to help farmers survive but not "just throwing money at the problem."

7. For Smith's latest venture, Jones said, "there is reasonably broad appeal. There may even be broad appeal. I think they have between a fairly good and an excellent opportunity."

EXERCISE 6-20

These paragraphs are examples of extended quotation. For a full discussion of extended quotation, see "News Writing," Chapter 9, pages 169 and 170.

Are these examples acceptable or not acceptable according to the guidelines in "News Writing"? Indicate your choice — to accept or not accept — by writing A or NA in the blanks at the right.

1. "As far as I am concerned, there's no such rule. I have to wonder about the motivation for this thing. It's a phony issue," Smith said.   _____

2. "I just walked away," Jones said. "It was easy to walk away. I had some personal problems at home to take care of."   _____

3. "As far as I am concerned," he said, "the company's probably doing it. I know our people aren't."   _____

4. "In order for classes to be on a full schedule, it was necessary to consolidate the smaller classes and eliminate some class offerings," he said. "This, in turn, reduced the number of teachers needed."   _____

5. "Farmers know how to deal with them, but your average backyard gardener is unprepared. I certainly wouldn't advise homeowners to spray either, because most of them don't know what they are doing," he said.   _____

6. "We've seen one good hit out there. I think you see by the empty seats that the fans are disgusted," Lesinski said.   _____

7. "I think it's terrible so far," a fan said. "They might just as well forget it. You're watching second-rate football but paying first-rate prices."   _____

8. "Frankly," Snyder said, "if the duck season were any better, I'd be hunting instead of sitting here. This game is the worst I've ever seen."   _____

9. "What happens to the complex doesn't affect our decision," Smith said. "We purchased the land in 1992. It's an excellent location and we plan to build in the future. But we have not decided just when."   _____

10. "He was selfless but ambitious. He felt strongly about a lot of things, but he never took it out on people," Armbruster said.   _____

Number Correct _____

Student _____

EXERCISE 6-21

This is an exercise in punctuating quotes within quotes. The words "hard to please" in these sentences are a direct quotation and should be enclosed in quotation marks. Make no other changes.

1. He said that the attorney general is hard to please sometimes.

2. He called the attorney general hard to please.

3. "The attorney general is hard to please," he told reporters.

4. Smith said the governor considered himself hard to please.

5. He told me the attorney general is hard to please.

6. "The governor says he's hard to please," Smith said.

7. "My opponent is being unfair," the attorney general said. "He said I am hard to please. I am not hard to please."

8. "I said he is hard to please and I meant it," Smith said.

9. Is the attorney general hard to please or not? people asked.

10. Editorials asked why the attorney general is hard to please.

11. Readers asked, "Is the attorney general hard to please?"

12. The attorney general said the governor is hard to please, too.

13. The lieutenant governor said Monday that both the governor and the attorney general are hard to please.

14. "They are both hard to please," the lieutenant governor said.

Number Correct _____

Student _____

EXERCISE 6-22

Verbs have been called the muscle of good writing. These sentences need a little more muscle. Rewrite them. Try to use a strong and vigorous verb. For example:

Weak   The economy experienced a quick revival.

Better   The economy revived quickly.

1. The governor cited a failed attempt in the legislature last year to create another state holiday.

2. He said that the school had made several accomplishments during his tenure as dean.

3. The Carolton VFW Post held an installation of officers Monday.

4. A two-car accident occurred Tuesday on Highway 30. Both drivers were injured.

5. John Baker pleaded guilty to speeding charges and received a $10 fine.

6. In a holdup Monday night, about $100 was taken from the cash register of the History Village Inn by an armed man.

7. An election was held Monday night in Carolton. Mayor Henry Clay Smith was re-elected.

8. Police are making an investigation of the bank robbery.

9. In an outdoor ceremony Monday, Mary Jones and Henry Simon were united in marriage.

10. Police have begun an investigation of what they called financial irregularities at the Carolton Country Club.

Student _____

141

EXERCISE 6-23

These sentences are defective. Delete *there is/are* or *there was/were* and revise
the sentences as necessary.

Weak   There were 82 cases reported during the school year.

Better   Eighty-two cases were reported during the school year.

1. There were 83 doors and windows found open.

2. There is already very little brain activity detected.

3. There are still some common interests found in the community.

4. There are several features which appeared in recent issues.

5. There are several magazines published for journalists.

6. There are also feature stories that profile women journalists.

7. There are also some features that do not appear in every issue.

8. There was a holdup Monday night in which $100 was taken.

9. There were some money managers who were quick to cash in.

10. There wasn't a lot of progress being made in the search, a police
    official said.

EXERCISE 6-24

Edit this news story. Correct errors in style. Use standard editing marks and practices. Do *not* rewrite or revise. There may be errors in spelling, grammar, usage or punctuation.

01   A Northwest college faculty member has been awarded

02   the coveted Mark Twain Prize for his history of the

03   Korean War.

04   Albert H. Sawyer, Jr., professor of history will

05   accept the award tomorrow in Charlotte, North Carolina.

06   Sawyer's history, The Forgotten War, was published by

07   the Northwest College Press. More than 4000 copies have

08   already been sold according to Miss Helen Wood, general

09   manager of the press who will accompany Sawyer to

10   Charlotte tomorrow.

11   Sawyer lives with his wife, two sons, and three

12   daughters at 640 East Nevada Ave.

13   Sawyer will be guest of honor at a reception in Old

14   College Hall on campus, Monday, at 4:30 P.M.

15   On Tuesday he will give the keynote address when the

16   Washington County Historical Society meets on campus.

17   The title of his talk is Wandering Through History.

18   Some two hundred historians are expected for the

19   meeting and Mayor Henry Clay Smith has designated next

20   week as "History Week" in Carolton.

21   Smith called Sawyer a likable chap but said that he

22   tends to exagerate things.

Number Correct _____

Student _____

EXERCISE 6-25

Edit this news story. Correct errors in style. Use standard editing marks and practices. Do *not* rewrite or revise. There may be errors in spelling, grammar, usage or punctuation.

01   The first of fifty-seven families whose homes are

02   sinking into a reclaimed swamp has been awarded more than

03   $400,000 in damages in a lawsuit against a local

04   developer.

05   The suit had asked for a million dollars in damages.

06   A jury in municipal court deliberated for more than

07   nine hours yesterday before informing judge Carol Brown

08   that it had reached a decision.

09   There are 7 other plaintiffs. They seek damages

10   ranging from $4000 to $63,000.

11   Many of the houses in Forest Lawn estates, a 105 lot

12   subdivision were built in the late 1960's.

13   Yesterday's verdict settled the claim of Harry and

14   Mary Johnson, 260 Washington Rd., whose two story home

15   settled and collapsed over a two month period in 1988.

16   Mr. Johnson is an insurance salesman with an office in

17   the Jollity building.

18   He is president of the Forest Lawn Neighborhood Assn.,

19   a member of the Northwest College Alumni club and father

20   of an 8 year old son by his 1st wife.

21   Mrs. Johnson teaches high school English and History.

Number Correct _____

Student _____

7 Hard News

Spelling

predator, dumbbell, sizable, salable, vacuum, picnicking, parallel, minuscule, miniature, inaugurate, embarrassment, admissible, innocuous

Usage

ravage/ravish, relic/relict, rend/render, delegate/relegate, doctoral/doctorate, complement/compliment, connote/denote

Newsroom Vocabulary

obit/obituary, second-day lead, breaking news/spot news, itemizing lead, wire, Fourth Estate, Guild/Newspaper Guild, reporter, legman, stringer, FOI/FOI Act, nut graph

149

Some Hard-News Stories

These topics are treated in detail in George A. Hough 3rd, "News Writing," fifth edition:

Chronology
Chapter 11, "Some Hard-News Stories," pages 206 through 210.

Obituaries
Chapter 11, "Some Hard-News Stories," pages 220 through 230, and model stories, Figures 11.6 and 11.7 on pages 223 and 224.

Itemizing Leads
Chapter 11, "Some Hard-News Stories," pages 213 and 214.

Libel
Chapter 10, "Legal and Ethical Considerations," pages 189 through 192.

Ethics and Professional Standards
Chapter 10, "Legal and Ethical Considerations," pages 181 through 202.

Attribution
Chapter 5, "Writing the Story," pages 82 through 85.

Hyphens
Appendix B, "Newspaper Grammar and Punctuation," pages 414 through 418.

EXERCISE 7-1

You were covering the police beat this morning when you were told about the rescue of a child who had fallen into the river. Write the story for tomorrow's paper.

From the report at police headquarters:

Boy saved from drowning this morning. Taken to Carolton General Hospital. Name: Mitchell Stephenson — age seven. Parents: William and Deborah. Address: 125 Indian River Place. Mother said boy had been playing near river.

From Carolton General:

Mitchell is in good condition. He will be held overnight for observation.

From Mercy Ambulance Service:

Ambulance and paramedics went to Indian River Place about 9:40 this morning. Took boy to Carolton General.

From (Mrs.) Kathy Gibbs:

I live next door. I heard Debbie scream and saw her run down to the river. I followed her. When I got there, she had pulled him onto the bank and was trying to bring him to. I'm not sure he was breathing.

From Mrs. Stephenson:

I was so nervous I couldn't do a thing. Kathy tried, too, but we weren't getting anywhere until John came.

From John Gibbs:

I followed my wife. She and Debbie were trying mouth-to-mouth resuscitation, but they weren't doing too well. I was a medic in the army, so I took over and got him breathing again.

From Russ Reimenschneider, Mercy Ambulance paramedic:

Mr. Gibbs saved the boy's life. If he hadn't known how to give mouth-to-mouth, the boy wouldn't have made it.

Verify names and addresses. Use direct quotes to help carry the narrative along.

EXERCISE 7-2

You were covering the police beat this morning. From the desk sergeant in the robbery squad office, you picked up the following facts:

```
Armed robbery — 8 last night — O'Malley's Restaurant and Bar
— $250 taken from cash register —

Restaurant owner — Floyd Scissors — age 38 — lives at 104
1/2 North Calhoun — shot in upper left thigh — taken to
Carolton General by police ambulance —

No one else hurt — restaurant busy at time — 50 to 60 people
eating dinner — plus the restaurant help —
```

Scissors gave police his account of the shooting this morning:

```
Man walked in and ordered dinner — finished his meal — came
up to cashier's counter — showed a revolver — told me quote
if you make any fuss, I'll kill you unquote — said he wanted
the money from register — I handed it over — man ran to door
— he looked back at me and fired one shot — hit me in the
leg — I don't know why he shot me — I didn't do a thing —
just gave him the money
```

The desk sergeant also tells you:

```
Description of robber: male — white — 25 to 30 — medium
height — blond hair — bushy mustache — wearing black leather
jacket — red and black running shoes —

Lt. Maher is in charge of the case — he called the hospital
a few minutes ago — Scissors is in good condition — resting
comfortably — a .38-caliber bullet removed from his leg this
morning and leg set — bullet had caused compound fracture of
the femur —
```

EXERCISE 7-3

The Record's city hall reporter called you with a story about a program to be held tomorrow night at the Adult Center:

```
Topic:       Alcoholism and the Elderly.

             How to recognize the signs and what to do.

Speaker:     Henry Burt, staff, Substance Abuse Program,
             Carolton General Hospital.

Time/place:  Adult Center, Room 210, 8 p.m.
```

EXERCISE 7-4

You were on the police beat today, where you picked up a story on a rape report. You learned:

From police desk sergeant:

```
Woman taken to Carolton General by police ambulance. Treated
and held for observation —
```

From Nancy Chin (police sergeant/women's bureau):

```
Victim — female — age  17 — was taken to hospital from her
apartment at 412 South Grant — multiple stab wounds — largely
superficial — I talked with her and she saw a counselor from
the Crisis Center —

Said she was asleep when a man woke her — held knife to her
throat — raped her — then stabbed her several times —

Said she fainted — came to and called 911 —

She describes assailant as white, about 30, around five ten
and weighing around 175 —

She didn't give a very helpful description of his clothing.
```

From desk sergeant in women's bureau (reading from crime reports):

```
Woman's name is Sally Kershaw.
```

You verify name from student directory. However, you have a dilemma. Should you report her name?

EXERCISE 7-5

You were covering police this morning. After checking at police headquarters, you stopped at the Central Fire Station and learned:

```
Fire about four this morning at 210 West Main. Smoke damage.
Electrical wiring burned out. Damage estimated at $6,500.

Cause given as quote faulty wiring unquote.

One pumper responded. Returned to station 4:45.
```

Remember, early estimates of damage and first thoughts about the cause of a fire may change after fire officials have had time to investigate. You should attribute opinions, even informed opinions. In this story, attribute to *fire officials*, since your information comes from official fire department records.

EXERCISE 7-6

When you stopped at the Carolton state police post this morning, you were told about a couple of drug busts last night. You talked with state police Lt. Jack Toy, head of the narcotics squad, and he told you:

In the first case, we're holding these men:

     James Earl March, age 26, St. Louis, Missouri
     John Lambert, age 24, East St. Louis, Illinois
     Harry Rogers, age 30, Kansas City
     Joseph Flag, age 27, Kansas City

Being questioned now. Expect to take them to county court this afternoon for arraignment. Charge will be possession of controlled substance with intent to distribute.

Arrest made by state police trooper Walter Hickok — on highway patrol — saw car pulling a boat trailer — trailer had no tail light — stopped car — checked car and trailer — found seven burlap bags of marijuana in boat — haven't been weighed yet. No estimate of street value.

Arrest was on U.S. 210 east of the city.

Another arrest on drug charges:

A Colombian national, Luis Calderon Carbajal, arrested at airport last night. Coming here from Mexico City on Capital Airlines flight. Customs agents found 2.2 pounds of heroin in his luggage. He is being held for questioning. He is at the county jail.

On second reference, refer to the Colombian as Calderon. Avoid police jargon. Find another word for *bust*.

You will have to write your story without waiting for details on the arraignment. Your city editor wants to get the story to the Associated Press right away. You can write an insert on the arraignment later.

EXERCISE 7-7

You were on the police beat today. One of your responsibilities on this beat is to cover the fire department. In checking with the fire department, you got a story about a fire in an apartment complex. The facts:

```
Fire at 347 West Arizona avenue this morning. Rubbish fire
in basement storeroom. One pumper and a ladder truck
responded. Alarm at 8:45. Equipment returned to central
station at 10:05.

Fire Lieutenant Jacob Strauss says building was filled with
smoke when firefighters got there. Some residents had left
their apartments and were standing outside in the parking
lot. Firemen went through the building and got the rest
outside.

Building pretty clear of smoke when they left the scene.
Occupants were able to go back in.

Strauss tells you it wasn't much of a fire. Maybe $1,500 in
damage to storeroom in the basement where fire apparently
started. Occupants may have some loss from smoke damage.

Fire marshal Clayton Evans assigned to investigation.
```

You ask Strauss about the building, and he tells you it is a 24-unit building. Three stories. Occupants are mostly elderly.

EXERCISE 7-8

There was a robbery this morning at the First National Bank, and since you were free at the moment, your city editor sent you to cover the story. At the bank, you talked with police, bank officers and witnesses:

From Detective Lieutenant John Begg of the robbery squad:

```
We've got an alarm out for the robbers — three men — two were
young — maybe twenty-five — third man was in his 50s — all
three medium height — slender — put on ski masks after they
entered the bank —

They left in a 1991 Toyota wagon — dark blue
```

From Mrs. Rita Hoffman, vice president of the bank:

```
I was with a customer at my desk. I looked up and saw a man
with a mask on pointing a gun at me. He said quote this is
a holdup unquote. I thought oh my god, this is it.

I saw three men. They ordered everybody to stand over against
the wall. They made me and my customer go with the others.
I think the older man was in charge. He held the gun on us.
```

continued on next page

From Mary Sue Wang, a bank teller:

```
I saw them when they came in. One had a can of spray paint
and squirted it at the camera. They were putting those masks
on as they came across the lobby. Scared? You better believe
I was.
```

From John Ashford, a bank teller:

```
I saw them in time to trip the silent alarm. One of them
jumped over the counter and grabbed the cash from the
drawers. The other went into the vault. They had canvas bags
to put the money in.
```

From Kenneth Stieber, 822 E. Nevada, an insurance agent:

```
I was in the bank to cash a check. It was over pretty fast.
They seemed nervous. The guy with the gun, his hands were
shaking. He had, I think, a .45 automatic.
```

```
We were facing away from them, but I could see a little in
a mirror on the wall at my left. The guy with the gun seemed
to be in charge. They hadn't been in the bank more than three
or four minutes when he yelled at the others to hurry. He
said quote let's get out of here unquote and they ran out
the door.
```

From Maurice Henderson:

```
I was just going into the bank when they were coming out.
They grabbed me and took my car keys. I'd parked right in
front of the bank. They jumped into the wagon and took off.
I sure hope I get my car back. It isn't paid for yet.
```

From Lieutenant Begg:

```
The alarm was sounded at 9:17. Uniformed officers in a scout
car got to the bank at 9:25. There were about a dozen
customers in the bank during the robbery and eight bank
employees. Nobody hurt. Several customers frightened and
upset. Others just angry. Quote robbers were amateurs, I
think unquote.
```

```
Spray paint did not cover camera lens completely. It may be
possible to identify the robbers — if the camera caught them
before they put on their masks.
```

From Mrs. Hoffman:

```
Robbers got about $100,000 — all bills — mostly $5, $10 and
$20 denominations.
```

You're writing this for page one, the city editor tells you. You've got some good quotes and some action here. Make it good.

EXERCISE 7-9

You answered the phone this morning when the Riley funeral home called with an obit. Write it for tomorrow's paper.

Deceased is Carolyn (Robb) Dwight. Born Nov. 1, 1920. Died yesterday at Holy Cross hospital.

Born in Winchester, Virginia. Came here in 1946 as a social worker with county welfare department. Worked later for county Council on Aging. Retired in 1985 as director of the agency. Served on the boards of the Family Counseling Center, American Red Cross and Salvation Army.

Graduate of Michigan State University school of social work.

Member All Saints Episcopal church, Washington County Democratic Women, National Organization for Women, Carolton Country Club. She was a veteran of WW II. Served in Europe with the Women's Army Corps.

When she retired she was honored at a dinner given by the Council on Aging. Mayor Smith said of her quote Mrs. Dwight has done a remarkable job in developing the Council (on Aging) — the city owes her a great deal for her work on behalf of the elderly unquote.

Services tomorrow at 10 a.m. at All Saints. Rev. Evers to officiate. Burial in Evergreen cemetery.

Survivors: husband, Robert, assistant general manager of Kelly Construction Co., sons, Robert, Jr., Newark, New Jersey, James, Williamsburg, Virginia, a daughter, Marion, Carolton; and a nephew, Harold Robb, Dothan, Alabama.

Funeral home said cause of death was cancer.

EXERCISE 7-10

You were in the office this morning when the Record's police reporter called in with an accident story. She told you:

One-car accident. Driver either drunk or asleep. Car went off road and hit a tree. Total loss.

Driver taken to Carolton General by Mercy ambulance. He is being held in the police ward.

Accident on Highway 30 about three miles southwest of the city near junction of 30 and County Trunk D.

continued on next page

No witnesses. Deputy Sheriff Larry Tate was on traffic patrol and spotted the car. Found driver near the car.

Tate says driver seemed dazed. Thinks he may have been drinking. Expects to ticket him for DUI.

Driver: Robert Willoughby, age 22. Lives in Carolton. Address 234 River Road. He has lacerations and contusions. May have a concussion.

———————

DUI, of course, means driving under the influence of alcohol. And from your own knowledge of police procedure, you know that the police ward at Carolton General is a locked ward where prisoners are housed.

EXERCISE 7-11

When your editor looked over your weather story (see Exercise 4-3), she asked you to get a little more on the house fire and write it as a separate story.

You have all that the fire department records show, so you call the Buchanans. Mrs. Buchanan tells you:

My husband and I had just gone to bed. It was raining hard and there was a lot of lightning. Suddenly there was the most awful clap of thunder and everything lit up like daylight. Then we smelled smoke and realized that the house had been struck. Harry went up in the attic and looked around. The attic was full of smoke so we were pretty sure the fire was somewhere up there or in the roof.

I ran to the children's room and got them up. Harry called the fire department from the kitchen. We got the car out and parked it in the street and sat there until the fire trucks came. The fire was in the roof at the back of the house. The firemen weren't here very long. We went back to bed about one. The house still smells a little smoky.

You ask about the extent of the damage and are told:

We've called a contractor to come look at it. I don't think there's much damage, but we'll know when we get an estimate for repairs. Harry checked this morning and our insurance will cover it.

———————

Write your story. Don't be misled by the amount of information you have. Be concise. Are you aware of the difference between *damage* and *damages?*

EXERCISE 7-12

You were in the office this morning when Door Brothers called with an obit. Write it for tomorrow's paper.

Deceased is Mrs. Esther (Keezing) Gold. Died early this morning at home. Born January 11, 1918, in Germany. Came to this country in 1933. She had lived in Carolton since 1948.

Husband: Morris Gold. They were married in 1946.

Two children, Harold, Carolton, and Dr. Ruth Gold Wells, Chicago. One brother, Charles, Palm Beach, Florida.

There are five grandchildren and one great-grandchild.

Member: Carolton Jewish Congregation, Hadassah, National Council of Jewish Women, National Women's Committee of Brandeis University, B'nai Jacob Sisterhood. Was on the board of the Carolton Public Housing authority.

Services tomorrow at Door Bros. at 4 p.m. Burial in Evergreen cemetery.

EXERCISE 7-13

Riley Brothers Funeral Chapel just called with an obit. Write it for tomorrow's paper.

Deceased is John Souza. Died this morning at Holy Cross hospital. In ill health for some time. Born June 19, 1908, in Funchal, Madeira. Came to this country as a child.

Attended public schools here. Foreman with county highway department forty years. Retired in 1978.

Communicant at St. Thomas church here. Member Holy Name Society. Member Carolton Senior Citizens Club.

Veteran of WW II. Served in army in Europe. Awarded bronze star and purple heart medals. Member Carolton VFW post and American Legion.

Wife, Mary (Costa); sons, Albert, Louis, Donald, Joseph, all of Carolton; a daughter, Linda, Monument Beach, Massachusetts; a sister, Mary, Tampa, Florida.

Funeral mass day after tomorrow at 11 a.m. at St. Thomas. Father Flynn will say the mass. Burial in church cemetery.

EXERCISE 7-14

While you were in the office today, your city editor asked you to get the details on the fatal accident on the river yesterday. You checked with various sources and found:

From the coroner's office:

Name of the dead girl is Kim Clarke. She was brought to the county morgue from Receiving hospital. Records show she died at 12:30 this morning. There will be an autopsy.

From the sheriff's office:

Accident happened about 6 yesterday afternoon at the boat dock on the Indian river west of Airport road. Rescue squad from the Carolton fire department was dispatched to the scene. Fire Captain Jack Hope may have more information. Talk to Deputy Medford.

From Captain Hope:

Rescue squad scuba divers found the girl in 20 feet of water near the boat dock. She probably had been underwater for 20 minutes. Rescue squad paramedics worked on her — CPR — then took her to Receiving. She was unconscious when they put her in the ambulance.

From Deputy Sheriff Jack Medford:

I was on patrol near the airport. Went right to the scene. Witnesses said the girl was climbing down a metal ladder to get into a canoe. Let out a yell. She just let go of the ladder and fell into the water.

The kids she was with tried to grab her, but she slipped underwater. The divers with the rescue squad got her out. She'd been underwater a while when they found her.

From Dr. H.L. Hirsch:

I was called a little after 6. Paramedics were working on her when I got there. I think she got some kind of electrical shock. Probably from something on the dock.

From Herbert W. Cooper, state department of natural resources officer:

We're investigating. The DNR is responsible for the park. The sheriff's people are also looking into it. If you call me tomorrow, I may have something.

From the dead girl's parents:

Kim a senior at Carolton Central. Age 18. Strong swimmer. They don't know anything at all about the accident. Kim had gone to the park with a group of friends from school.

EXERCISE 7-15

When you came to work this morning, your city editor handed you this wire story and asked you to check on it and write something for tomorrow's paper. The wire story isn't adequate, so you make a couple of phone calls to fill in the gaps:

The wire story:

> ROGERS CITY — (today's date) — Three people were shaken up but uninjured this morning when their light plane overshot the runway at the Rogers City Airport and overturned in a ditch.
>
> Treated and released at Rogers City Community Hospital were Hugh Morgan, Monroe; John Lodge, Carolton; and George A. Rogers, Carolton.

From Rogers' office at city hall:

> Rogers is in Rogers City for a meeting of the state Municipal Officers Association. He is expected back tomorrow. No one in his office has heard about the accident.

From Mrs. Rogers:

> George called me just now. He's fine. He's got a bump on his head, but nothing serious. He said he's going to the meeting and will be back tomorrow. If the plane can't fly, he said he will take the bus.

FYI: The plane belongs to the city, and you know that Rogers, who is in the Air National Guard, frequently flies it.

EXERCISE 7-16

You were asked to cover city council last night. Among other things, the council approved a gun control ordinance. Your notes:

> Ordinance proposed at last week's council meeting by John Clark. Clark responding to a petition submitted to council with several hundred signatures —
>
> Ordinance would ban possession of a firearm — or sale to — anyone under 21.
>
> Ordinance needs approval of state legislature and the governor.

Carolton is a home-rule city, and the city council can legislate in matters like this with state approval.

161

EXERCISE 7-17

You were on the police beat this morning, and after making the rounds at police headquarters, you stopped in at the public safety office on campus. You were told that Lieutenant Kelly has a case involving a group of students arrested last night.

From the desk sergeant:

These were arrested last night:

```
Richard Allen, 20, 540 S. Mead
Will Henderson, 19, 540 S. Mead
Daniel Roberts, 21, 540 S. Meade
Gregory Gould, 18, Hallowell Hall
Quimby Lawrence, 19, Hallowell Hall
Harry Matthews, 20, Hallowell Hall
```

From Lt. Sean O'Kelly:

They've admitted they cut down the big fir tree on Circle drive on campus night before last. They have been released on $500 bond each. Charge is criminal trespass.

Tree was a 30-foot fir in front of Forestry school building on Circle drive. Valued at $750. Was cut down and taken away night before last. A campus police officer found it yesterday in front of fraternity house, set up and decorated with lights.

Fraternity is the Alpha Zeta Omega fraternity house.

From Beatrice Wetherbee, assistant dean for student affairs:

The students have been referred to the student judiciary. They are pledges and were sent out to get a Christmas tree.

———————————

Write your story. Attribute carefully.

EXERCISE 7-18

You were in the office this morning when the Record's police reporter called this story in. Write it for tomorrow's paper.

Auto accident on Old Meetinghouse road near bridge. Two cars involved — accident about 2 a.m. Ambulance called at 2:25 am.

Car No. 1 — driven by Horace Gilmore — accident report gives his address as 335 W. Oregon — car had been stopped at side of road — driver was attempting to return to pavement — collided with approaching car.

Car No. 2 — driven by Branson Porter, 506 S. Sherman — heading north on Old Meetinghouse Road.

Sergeant John Talcott (Carolton police accident prevention bureau) is officer in charge of investigation. He says that Porter had been drinking. Blood test taken at hospital. Neither driver has been ticketed.

Gilmore taken to Carolton General. He has fractures of left arm and leg. May have a concussion. Possible internal injuries. Hospital says his condition critical.

Porter also at Carolton General. Abrasions and contusions. Being held for observation.

Virginia Main, 804 N. Sherman, also injured. Fractured left arm. Abrasions and contusions. Possible concussion. Held for observation.

Accident report on file at police headquarters shows Virginia Main was a passenger in car No. 1.

Report gives Gilmore's age as 45; Main, 40; Porter, 52.

No one involved in the accident has been able to give police a statement.

Attribute as appropriate. Police reports are notoriously careless about spelling of names and about addresses. Please verify all names and addresses before you write.

EXERCISE 7-19

You were on the police beat this morning. At the Accident Prevention Bureau, you picked up this story about a fatal accident last night. Write it for tomorrow's paper. Use an itemizing lead.

From accident report at police accident bureau:

Accident was at the railroad crossing on Western avenue. An eastbound freight hit a 1993 Dodge Spirit. Dragged car hundred yards before train stopped.

Four occupants of vehicle taken to St. Luke's hospital. Three were DOA.

Vehicle was going north on Western avenue.

APB officer John Talcott got a statement from the survivor. He said they all had been drinking. He was in front passenger seat. He saw the train. Thinks it was going about 40 miles an hour. Ferreira was driving. He tried to beat the train.

In the car:

        Ricky Ferreira, 16, 127 Maple
        Lawrence Carew, 17, 221 Sycamore
        Stephen Dawson, 15, 308 South Houston
        Anthony Carter, 16, 212 East Florida

Carter is at Receiving Hospital. Has abrasions and contusions, sprained left wrist, a concussion. Hospital says his condition is satisfactory.

Bodies are at Door funeral home. Talcott says there will be an autopsy.

From Ray Vanderpol at the railroad:

Crossing signals were working at the time. Train was probably going about 45 miles an hour — normal speed when traveling in a congested area. Engineer of the train, Walter Stroh, is at police headquarters to give his statement.

FYI: *DOA* is police jargon for *dead on arrival.*

EXERCISE 7-20

You were on police today. You heard about a holdup at the Holiday Inn just after it happened and went to the scene. During the morning, you learned the following:

From police officer John Chin:

The injured man was lying on the floor in the middle of the lobby when I got there. He appeared to have a chest wound. There was a lot of blood. I called the ambulance. They took him to Carolton General. I don't know his name. He appeared to be about 40 years old. He was staying at the hotel, I understand.

From Detective Willis Barke:

The desk clerk and his assistant have just given us statements. We have a pretty good description of the suspects, and hopefully we'll find them fast.

From Charles Watson:

I'm the night clerk. I go off duty at 6. It was about 10 to and Frank was just getting ready to take over the desk. I was showing him some new registrations when I heard someone come in. I looked up and there were these two guys with masks on. Ski masks, you know. One of them had a shotgun. The tall one. The other guy had a pistol. That's what he slugged me with. He jumped right over the desk and shoved us back. He hit me with the gun . . . I just went out like a light. That's all I remember till the cops were there. I'm going over to the hospital for a check. My head hurts.

From Franklin Swift:

We looked up and saw these two guys. The tall one had a rifle or shotgun. The other one is the one that slugged Charlie. He hit him, then grabbed at the cash drawer. He just pushed me, that's all. He wanted me to open the safe, but I couldn't. We don't have keys. It's locked at night. They were in a hurry. They were running back to the lobby door when this man came in off the street . . . a guest . . . I don't know his name. They just shot him and ran out the door. I don't think he really saw them. He was heading to the elevators. I called the cops.

From Carolton General:

Injured man is in serious condition. He has a gunshot wound in the upper left chest. He is still unconscious.

continued on next page

165

From Gerald Olds, manager, Holiday Inn:

The guest's name is Gerald Blaine. He checked in last night.
I think he's an engineer. From what Frank and Charlie told
me, I think he was shot by mistake. He just showed up at the
wrong time. I think the robbers reacted before they had a
chance to think. This is the first time we have been robbed.
I don't think they got more than $150. We never have much
money in the cash drawer. The night clerks don't have a key
to the safe. I open it in the morning when I come in.

From Detective Lieutenant Pinky Maher:

We have a description of the suspects. First one is about 6
two. Maybe 40 years old. Wearing a plaid shirt and corduroy
pants. The other is about 5 six. About 175, we think. Same
age, about 40. Had on a tan work shirt and pants. Wearing
army combat boots. Both had ski masks on. Both were white.

We don't think they're local. No similar descriptions from
recent holdups. Don't know how they got away.

Injured citizen is Gerald Blaine. Papers in his wallet
indicate he is 48. Home is Oak Park, Ill. He is with Great
Lakes International, Oak Park, Illinois.

From Mrs. Myrtie Watson, 107 Maple:

You can't talk with Charles. He's in bed. He doesn't feel
well. He has a headache and a big lump on his head. The
police took him to the hospital, but they let him come home.
He says he'll be all right and is going to work tonight. I'm
not sure he will. What? No, I'm not. I'm his mother.

Slug your story *holdup/page one*. Use direct quotes. Attribute carefully. There's
a lot of action here.

EXERCISE 7-21

Jenkins Funeral Home just called with an obit. Your city editor saw that you
weren't busy and asked you to take the call. She wants the obit for the first
edition of tomorrow's paper. The deadline is fast approaching.

Deceased is Mrs. Mary Theresa Marks. Born in Carolton on
December 11, 1926. Died yesterday at home. Had been ill for
some time. Husband, Peter; daughters, Mrs. Horace Meade
(June), Mary, Patricia and Ellen, all of Carolton; brothers,
the Rev. Patrick McGuire, Providence, Rhode Island, John,
Harold, Edwin McGuire, all of Carolton.

Cause of death was lung cancer.

continued on next page

Her parents were the late Patrick and Kathleen (Grogan) McGuire of Carolton.

Educated in public schools here. Bachelor of Arts from Boston college, master's of medical social work from Catholic university, Washington.

She helped establish the Holy Cross Medical Center here and served as a member of the board of the center for many years.

Member Boston college alumni society; Daughters of Ancient Order of Hibernians; Washington County Democratic Women; board of directors of Washington County historical society; Carolton Professional Women's club.

Communicant at St. Thomas church. Mass of Christian Burial will be celebrated day after tomorrow at St. Thomas at 11. Burial in church cemetery. Father Flynn to celebrate the mass.

Rosary at funeral home tomorrow night at 7.

Family suggests that memorial gifts be made to the Washington County Cancer Society.

EXERCISE 7-22

While you were in the office this morning, you took a call from Jim Riley at Riley Funeral Home. Riley gives you an obit. Write it for tomorrow's paper.

Deceased is Walter Edsel Page, 34, address 782 North Jackson. Died last night at Carolton Hospice. Lengthy illness. Cause of death pneumonia. He had AIDS.

Survivors:

Parents, John and Ethel Page, 400 East California. Two sisters, Margaret Johnson, Seattle, and Christine, Carolton. One brother, Robert, Jacksonville, Florida. His companion, Henry L. North, Carolton.

Page was an interior decorator. Had own business here. Graduate of New York University. Studied fashion, textiles and design.

An accomplished artist. Work shown recently at city hall.

He was a technical sergeant in the air national guard. Was in Middle East during the Gulf war.

Services day after tomorrow at First Methodist church. Rev. Alison Carter will officiate. Burial: Evergreen cemetery.

Family has asked that memorial gifts go to the Carolton hospice.

EXERCISE 7-23

You stopped at Central Fire Station this morning and picked up the following:

Fire early this morning — 3:50 a.m. — family burned out — several injured — fire fighters rescued parents and two children from second floor of house —

all taken to Receiving — Ivan Snook, 36, and Ellen Snook, 35 — their two children — Christian, four, and Mitchell, two —

both boys suffering from smoke inhalation — condition stable — parents have second and third-degree burns — both serious —

house gutted — cause of fire not known yet —

house is at 540 West Lexington Road — two story frame house —

———————

This story will require an itemizing lead.

EXERCISE 7-24

You took a call this morning from the Record's police reporter. She gives you the following about an incident at the junior high school:

14-year-old taken to Receiving this morning from the junior high. Bullet wounds left hand and left thigh.

Boy's name is Roger Booker. He was treated and released. Injuries not serious. An eighth grader.

Police say he had a .25 caliber pistol in his pocket and it accidentally fired.

No one else hurt. Larry Berg, school security officer, called police and for an ambulance.

———————

Write this for tomorrow's paper. In this state you may not identify by name a child under 17 years of age.

EXERCISE 7-25

You were on police today, where you picked up a story about a shooting. You learn:

From desk sergeant:

```
Victim is Jason Kirby. Taken to Receiving hospital. Gunshot
wound in left shoulder.
```

From Lieut. Begg:

```
We are holding Larry Snodgrass, age 35, Aiken, South
Carolina.

Snodgrass driving east on interstate south of city — fired
at Kirby — says Kirby cut in front of him — shot went through
driver side window — hit Kirby —

We have confiscated a .22 caliber rifle and some other guns
that were in Snodgrass's car — he was driving a 92 Ford
pickup —

We are still checking things. Have more for you later.
```

From the hospital:

```
Kirby being held for observation. Resting comfortably. Bullet
removed. Wound not serious.
```

That's all you were able to get. Write it.

EXERCISE 7-26

While you were in the office this morning, you took a call from the Record's police reporter who tells you about a holdup. Write it for tomorrow's paper:

```
robbery last night — convenience store at service station at
511 South Territorial Rd. — suspect is a black male in his
30s — six feet two — 180 pounds — wearing blue jeans, army
jack, red cap —

robbery reported by female clerk, Mrs. Henry Hall, age 40 —
says robber told her quote gimme the money, I've got a gun
unquote —

she gave him $60 from cash register — cops say there was a
similar robbery at the same location last month —
```

EXERCISE 7-27

Edit these sentences so that hyphenation conforms to the rules given in "News Writing," pages 414 through 418 and pages 440 through 442. You may also want to consult Webster's New World Dictionary. Use standard editing marks to insert or delete punctuation.

1. The expresident called the action unAmerican and said that it was unbecoming to a well known political figure.

2. The seven year old girl traveled alone on a nonstop transAtlantic flight.

3. The chairman was reelected despite the charge that he was antiintellectual.

4. "I'm 7 years old," the boy said. "And in 69 years I will be seventy-six."

5. The 11-year-old child was gravely ill but rallied when she was given an antivirus vaccine.

6. Everyone has a right to work, but in some states the right is spelled out in right to work laws.

7. The antiBritish elements in the audience booed at the speaker's off-the-cuff remarks.

8. The accused, a two time loser, was quickly sentenced to a ninety nine year prison term.

9. Northwest won 21 to 7 in the final game of the season.

Number Correct _____

Student _____

EXERCISE 7-28

Rewrite these sentences to avoid using *alleged* or *allegedly*. For example:

> The utility was fined $5,000 after the commission determined that it had *allegedly* violated safety regulations.
>
> The commission determined that the utility had violated safety regulations and fined it $5,000.

1. Police arrested the man they saw allegedly attacking two women students.

2. Police said they found that the man's alleged address was false.

3. Police said drug deals were allegedly discussed in the conversations they recorded.

4. A prisoner who allegedly fled from the county jail was recaptured two hours later.

5. John Doe went on trial Monday for an alleged attack on a guard at the county jail.

6. A nurse at Carolton General Hospital was charged with murder Friday for allegedly injecting a patient with a fatal dose of potassium chloride.

7. A 23-year-old woman was indicted Wednesday for her alleged role in a statewide drug ring.

8. The FBI has launched an investigation of alleged misuse of Family Court funds.

Number Correct _____

Student _____

EXERCISE 7-29

Edit this news story. Correct errors in style. Use standard editing marks and practices. Do *not* rewrite or revise. There may be errors in spelling, grammar, usage or punctuation.

01   Three heavily armed men burst into O'Flynn's last

02   night, robbed some 50 customers of the popular nightclub,

03   took 2 hostages, and escaped in a limousine driven by a

04   uniformed chauffeur.

05   One man was shot, apparently accidentally, during the

06   holdup.

07   John T. (Knuckles) Shonsky, state middleweight boxing

08   champion in the 1960's, is at Carolton General hospital.

09   His physician says he has a subdural (ok) hemorrhage.

10   A four man team of detectives headed by police

11   Lieutenant Jacob C. Bernstein is directing the search for

12   the holdup men and their hostages.

13   Taken hostage were Kermit Frogge, sixty, a retired

14   industrialist and the inventor of scotch tape, and Rodney

15   King, 18, an employe of the nightclub. King had worked

16   at the club for only ten days.

17   O'Flynn's is at 104 River Rd. in a renovated brick

18   mill overlooking the Indian River.

19   Harold Hill, manager of O'Flynn's, said the robbers

20   took about ten thousand dollars from club customers.

Number Correct _____

Student _____

EXERCISE 7-30

Edit this news story. Correct errors in style. Use standard editing marks and practices. Do *not* rewrite or revise. There may be errors in spelling, grammar, usage or punctuation.

01   The husband of a Carolton woman who was killed

02   yesterday in a shootout between police and a trio

03   suspected of selling drugs has asked for an inquest.

04   Dr. John E. Boomershine said he wants a complete

05   investigation into the death of his wife, Madeline, 27.

06   Boomershine is a veteranarian. He has an office in

07   the Oglethorpe building at 17 West Main Street.

08   The shooting occured in front of The Morning Reccord

09   Publishing Co. offices at 312 E. Main Street.

10   Boomershine, a "Morning Record" bookkeeper, was on

11   her way home from work. She was crossing the street when

12   the gunfire started. She was the only person on Main

13   to be hit.

14   The Morning Record Publishing Co. occupies a

15   three-story building in the heart of the city's historical

16   preservation district.

17   Dr. W.T. Door, Washington County Coroner, will

18   perform an autopsy tomorrow.

19   Carl Manners, 40, the Fla. man who was wounded in the

20   shooting is in serious condition at Carolton General

21   hospital. The police balistics lab is testing the gun

22   used by Manners.

Number Correct _____

Student _____

8 Second-Day Stories

Spelling

skillful, sacrilege/sacrilegious, permissible, miscellaneous, deity, colloquium, bizarre, awful, commitment, disastrous, lien

Usage

tenet/tenant, tortuous/torturous, uninterested/disinterested, venal/venial, couple of, type of, allege, allegation

Newsroom Vocabulary

background/backgrounder, insert, add, round-up, second-day story, update, follow, shirttail, sidebar, alive/live, kill/dead, hold

Second-Day Stories

These topics are treated in detail in George A. Hough 3rd, "News Writing," fifth edition:

Backgrounding/Tie-back
Chapter 12, "Second-Day Stories and Other Organizing Devices," page 239.

Second-Day Stories
Chapter 12, "Second-Day Stories and Other Organizing Devices," pages 236 through 240.

Follow-up Stories
Chapter 12, "Second-Day Stories and Other Organizing Devices," pages 240 through 242.

Round-ups
Chapter 12, "Second-Day Stories and Other Organizing Devices," pages 242 and 243.

Errors in Reporting
Chapter 6, "Be Clear, Complete and Accurate," pages 112 and 113.

Libel
Chapter 10, "Legal and Ethical Considerations," pages 189 through 192.

Before you begin work on assignments in this section, review these topics: summary leads, identification, attribution, obituaries, quotation, paired commas, hyphens.

EXERCISE 8-1

You answered the phone this morning when the Record's police reporter called in with a tip on a story. The city editor asked you to take it and follow up. You take the information and make a couple of phone calls to flesh out the story.

From the police reporter:

```
Police records show an ambulance run from 347 West Arizona
to Carolton General. Time: 9:45 this morning. Patient:
Harriet Ormsby.
```

From the hospital:

```
Harriet Ormsby admitted today — she is in the cardiac care
unit — no other information.
```

From Zelig Ormsby:

```
Wife has been in ill health for a couple of years — since
the fire yesterday, she hasn't felt well — she collapsed this
morning after breakfast, and I called the ambulance — she's
got a bad heart.
```

Look up the story about the fire (Exercise 7-7) and write a brief story for tomorrow's paper.

EXERCISE 8-2

While you were in the office this morning, the Record's police reporter called with word that the getaway car in yesterday's bank robbery had been found. She told you:

```
Car recovered in Green county this morning. Was parked at
side of a dirt road a mile or so off U.S. 210 about 20 miles
east of Carolton. State police have taken car to state police
station here.

Nothing yet from police crime lab. Technicians are going over
the car now.

Lieutenant Begg says a ski mask was found under front seat
that appears to match description of masks the men were
wearing when they robbed the bank.

He says he's hoping to find fingerprints.
```

You'll have to check the original robbery story before you write (Exercise 7-8).

181

EXERCISE 8-3

This morning you took calls from the funeral homes in charge of arrangements for the teen-agers killed day before yesterday in the accident at the grade crossing (Exercise 7-19). Pull the three stories together under one lead. Obituaries with biographical material and lists of survivors ran in today's paper, so the only new information is the funerals. The three services will be held day after tomorrow.

From Door Brothers:

```
Carew services — 11 a.m. at First Congregational church —
Nightingale to officiate — body will be at church from 8:30
a.m. until the services  — burial in Forest Lawn.
```

From Jenkins:

```
Dawson services — Liberty Baptist church — Duttweiller — 10
a.m. — burial in Evergreen cemetery.
```

From McKay:

```
Ferreira services — rosary tomorrow at 7 o'clock at McKay —
services at 11 — at St. Thomas — Father Flynn  to officiate
— burial in church cemetery.
```

Write your story. Provide adequate background.

EXERCISE 8-4

The Record's police reporter has called in with a follow on the robbery at O'Malley's. You recall the earlier story (Exercise 7-2) that you wrote, which was published last week. The police reporter told you:

```
Police have a suspect in the O'Malley robbery. He was
arraigned this morning in municipal court. Charge is armed
robbery and assault with a deadly weapon. He pleaded not
guilty, and Judge Hughes ordered him held for a preliminary
hearing. He's got a public defender.
```

```
His attorney asked for bail. Hughes set it at $5,000, and
Wood has no hope of raising it.
```

```
Name: Milford Wood. Age 30. No address.
```

```
I just checked at the hospital and Scissors is in good shape.
He's going home tomorrow.
```

Check the clips on the earlier story and bring things up to date for tomorrow's paper.

EXERCISE 8-5

After you had written your holdup story (Exercise 7-20), you got a call from your police reporter, who has new information about the holdup. She tells you:

Blaine just died. Hospital called Maher, who told me.

Watson is back in the hospital. He has a concussion and is being held for observation.

Swift is also in the hospital. He says his back was injured when he was shoved by one of the robbers. Hospital says he may also have a broken rib.

Cops think the robbers escaped in a stolen car. A hotel guest, Hubert Hawkins, 35, of Phoenix City, Alabama, told the hotel that his 1988 Olds is missing. He had left it parked in front of the hotel.

Police have disseminated a description of the car as well as the descriptions of the robbers.

Write a new lead on your holdup story. Slug it *new lead holdup*.

You may have to make other revisions in the story. After you complete your new lead, check the entire story over carefully for coherence.

EXERCISE 8-6

You were in circuit court this morning for the arraignment of the man involved in the drive-by shooting yesterday. Your notes:

Snodgrass charged two counts of reckless endangerment — one count attempted murder — pleaded not guilty — public defender represented — Greg Kelley —

Lt. Begg testified to arrest — says S. had quote small arsenal unquote in pickup — listed 2 9mm semiautomatic handguns — 12-gauge shotgun — .22 caliber rifle — 500 rounds ammunition —

S. on stand — says he was on way home from S. Dakota — been hunting — quote shooting varmints unquote — says he fired in self-defense — says Kirby trying to run him off road —

continued on next page

183

```
Kirby testified — passed pickup — returned to right lane —
suddenly pickup came up alongside — shot fired — only going
55 — wasn't aware of pickup until it came alongside —

Prosecutor — Boylan — asked for high bail — $100,000 —

Judge Gordon set bail at $50,000 — no trial date set.
```

Before writing your story, you check the earlier story on the shooting (Exercise 7-25) and you check with the clerk of court. Snodgrass has not made bail. He is in the county jail.

EXERCISE 8-7

You were in the office this morning taking calls from suburban and rural correspondents. A few minutes ago, your stringer from Brewster called with a fatal accident. She had just been to the sheriff's office, where she got the following:

```
Victim is Barbara Helen Johnson, age 17.

She was driving home from a dance at West Branch with Harold
Faver, also 17. Car left the road and struck a tree. Barbara
was thrown out of the car. She was dead when sheriff's road
patrol arrived. This was about one a.m. Faver was alive. He
is at Carolton General in serious condition. Multiple
fractures of both legs, possible internal injuries.

Accident was on County Trunk D about five miles east of
Brewster. Sheriff doesn't know what caused the accident.
Faver hasn't been able to make a statement.

Barbara is the daughter of Mr. and Mrs. John L. Johnson. He
is cashier at the First National Bank of Brewster. Faver is
son of Mr. and Mrs. Charles Faver. He is Brewster high school
principal. Besides her parents, Barbara has one brother, John
Jr., a lieutenant in the Marines. He is stationed at Parris
Island, South Carolina. Family is trying to reach him.

Funeral services day after tomorrow — Rev. Eli Baker will
officiate — 1st Methodist Church in Brewster — burial in
Mount Olivet cemetery in Brewster.
```

Your correspondent has no other information. Write the story. First edition deadline is approaching. Put a Brewster dateline on the story.

FYI: Brewster is the county seat of Madison County, just west of Washington County. The Record has a substantial circulation in the region between Carolton and Brewster.

EXERCISE 8-8

While you were in the office today, you took a call from the Door funeral home with a late death. You are told:

Died at hospital this morning — Harriet Ormsby — address is 347 West Arizona — No arrangements yet.

———————————

The name seems familiar, so you check this morning's paper and find the story (Exercise 8-1) that fills in a few details. You are on deadline, so write what you have.

EXERCISE 8-9

Your city editor has asked you to follow up on the Clark fatal (Exercise 7-14). You made a few calls and learned:

From the coroner:

A pathologist called in to perform an autopsy has decided cause of death was drowning. Coroner says both he and the pathologist believe an electrical shock contributed to her death.

From Deputy Medford:

Girl was knocked into the water by a shock from an electrical charge she received when she touched a metal ladder on the dock.

Not sure yet of the source of the electrical charge. Sheriff's detectives and DNR are still investigating.

Quote another swimmer said he felt a tingling sensation in the water a few seconds before the girl fell unquote.

We're pretty sure there was enough electricity running through the ladder to knock the girl off her feet.

———————————

You must provide enough background in your second-day story to fill in readers who did not see the accident story in this morning's paper.

Practice Exercises in News Writing

EXERCISE 8-10

The Record's police reporter has just called you with news that a prisoner is missing from the county jail. He tells you:

```
Prisoner apparently walked out of the jail this morning with
a group of visitors. He wasn't missed until a few minutes ago.

Sheriff says he is sending description to police and sheriffs
departments in nearby counties and expects to have the man
back in custody before long.

Description: white, five 10, 170 pounds, blond hair cut
short. Mustache. Wearing blue shirt and blue denim pants. Red
and black running shoes. Age 30.

Name: Milford Wood.

He was in jail waiting a preliminary hearing. Not armed, but
may be dangerous.
```

Check the clips for an earlier story (Exercise 8-4). You have only a few minutes to catch the first edition with this story.

EXERCISE 8-11

When you returned from lunch today, the city editor handed you a memo. It reads: Follow this up. Ormsby has been at city hall this morning, raising hell. He told the mayor the city is responsible for his wife's death.

A clipping was attached to the memo (Exercise 8-8).

You call Mr. Ormsby and he tells you:

```
She'd be alive today if the ambulance hadn't taken so long
to answer my call.

Slow service by the ambulance is directly responsible for my
wife's death.
```

You're the cautious type, so you call the Record's police reporter and ask her to check on the ambulance call. She does and tells you:

```
Police department records show the ambulance responded in 50
minutes. This is average — according to the records — for
non-emergency service.
```

Write your story. Explain the background carefully.

186

EXERCISE 8-12

Riley Brothers Funeral Home called in the Blaine obit just now, and you took the call. Write it for tomorrow's paper.

Blaine was a native of Carolton. Born here. Parents Harold E. Blaine, on Northwest faculty, professor of history, and Marilyn (Love) Blaine. Parents live at 708 West California.

Born 1946. Home was in Oak Park, Illinois.

Blaine a graduate of Central high and Northwest college. Majored in business. He has an MBA from Georgia State.

He is a veteran of the Viet Nam war. Served four years in Air Force. Released from active duty as a major. Has Air Medal and Silver Star.

After war, Blaine went to work for General Motors in Detroit. In 1988 he left GM and went to work for International Harvester. Now works for Great Lakes International in Oakbrook, Illinois, as a regional representative.

His wife, Analoyce Spaulding, also native of Carolton. They were married in 1978. They have two children: John, sixteen, and MaryBeth, age eighteen.

Blaine has two brothers, Albert, who lives in Kansas City, Missouri, and Randolph, who lives in Honolulu, Hawaii. He also has a sister, Susan, who lives in Atlanta. She is married to Belmont E. Downs.

Blaine will be buried here in Evergreen cemetery. There will be a service at the First Methodist Church the day after tomorrow at 3 o'clock. The family has always attended this church. Rev. Hardy C. Boise, the 1st Methodist minister, will officiate at the services.

The funeral director tells you that Blaine's family will be at the funeral home from seven to eight tomorrow night.

Memorials: college scholarship fund at Central high.

Other: member, VFW, Northwest College Alumni Society of Chicago, 1st Methodist Ch., Oak Park, Illinois, World Trade Club (Chicago), Chicago Press club.

Write the obit. It requires a second-day lead and must include cause of death.

EXERCISE 8-13

The Record's police reporter called in with this story. Your city editor asks you to take the call and write the story for tomorrow's paper. You talk with the reporter and learn:

```
Carolton fire department got a call at 5:45 about a fire in
a building near the airport. Fire was in the Acme Fire and
Accident Insurance Co. building. Building has six stories.
Fire apparently started in an office on first floor,
according to the fire marshal. There was smoke damage
throughout the building. Loss was substantial on first floor.
Nothing but offices on first floor.

The fire marshal thinks the fire was set. Some physical
evidence, he says. He also thinks it was a professional job.
He has the description of a man seen near the building early
this morning shortly before the fire was reported. He has
sent the description to authorities in six nearby states.

Firemen fought the fire for two hours before they had it out
and were sure it would not start up again.

Fire equipment from West Side station responded. Central
Station equipment went to scene when second alarm sounded.

Fire chief estimates damage as quote possibly hundred
thousand dollars unquote.

Night watchman named Peters turned in the alarm.

Company spokesman Harold Spizman, vice president for public
relations, says building closed today. No idea when mess will
be cleaned up and employees can return to work. Lost time
will add to fire and smoke damage loss.
```

EXERCISE 8-14

Your editor reminds you that earlier in the day you wrote a story (Exercise 5-27) about a fatal accident in which a Carolton man was killed east of the city. "Get that story back," she tells you, "and add it to the other fatal (Exercise 8-7)."

You now have two fatal accidents to handle in one story. Use an itemizing lead.

EXERCISE 8-15

A story you wrote yesterday (Exercise 7-10) about the auto accident on Highway 30 was in today's paper.

This morning your city editor had a call from a local attorney, Sue Dendramis. She was upset about the story. Roger Willoughby is her client. She has been to see him in the hospital and says your story about the accident does not jibe with the facts.

She told your editor:

```
After Willoughby was given first aid at the hospital, a blood
sample was taken at Willoughby's request. No trace of alcohol
in his blood.

Willoughby has had the flu and has been taking medication
ordered by his doctor. He says the medication makes him
drowsy. He had taken medicine just before leaving home
yesterday. He says he fell asleep at the wheel and that was
the cause of his accident.

Willoughby has been taken out of the police ward and is in
a private room. He will be released this afternoon. He has
minor cuts and bruises and a bump on the head. No concussion.
```

Your editor tells you:

```
She's talking libel and she may have a case. Drunk driving
is taken pretty seriously right now. However, I think she'll
be satisfied with a correction. Fix something up. And for
gosh sakes, don't believe everything you're told.
```

Write a correction for tomorrow's paper. Be contrite. You made the error.

EXERCISE 8-16

You took another call from the Record's police reporter and were told that she had an odd accident story that you might be interested in. Use these notes to write a story for tomorrow's paper.

```
Accident about 7:30 this morning on Airport Road in front of
the Acme building. Road is narrow here — two lanes — and fire
trucks were parked along side of the road, blocking one lane.
There's a lot of early-morning traffic on this road — people
on their way to work in the city and on the campus.

Two cars collided. One driven by John Ely, age 40, of
Madison. He was alone. Other car driven by William Sears, age
37, of rural Carolton. His son Richard was in the car with
him. Richard is ten. He was injured and taken to Carolton
General hospital by ambulance.
```

continued on next page

189

Richard's father went to the hospital with him. Boy was treated for abrasions and contusions and a sprained left knee. Released after treatment.

Carolton police accident prevention bureau officers investigated the accident. Officers arrested Ely after they found a .32 pistol in the glove compartment of his car. Pistol was loaded. Penalty in Washington county for an unregistered gun is 12 months in jail or a $500 fine or both. Police are checking to see if gun is registered.

Police also found a bundle of marijuana weighing 25 pounds in the trunk of Ely's car.

Ely is being held for investigation.

EXERCISE 8-17

This morning you were working in the office when Door Brothers called with an obit. Write this one for tomorrow's paper. It will require a second-day lead, since there was a brief story in this morning's paper about Mrs. Ormsby's death.

Deceased: Mrs. Harriet Ormsby — died at Carolton General yesterday — in ill health for some time
Survivors: husband
two daughters: Mrs. Otto Twardzynski — Carolton
Mrs. James J. Sullivan — Carolton
one son: Harold, Cincinnati, Ohio
granddaughter: Laura Twardzynski
sister: Mrs. Henry Quill — Carolton
Services: First Congregational church — tomorrow 2 p.m. with Rev. H.L. Nightingale in charge of service — burial in Forest Lawn cemetery

Other:

Mrs. Ormsby lived in Carolton all her life. Public schools, Carolton Central grad, Northwest college grad. Was a public school teacher 32 years. Retired in 1982.

Mrs. Ormsby born May 15, 1917. Member VFW Auxiliary, Professional Women's club, Carolton Senior Citizen's Organization, attended Congregational church.

Husband retired vice president of First National Bank.

You recall that she was hospitalized a day or so after the fire in the apartment building where the Ormsbys lived. She was in the cardiac care unit at the hospital. Her husband complained about delay in ambulance service when she was taken to the hospital. Because of his complaint, there was an autopsy. Medical examiner decided death was from natural causes. You can check your clips on the earlier stories.

EXERCISE 8-18

While you were in the office today, the Record's police reporter called in with a story. Your city editor asked you to take it. You were told:

```
The coroner's office has the toxicology results on the
teen-agers killed a couple of weeks ago in an automobile
accident at a grade crossing here (Exercise 7-19).

No evidence of drugs.

No report on the survivor. Hospital took blood sample but
will not release results.

Blood alcohol content of the three who were killed:

Ferreira, .11 percent; Carew, .07 percent; Dawson, .06
percent.
```

Under state law, a driver is considered impaired if blood alcohol content is .05 to .09 percent, and under the influence if blood alcohol content is .10 percent or higher. You check the clips before writing your story (Exercises 7-19 and 8-3).

You also find another story published several days after the accident, in which family members were quoted. You can use these quotes if you wish:

From Richard Ferreira, father of the driver:

```
Ricky used to drink beer at home while he watched television
with his friends. I don't think he was a heavy drinker. Just
an occasional beer. He didn't drink much away from home. He
never touched hard stuff.
```

From Frances Ferreira, mother of the driver:

```
He would have a few beers at the house. But you don't know
what they do when they are out.
```

The Morning Record has been campaigning against drunken driving, and your editor wants a complete story on this. Background your story.

191

EXERCISE 8-19

You were in the office again today and have been taking calls from funeral homes and writing obits. The last call was from the Jenkins Funeral Home with the Boomershine obit. A story about Mrs. Boomershine's death was in the paper yesterday (Exercise 5-32). Write the obit for tomorrow's paper. The facts:

Boomershine, Madeline Mary, born January 30, 1959. Services tomorrow at 11 at St. Thomas church. Father George Flynn will say a mass of Christian burial. Burial in church cemetery. Rosary at funeral home tonight at 7.

Survivors: mother, (Mrs.) Bridget Murphy, Winston-Salem, North Carolina — sister, Margaret Murphy, Ashtabula, Ohio — two brothers — Ian and Jack Murphy, North Andover, Massachusetts — husband, John E. Boomershine, Carolton — two sons, Brian, age six, and John, Jr., age eight.

Mrs. Boomershine died day before yesterday.

She was born in North Andover, Mass. Graduate of Holy Cross College. Majored in accounting. She worked here for The Morning Record.

Member daughters of the American Revolution, the St. Thomas church PTA. She did volunteer work at Holy Cross hospital.

Boomershine family lived at 386 West Nevada. They have been in Carolton five years. Came here from East Lansing, Michigan. Dr. Boomershine studied vet medicine at Michigan State.

You check with the Record's business manager and learn that Mrs. Boomershine's job title was assistant controller.

You review the clips on the shooting in which she was killed.

You check with the coroner and are told that the cause of death was a single gunshot wound to the head and that the coroner considers it a homicide.

EXERCISE 8-20

While you were answering the phone in the office today, the Record's police reporter called in these stories. The times referred to are this morning. Pull all three stories together into one story. Be concise. This is for tomorrow's paper.

8:05 a.m. Carolton police received a call from Don Waldron, 115 E. Main. He is owner of Duke's Shell Service, 511 Territorial Road. He reported that his station had been broken into during the night. A cash drawer in the station office was pried open and some change is missing. About $35. The cigarette machine was also pried open and about $50 worth of cigarettes is missing. Waldron says he can't find a .32-caliber pistol, which he keeps in the top drawer of his desk.

He thinks the back door was pried open with a crowbar. He left the station at 11 last night and locked up himself. Everything was okay then. He opened at 7:55 this morning and discovered the burglary.

8:15 Police get another call. From Jack Snell, 252 West New York. He says that his Texaco station at 585 S. Grant — at the corner of Lexington Road — has been broken into. He's on his way over there now.

8:20 Police car calls in from 585 S. Grant. Officer says he has talked to the station attendant who discovered the break. Her name is Paula Simpson. She found the back door to the station open when she arrived about 8:00 o'clock. Officer says Mr. Snell has just arrived. He closed up last night and everything was secure when he left at midnight. Snell says $100 is missing from the cash register. Ms. Simpson says she called Snell as soon as she discovered the open back door.

8:30 Desk sergeant at police headquarters says he had a call a little earlier from College Standard Service, corner Newton Road and Territorial Road, report of an attempted robbery. Call was from station owner, Jack Delnay, 202 Maple. He said that when he opened up this morning he found evidence that someone had tried to pry open the back door of the station. There are pry marks on the door and door frame, he said. Station was not broken into. Nothing missing.

EXERCISE 8-21

You took another call from the Record's police reporter. She gave you facts on a minor accident that happened this morning at the airport. Your city editor told you to shirttail it to the accident story you have been working on (Exercise 8-16).

At 9:15 there was a minor accident at the Washington county airport.

A light plane overshot the east-west runway and tipped over in a ditch.

No one was hurt. Two people in the plane.

Occupants were Marshall Parks and John O'Byrne.

First accident of any kind at the airport this year.

EXERCISE 8-22

You were in the office this morning and took a call from the Record's city hall reporter. She told you that the mayor has just signed the gun control ordinance and gave you the following:

Mayor signed the ordinance — said it was a milestone in city's efforts at public safety — said gun incident at junior high the other day one of reasons ordinance a good idea.

All council members there for signing — other city officials — some high school students — some parents.

Mayor said:

quote — this sends a message we are serious about getting guns off the street — I will sign almost any piece of legislation intended to control guns — I hope the governor and the legislature will follow Carolton's lead — unquote.

Mayor also said he is sure state will at least approve Carolton gun ordinance.

Check earlier stories on this: Exercises 7-16 and 7-24.

EXERCISE 8-23

Carolton has had a minor crime wave, if you can believe the stories published in The Morning Record: a shootout on Main Street that resulted in the death of a passer-by, a bank robbery, a couple of other armed robberies, a rape, drug arrests and even a junior high student who took a gun to school.

Your editor thinks that the Holiday Inn robbery needs a sidebar reprising the crime situation in the city and asks you to handle it.

From records at police headquarters, you learn:

```
Arrests reported since January 1:

          violent crime                  89
          property crime                326
          murder, negligent homicide     10
          forcible rape                   4
          robbery                        91
          burglary                      108
          larceny, petty theft          314
```

From FBI Uniform Crime Reports, on file at police headquarters, you find comparable national figures.

You talk with Herb Callendar, Carolton chief of police, and he tells you:

```
    I don't think crime is any worse here than anywhere else.
Sure, we have had homicides and robberies. But we are holding
our own. We have a handle on drugs and our streets are as
safe as any streets anywhere.

    We are working closely with the FBI on the bank robbery.
```

Recent crime statistics from the FBI's Uniform Crime Reports can be found in the current edition of The World Almanac.

Are Carolton crime statistics — so far this year — out of line?

EXERCISE 8-24

Revise these sentences so as to avoid the use of the present participle. For example:

> They contended the meeting was one-sided, *refusing* to participate.

> They contended the meeting was one-sided and *refused* to participate.

For a discussion of present participles, see "News Writing," Appendix B, "Newspaper Grammar and Punctuation," pages 411 and 412.

1. Fire broke out in the basement, filling the building with smoke.

2. The emphasis on rules eliminated debate, making participation a passive activity.

3. A man poured paint thinner on a woman and set her on fire with a match, critically injuring her.

4. A storm spread snow and freezing rain over the area Monday night, contributing to at least four deaths.

5. High winds and blinding snow battered the area Monday, leaving hundreds of people stranded in cars or trapped in their homes.

6. A severe thunderstorm rolled across the Carolton area Monday night, causing one pedestrian to be struck by a falling tree.

7. A freight train carrying toxic chemicals was wrecked near Carolton Monday, forcing nearly 1,000 people from their homes.

8. Spectators of all ages turned out for the parade, lining the street five deep along the way.

9. The drill team marched briskly along, stopping occasionally to perform a snappy routine.

10. The driver lost control of the car, skidding more than 100 feet before coming to a stop.

Number Correct _____

Student _____

EXERCISE 8-25

Many editors object to the offhand creation of verbs from nouns. Although this is a normal and useful way of creating words, sometimes the results are awkward. Objections have been raised to the verbs underlined in these sentences. Revise the sentences to get rid of the underlined verbs:

1. Mrs. Smith was taken to the hospital and <u>sedated</u>.

2. The television personality <u>hosted</u> a late-night talk show.

3. New technology has <u>antiquated</u> many practices.

4. The company is <u>headquartered</u> in New York.

5. The candidate <u>motorcaded</u> through downtown streets.

6. The prisoner <u>suicided</u> in his cell at the city jail.

7. Smith <u>guested</u> on the network talk show.

8. The pilot <u>messaged</u> her destination to the control tower.

9. The judges <u>medaled</u> the winners of the track meet.

10. They <u>elevatored</u> to the top floor of the new hotel.

11. Councilman Montgomery <u>motioned</u> for adjournment.

12. Jackson, a reporter, <u>authored</u> the book in his spare time.

Student _____

EXERCISE 8-26

Edit this news story. Correct errors in style. Use standard editing marks and practices. Do *not* rewrite or revise. There may be errors in spelling, grammar, usage or punctuation.

01   Two Carolton residents were injured yesterday in a

02   one car accident at Lexington Rd. and Scott Street.

03   They are:

04   Michael Blodgett, nine, of 215 S. Grant Street.

05   Helen M. Hays, 70, of 109 East Ohio Avenue.

06   The two were passengers in a car driven by Mrs.

07   Marianne Blodgett, 215 S. Grant Street.

08   Police said Mrs. Blodgett lost control of her car

09   when a bicycle ridden by Sally E. Walker, 11 swerved in

10   front of her. The accident occured at 9:00 a.m.

11   Mrs. Blodgett braked to avoid striking the bicycle.

12   Her car struck the curb and hit a 60 foot utility pole.

13   A crowd collected, but police managed to disperse them

14   before they became unruly.

15   Mrs. Hays at first refused medical attention but was

16   eventually convinced to go to the hospital. She was

17   taken to Holy Cross Hospital, treated, and released.

18   Sally Walker did not seem effected by her narrow

19   escape from injury.

20   "I'm alright," she told police Lt. James Smith, Jr.

Number Correct _____

Student _____

EXERCISE 8-27

Edit this news story. Correct errors in style. Use standard editing marks and practices. Do *not* rewrite or revise. There may be errors in spelling, grammar, usage or punctuation.

01   Walter Bettencourt, Jr., 84, former publisher of

02   The Morning Record, died yesterday (date) in

03   Bal Harbor, Florida. He had been ill for some time.

04   Mr. Bettencourt retired in 1970. He made his home

05   here but spent the winter months in Fla.

06   Services will be held tomorrow at 11:00 a.m. at All

07   Saints Episcopal Church at 680 North Jackson Street.

08   Rev. Edward E. Evers, pastor of all Saints will

09   officiate. Burial will be in Evergreen Cemetary.

10   Survivors include his wife, the former Elizabeth

11   Morley Wilson; two daughters, Anne Courtwright and

12   Mrs. John (Margaret) Cowles; a son, Walter E., of

13   La Jolla, California; and a sister, Mrs. Harriet Wills,

14   of Dallas, Tex.

15   Mr. Bettencourt attended the Lenox School and earned

16   a B.A. at Harvard college. He was a veteran of WW II.

17   He enlisted after Pearl Harbor, went on active duty as

18   a sergeant and retired from the United States Army

19   Reserve in 1955 as a lieutenant general. He was recalled

20   to active duty for ten months in the early 1960's.

21   He started his newspaper career in Chicago, Illinois.

22   He bought "The Morning Record" here in 1961.

Number Correct _____

Student _____

203

9 Speech Stories

Spelling

desiccate, accommodate, ax, phony, naive, drunkenness, questionnaire, paraphernalia, tendon/tendinitis, argue/argument, lighten/lightning, nuclear

Usage

kudos, destroy/demolish, unique, after/following, court martial/courts martial

Newsroom Vocabulary

paraphrase, Q. and A., bridge, swing paragraph, transition, editorial, editorialize, op ed, journeyman, must

Speech Stories

These topics are treated in detail in George A. Hough 3rd, "News Writing," fifth edition:

Speech Leads
Chapter 13, "The Speech Story: Leads," pages 251 through 266.

Speech Story Development
Chapter 14, "Reporting the Spoken Word," pages 269 through 301.

Quotation
Chapter 9, "Quotation," pages 157 through 179.

Panel Discussions
Chapter 14, "Reporting the Spoken Word," pages 277 through 281, Figure 14.4 on page 279 and Figure 14.5 on pages 280 and 281.

Trials, Hearings and Public Meetings
Chapter 14, "Reporting the Spoken Word," pages 281 through 285, including Figures 14.7 and 14.8.

EXERCISE 9-1

1. Using this statement and speech tag, write a Type A and a Type B lead in the blanks.

    statement: The Administration is going to see that U.S. cities get more federal aid.

    speech tag: HUD Administrator Urban T. Beach said today.

    Type A _____ (that) _____

    _____

    _____

    Type B _____

    _____

    _____

2. Using this statement and speech tag, write a Type A and a Type B lead in the blanks.

    statement: The ability to read is the most basic and essential ingredient in education today.

    speech tag: State Superintendent Harold North said here today.

    Type A _____ (that) _____

    _____

    _____

    Type B _____

    _____

    _____

    How do Type A and Type B sentences differ? Is the connector *that* essential to a Type A sentence? What is the purpose of the comma in the Type B sentence?

Student _____

EXERCISE 9-2

1. Using this statement and speech tag, write a Type A and a Type B lead. Note that the statement appears as a direct quotation. Change it to indirect and edit it to make it more concise.

   statement: I strongly believe that we in government have an obligation to monitor our own advertising as carefully as we review the advertising of the private sector.

   speech tag: Henry E. Hopgood, director of the state consumer affairs department, said here today.

   Type A _____

   _____

   _____

   Type B _____

   _____

   _____

2. Using this statement and speech tag, write a Type A and a Type B lead in the blanks. Note that the statement appears as a direct quotation. Change it to indirect and edit it to make it more concise.

   statement: I think that all Americans must be allowed to vote, even if it means registering illiterate persons.

   speech tag: Christine Harris, Washington County Democratic Committee chairman, said here today.

   Type A _____

   _____

   _____

   Type B _____

   _____

   _____

Student _____

EXERCISE 9-3

Indicate in the blanks at right whether the lead is a Type A lead, a Type B lead or neither. Use the letter A, B or N to indicate your choice.

1. The print media are alive and well and in no danger of demise, John H. Sitco said here today.   _____

2. John H. Sitco gave a talk here today about the problems of the print media.   _____

3. The print media are in no danger of imminent death, the publisher of Flags magazine told the Adcraft Club today.   _____

4. John H. Sitco said here today that the print media are in no danger of demise.   _____

5. "The Print Media: A Healthy Industry" was the subject of a speech given here today by the publisher of Flags magazine.   _____

6. John H. Sitco, publisher of Flags magazine, discussed the health of the print media here today at a meeting of advertising executives.   _____

7. The print media are in no danger of imminent demise — they're alive and well, John H. Sitco, publisher of Flags magazine, said here today.   _____

8. We should hang on to our better-educated workers and retrain those who are poorly educated, the state labor commissioner said here Monday.   _____

9. The state labor commissioner said here Monday that the state should hang on to its better-educated workers and retrain those who are poorly educated.   _____

10. The state labor commissioner discussed employment in a speech here Monday.   _____

11. "Full Employment Now" was the title of a talk given here Monday by the state labor commissioner.   _____

12. The state labor commissioner told the directors of the Washington County Chamber of Commerce here Monday that the state must hold on to its better-educated workers.   _____

Number Correct _____

Student _____

Speech Lead Form

Use this form for the lead for Exercise 9-4. Read the text of the speech in Exercise 9-4 and tailor it to this three-paragraph form.

First paragraph: a concise summary statement, a paraphrase — your own words.

Second paragraph: details that add to what was said in the first paragraph — again, in your own words.

Third paragraph: a follow-up of the first two paragraphs, with a direct quote that adds to and completes the ideas expressed in the first and second paragraphs.

```
    Charles E. Lafferty, professor of economics at Northwest

College, said here Monday that _____

_____

_____


    Lafferty said that _____

_____


    "_____

_____

_____," he said.

                        (more)
```

Student _____   213

Speech Lead Form

Use this form for another version of a lead for Exercise 9-4.

First paragraph: a concise summary statement, a paraphrase — your own words.

Second paragraph: details that add to what was said in the first paragraph — again, in your own words.

Third paragraph: a follow-up on the first two paragraphs, with a direct quote that adds to and completes the ideas expressed in the first and second paragraphs.

A Northwest College economist said here Monday that

_____

_____.

Charles E. Lafferty said that _____

_____

" _____

_____

_____," he said.

(more)

Student _____

EXERCISE 9-4

Charles E. Lafferty, professor of economics at Northwest College, gave a talk last night on employment policy. You may say that he spoke to faculty and students of the School of Business on campus. Write a three-paragraph speech lead based on this excerpt from Lafferty's speech. You may use either a naming lead or a blind lead.

Despite federal legislation that bans sex-based discrimination in employment, the female-male earnings gap remains significant and pervasive. Demands for pay equity will continue, therefore, to be heard in the courts, in the halls of state legislatures and the Congress, and at the bargaining table.

For the past two decades, the median earnings of women working full-time throughout the year has fluctuated between 57 percent and 64 percent of the median for men.

Occupation appears to account for more of the earnings gap than any other factor, and the level of pay in any given occupation appears directly related to its sex composition. Overall, "women's work" pays an average of roughly $4,000 less per year than "men's work."

EXERCISE 9-5

Write a story based on these remarks by Arnold Nguyen, director of placement services at Northwest College. He spoke at a conference of college placement directors today on campus.

A while ago, the job market was a seller's market. All you needed was a college education — almost any kind of an education — and someone would hire you.

Today, however, and tomorrow and in the 21st century, the job market has and will have a very different look.

The job market our college seniors seek to enter is competitive, it is global. It is a turbulent world where no job is secure and no job title adequately describes what the position requires.

Job seekers will require expertise that includes attributes like versatility, imagination, reliability and inventiveness. They must be committed to ideas, to the development of critical intelligence, and be willing to ask difficult questions and seek unsettling answers.

continued on next page   217

The French have a saying that the more things change, the more they are the same. Well, that's not true today. The world has changed, it will continue to change and nothing is going to stay the same for long.

College graduates who want rewarding careers in this changing, unstable job market must seek the kind of liberal education, develop the kind of attitude, the intellectual reflexes that will enable them to change and cope with change in a world where nothing is the same for more than a few months at a time.

EXERCISE 9-6

Using this text, write a three-paragraph lead for a speech story. You may write a naming lead or a blind lead.

The speaker is Aaron Blakewell, executive director of the state Chamber of Commerce. He spoke last night at a meeting of the Rotary Club.

The text:

We in the business community have got to assume more aggressive leadership if we are going to improve the nation's educational system.

Business and industry must, of course, continue to invest heavily in research and development. But business and industry must put even more dollars into education.

There's no point in developing a higher technology and a more sophisticated means of production if we won't have educated workers.

We can improve our schools and our educational system. We can have a better educated work force.

Education is a local matter. And business and industry have a great influence on the local level. Let's act now. It will be too late when we can't find qualified people for new and replacement jobs.

EXERCISE 9-7

James Vorenberg, former dean of the Harvard Law School, was on campus yesterday to give the Law Day address at Northwest College. He spoke in the LaFollette Auditorium to Law School faculty and students, but his remarks, as you can see, were directed primarily to the students. Write a story for tomorrow's paper based on this excerpt from his speech.

As lawyers, you will be the objects of admiration and cynicism. The legal profession today offers ample justification for both. One thing is clear: It needs the best you can give it. Those to whom being a lawyer is just the means to personal wealth and power may gain both, but they will miss many of the satisfactions the profession offers.

Think about yourselves as lawyers in three different, but closely related, roles.

First, you will represent people with difficulties and fears that overwhelm them and who will turn to you for help in making their way through a maze of rules and institutions. For the poor, this means confronting the landlord who will not provide heat or remove lead paint, the local welfare office that has cut off benefits or a social service agency that threatens to remove a child from a parent who lacks the knowledge or strength to fight back. Even for those who can pay a fee, the events that call for a lawyer can be intimidating — a nasty lawsuit, the potential loss of one's business, a marital breakup or trouble with a government agency. Whether you are in private practice, government or a legal service office, you will have the special responsibility of dealing with people when they are most vulnerable, and will enjoy the special satisfaction that comes from providing help when it is most needed.

Second, as a lawyer you can be an adventurer, or joint venturer with others, in seeking needed changes in laws, legal processes, the legal profession — and in society. Almost every major public issue involves law, and some of your predecessors have played heroic roles in such quests as those for racial equality, for arms control, for children's rights, for environmental protection and for international human rights. None of those issues is behind us.

Within the legal system, your generation must deal with courts that are increasingly overwhelmed by caseloads and with the need, as a matter of simple fairness, to provide legal assistance to the poor. And the legal profession itself is undergoing fundamental changes as large law firms get larger, the competition for legal business gets fiercer and pressure increases to find alternatives to litigation for resolving disputes.

continued on next page

219

Third, think of yourselves as intellectuals who bring creative abilities and imagination to the solution of difficult problems. One of the great pleasures of being a lawyer is seeing hard thinking translated into the results you are seeking for your clients. Whether you are planning a complex corporate merger, writing a brief for an appellate court or seeking to persuade a judge to place a convicted defendant on probation, you should bring to your task all the intellectual power and craftsmanship of which you are capable.

I hope your life in the law will enable you to see yourselves as respected and independent professionals. During the recent controversy about whether a lawyer must divulge a client's commission, or planned commission, of a crime, it was asked whether a lawyer is just a "hired gun." That expresses the issue too narrowly.

What is really at stake is your integrity. You will have to develop your own standards of what you will and will not do, and be ready to be judged by them. Some of the issues will be agonizingly difficult. In particular cases, you may find that the interests of a client conflict with your view of the public interest or your sense of justice. More broadly, you will have to decide to what you are willing to devote your talents.

Whether you are working in private practice or public service, in small or large offices, you will share responsibility for the processes of justice that are a measure of the decency of a society. It is only fair that you carry this responsibility, for if lawyers who build their livelihoods on those processes are not morally obliged to serve as their guardians, who does have that obligation?

Vorenberg is a rather distinguished man. Perhaps you ought to include in your story something more about his background. He's listed in Who's Who.

EXERCISE 9-8

Write a news story based on this speech by Edward T. Foote 2nd, president of the University of Miami. He spoke today to the faculty of the School of Education at Northwest College.

Higher education is becoming increasingly commercialized. Colleges and universities are big business. That much is clear. What is not clear is how they will survive as educational institutions.

Until recently, higher education occupied a special, quiet place in our culture. A college education, after all, was central to the American dream. The decade of the 1960s burst this cocoon, spun for generations by a respectful public. The developing commercialization of higher education has its roots in the politicization of higher education during those years.

Students became the focus of political resistance to the Vietnam War; campuses swirled in controversy. The older generation winced. Even without the social upheavals of the 1960s, universities would have commanded more public attention because of their swelling size. With those upheavals, they got a lot more than they wanted.

Meanwhile, higher education became a magnet for new laws and increased litigation. Such issues as affirmative action, draft registration, and faculty tenure gave lawyers a field day in academe. Federal auditors swarmed over university research accounts.

Along with Government penetration came the conviction that colleges and universities, now immensely complex institutions, were outgrowing the old ways of doing business. Computers, among a host of technological advances of the 70s, opened new worlds to educators and changed traditional management practices. Trustees, often from the arena of big business, exerted more control. Professors formed unions to win more economic power. Their innocence fading, universities flexed their own muscles in the larger world.

[In the 1980s] . . . the number of college-age students declined for the first time in a generation, a trend expected to continue into the 1990s. The shrinkage of the student market and Federal support forced higher education into a spirited search for new sources of funds, accelerating further the drift toward commercialization.

There is now a fierce competitive scramble for the available students. At a gathering of college presidents, one is likely to hear more talk of marketing techniques than of Shakespeare. Educators turn increasingly to "commercial"

continued on next page

221

practices like advertising. Universities undertake joint ventures with entrepreneurs. Scientists become rich from patents. Trustees experiment with venture capitalism.

The demand for marketable skills presses heavily on the curriculum. Threatened increasingly are rigorous courses in the arts and sciences, the core knowledge of what has traditionally been considered the educated person. Professional programs proliferate at lower and lower levels, channeling interest too early for truly educating anyone, including professionals, well.

Some changes, such as sophisticated strategic planning, are beneficial, but many are not. Temporary market conditions should not dictate the curriculum. An education is for life, for a person's last job as much as his first.

The question for most colleges and universities is not one of survival. Most are tough survivors. Education itself is not. It is a fragile process requiring not only constant attention, but deep reverence for its root principles. Among these principles is the requirement that thinkers — students and scholars — be free to experiment, create, learn, dream in their own way.

The marketplace cannot afford such short-term luxuries. Yet America cannot afford to abandon them, for long-term they are not luxuries. Learning is not to be rushed. Research leading to new discoveries takes time. Profitability is fundamentally incompatible with the essence of a university. A department of philosophy will never be profitable, but without one there is no university.

Maintaining a strong, independent system of higher education is a task too important to leave to the whims of the marketplace. This is no time to be preparing half-educated leaders or failing to invest for the 21st century, whether the challenge is cancer, robotics or a weapons system. Much needed — and soon — is a national commitment to rebuild our strapped universities, buy the necessary computers, bring our outmoded laboratories up to date, encourage our students to learn to the limits of their capacity. The commitment must include private philanthropy and collaboration with industry, of course, but it will fail if it does not also include sustained, heavy investment of public funds.

EXERCISE 9-9

You covered a speech last night on the Northwest College campus. The speaker was John B. Parrish, professor emeritus of economics, the University of Illinois. The occasion was the annual faculty and student convocation of the School of Arts and Sciences. Write about 400 words for tomorrow's paper. The text of Parrish's speech, given to you in advance, follows:

Critics argue that women, despite strong gains in the business world, have been kept out of the board rooms by continuing male prejudice. They usually point out that of the 500 largest industrial companies, only one has a woman as top executive (Katharine Graham of the Washington Post Company).

That picture may be accurate, but it hardly tells the whole story. It takes a generation for a man who starts at the bottom of the corporate hierarchy to reach the top. It has only been 10 years since women began entering the business world in large numbers. Clearly it is too early to say how far or high they can go.

But other things are changing, too. Now, when they find the ladder to the top blocked, women are increasingly leaving to start their own businesses. The estimated 20 newly minted, self-made millionaires who are women would seem to offer proof that the switch is being accomplished with considerable success.

[Former] President Reagan has called this the "Age of the Entrepreneur," and he might well have added "especially for women." Their participation in the most dynamic segment of the United States economy — small entrepreneurial businesses — is particularly impressive.

In 1960, women owners accounted for only about one of every ten start-up companies. By 1985, their share of these enterprises had risen to one in three, and if present trends continue, women will start half of all new businesses by 1995. For a number of reasons, it seems likely that the trend will continue.

First, women today exercise much greater control over the timing and number of children they have. In addition, it is now much safer to have children after the age of 30. These two developments enable women to pursue several paths — marriage, childrearing, school, a career — and to a greater extent than ever before.

Second, more women are getting college degrees, which tends to enhance upward economic mobility. In 1950, women made up about 30 percent of college students. In 1982, 52 percent of the nation's college students were women. This trend has been

continued on next page

reinforced by a shift away from the liberal arts toward business and professional training.

In addition to being better prepared, women who run their own businesses today can also find more supporting services than they could a decade earlier. Dozens of "women in business" books and magazines are now available. A number of professional associations, such as the National Association for Female Executives, have been created to provide special counseling to women.

Federal equal credit laws and changing attitudes have given women greater access to credit by making it easier for women to borrow money and to establish credit in their own names. And the activities of women's equal rights organizations, although difficult to quantify, have probably encouraged women to strike out on their own in business.

The final development that should accelerate women's participation in business involves the changing structure of the American economy. Women have been attracted particularly to service industries, which have enjoyed a robust expansion in jobs since World War II.

Women's start-up businesses will be concentrated in the service areas, thus expanding this sector even more. Most college women will marry, and have children as well as careers. Their husbands will probably also have demanding careers. These high-income, low-time families will need and be able to pay for an ever widening range of services — child care, travel, cleaning, investment and accounting — creating more demand for new service jobs and businesses.

These portents may be ironic. The high-income, two-earner families will enjoy a rising standard of living, leaving behind the poorly educated, single-earner families. The new freedom for women may create a wider spread between the haves and have-nots.

EXERCISE 9-10

Here is an excerpt from a speech given on the Northwest College campus last night by Gilbert Fite, professor emeritus of history at the University of Georgia. He was on campus to address the college's annual alumni dinner. The text:

Higher education has a function that goes beyond that of providing professional competence, however important that may be. At least we talk about those other benefits and virtues that are somehow supposed to be connected with a college education. These include such things as love of learning, intellectual growth, cultural awareness, personal

continued on next page

development and many other benefits. Indeed, if we surveyed college and university catalogues published over the last century, we could make a long list of the outcomes purportedly associated with a college education, all in addition to preparation for a profession.

I submit, however, that the true function of higher education is to foster intellectual activity and creativity. College has to do with the mind, with thinking and with a student's thought processes. It should deal with the matter of how we look at problems and how we weigh and handle evidence. A college education should be concerned with gaining perspective on ourselves and the world around us. Let me repeat, the university experience should be concerned primarily with thought, with thinking.

It is clear enough that the activities that go on in the halls of colleges and universities have greatly increased our store of knowledge, but the important question is, have we achieved greater understanding, or to put it another way, do we use that knowledge in a rational and reasonable way? Are college graduates more rational, more reasonable, more understanding, more analytical in their approach to problems, more humane, more civilized and cultured in the best sense, more decent in human relationships, and do they have a greater love of learning than those who have never had a formal course in history, literature, science or mathematics? In short, has college affected their behavior? Is there evidence that our graduates think better than non-college people?

During the years since the end of World War II literally millions of Americans have attended colleges and universities, and graduates have flooded into our society in ever increasing numbers. We are the most highly credentialed and degreed society in human history. What kind of leaven, so to speak, have these millions of college graduates provided in our society? Have they led the way toward a better political, social and economic system, and improved the standard of human relationships? Have these college graduates been an influence in raising the level of civility, refinement, reason and culture? Have they brought wisdom and enlightenment to the affairs of men? I think the answer to these questions is fairly obvious. It is mainly "no," and at the most "maybe."

College trained individuals seem to be as emotional, indeed even at times hysterical, and as lacking in rationality and reason in dealing with other people, and with various problems, as individuals who have never been exposed to higher education. They act on emotion rather than reason, which is just the opposite of what we think we are teaching in our mathematics, science, history and other courses where we apply reason to objective evidence. A decade or so ago, many college students even turned to mysticism and

continued on next page

spiritualism of one kind or another. They were more concerned with feeling than with thinking. While such people may find a certain amount of personal relief and satisfaction sitting under a banyan tree in contemplation, it is no substitute for thinking and reason.

There is, of course, nothing wrong with emotion. It is important in our lives. But as Gordon N. Ray, [former] president of the Guggenheim Foundation, wrote some years ago, "Powerful emotional responses become socially valuable only when they are combined with trained intelligence and a firm grasp of reality, and it is precisely these things that students should get from the university."

What I am getting at is simply this: Universities have become the center of a great knowledge industry, and in our highly technical society knowledge is the basis of power. The people who hold knowledge and power are mainly college graduates. But knowledge and power, uncontrolled and ungoverned by reason and by decent human values and high moral standards, are a source of terrible danger to us as a people and to a free society.

It is not enough for our universities to produce knowledge, a task at which they have been remarkably successful. They and their constituencies must point the way for the best use of that knowledge. Besides promoting reason, self-restraint, humane and civilized behavior, the University must always operate itself in promoting high moral and ethical principles. You may say that the University can only be a reflection of the society in which it operates. I say that the standards, principles and behavior on a university campus should be higher than those in the general society. Why? Because we claim to be educated. The same should be true of a society with large numbers of college graduates.

Somehow higher education needs to make a greater difference in human affairs than it has in the past. In producing knowledge we have achieved huge successes; in applying that knowledge to human relationships, in providing the leaven for a more just society, and in supplying a humanizing and civilizing influence our record is poor. This is the challenge before us. I do not pretend to know how this is to be done, but I know that it must be done. Believing in the rational approach to problems, I believe that our first task is to identify the problem. Somehow we must combine the vast knowledge that students are accumulating on campus with appreciation of, and commitment to, the highest humanistic and social values.

EXERCISE 9-11

You were assigned last night to cover the monthly meeting of the Carolton planning board, the city board that is responsible for planning and zoning. All members of the board were present: Richard Daggett (chairman), Harold Gold, Nancy Johnson, Lorraine Worthington and George Rogers. Rogers is an ex officio member.

Your notes:

```
Bob Dwight appeared to talk about his plans for a subdivision
on West Wisconsin.

Dwight wants approval of his sub/div plans: quote I don't
want to go to all the expense of submitting an application
if the board is going to turn the plan down unquote.

Sub/div will include 40 single-family, brick veneer homes on
half-acre lots — land he wants to develop contains about 50
acres — expenses mean site plans, architectural renderings
and so on.

Dwight wants a waiver to allow all the houses to be built in
one year. (City now limits building in any new subdivision
to 20 units a year.)

Worthington:   On what grounds do you want a waiver?

Dwight: Too expensive to stretch building out over 2 years.
The city needs housing now. I'd like to get this all done in
one operation.

Rogers: We've got to have some limits on growth. We can't
accommodate that many new homes in one year.

Dwight: I can't see phasing in this project. It doesn't make
any sense to do it over 2 years. If you can see your way
clear to granting a waiver, I'll include eight units of
affordable housing in the project.

Daggett: That's not going to qualify under the state program.

(To qualify for the state Housing Opportunity Program, the
number of affordable housing units in a development must be
25 percent.)

Gold: Can't you increase that to ten units?

Dwight: Can I get a waiver?

Daggett: Can we get the affordable units? Without those ten
lots, I'm opposed to the plan.
```

continued on next page

Dwight: I'll guarantee it. What kind of a guarantee do you want? I'll work with the board.

(Issue here is the affordable housing. Under state guidelines, families with incomes of $17,000 to $35,000 can qualify for five and one half percent mortgages.)

(After some discussion, Dwight says he'll include ten units of affordable housing.)

Worthington: You are suggesting five units to be sold for no more than $80,000 and five for no more than $110,000. I think that should be cut to no more than $100,000.

Dwight: I can't do it. You're asking me to lop $50,000 off the top. That's a lot of money.

Rogers: I don't think $110,000 homes are affordable housing.

Daggett: I think we have to see a site plan and some drawings before we can do anything for you.

(No vote, but board members told Dwight they wanted to be helpful, and would be as cooperative as possible when he brings in a concrete subdivision proposal.)

Dwight: (to reporters after the meeting) I've tried to work with the board — I'll continue to work with the board — but I can't just pour money into this thing until I know where I stand.

The board told Dwight it needs to see:

> plans for improvement of the intersection of Wisconsin and Territorial road —
>
> designation of units that will be affordable housing —
>
> building plans, architectural renderings and landscape plans —

Daggett, Gold, Johnson, Rogers indicated they would go along with Dwight. Worthington holds out — says quote I'm not willing to waiver the phasing unquote.

Write your story. Your lead ought to summarize the results of the meeting. Use direct quotes where you can. Zoning is a touchy question in Carolton, so this is a story with high reader interest.

EXERCISE 9-12

You covered a speech on campus last night. Speaker was John Chancellor, former senior commentator for NBC News. Mr. Chancellor spoke at the annual convention of the state press association at the conference center on campus. Write a story based on this portion of his remarks.

Ideas need careful care and feeding, and that has never been as true as it is today. We live in a world stuffed with information, groaning and creaking under the biggest load of facts and statistics in history. Can good ideas get lost in all this? They certainly can.

It is hard these days for an idea to get a hearing — from the university or the press or a foundation. There is a clamor of ideas — a cacophony. There is intense competition for chances to develop ideas. We have reached a stage in this country where we are generating ideas at a faster and faster rate, and society's ability to deal with the flow and pay for the development of ideas is in danger of being overloaded.

Ideas, especially in the sciences, are expensive. Long ago in history, ideas came virtually without cost. Newton didn't have much of an expense account. By the time Tom Edison and Henry Ford came along, the ideas cost a little more, but not much. Yet I wonder how much money went into the discovery of DNA, which contains our genetic code. DNA itself — the acid — was discovered in 1870 in a process that cost little. It was almost 100 years later when Watson and Crick began to break the code. I wonder how much money went into that.

We need ideas more than we ever did before. Things are changing. The kind of changes we are going through requires a steady, uninterrupted supply of fresh ideas and innovative techniques. Americans are as good at that as any people in the world.

One of the challenges we face is to sustain that great momentum in the discovery of the new, in the finding of new ways to do things and make things. It's not going to be easy. It is a contest with other countries that may be decided by the end of the century. Its outcome will shape the United States in the next century.

If you want to give more background on Chancellor, he is listed in Who's Who.

EXERCISE 9-13

The School of Law is holding a conference on crime and criminal justice, and today you were asked to cover a panel discussion on gun control. One of the panelists was Ralph C. Martin 2d, district attorney for Suffolk County, Mass. Write a story for tomorrow's paper based on these excerpts from his remarks:

We have so much stricter controls, so many more checkpoints for many things far less dangerous than guns. There is no reason why we cannot do it for guns. We have meat and drug inspectors. We have pharmacies where you cannot get controlled substances without prescriptions.

At the moment we can trace guns easily from factory to distributor to dealer. But after that we have a situation where, say, it is much more restrictive to buy a gun in the Northeast, but very permissive in the Southeast. Why can't we get the federal government to ban sales to anyone who is not from that state? Why can't we get a system that would make it harder to use fake in-state IDs?

Ideologically, I could be for a handgun ban.

(He suggests making it illegal to purchase any automatic or semiautomatic firearm. He says he advocates serious, uniform national gun control.)

We have plenty of evidence that shows that carrying a gun for self-defense is an illusion. The tragedies of getting killed far outweigh the success stories of self-defense. There are few cases where a robbery failed because the person being robbed whipped out a gun. The police tell shop owners, even if you have a gun, don't pull it out if you're getting robbed. Just give up the money. I know police officers who never bring a loaded gun into their homes because they don't want their children to play with them.

But I'm not calling for a complete ban because I don't want to spend 10 years fighting a battle I don't have a chance to win, especially when all the signs say that we must do whatever we can to keep the problem from getting immediately much worse. I think the controls I've mentioned will tighten up the supply of guns to a point where we will see an effect in a couple of years.

_____

Suffolk County is metropolitan Boston, and you know from this and other things Martin said that shooting deaths are an everyday occurrence in that city. Carolton, too, is not immune. Martin's remarks should be taken seriously.

EXERCISE 9-14

Dr. Shanks of the college medical center spoke today at a conference on alcohol abuse on campus. Write a story based on these excerpts from his remarks.

I don't think we can put a stop to teen-age drinking any more than we can put a stop to adult drinking. Beverage alcohol has deep roots in our culture. No amount of talking, of slogans, of public service advertising will halt or even slow the drinking in sports bars, at cocktail parties, at football games or at fraternity houses.

Teen-agers do what adults do. They drink because they see that adults drink. They see drinking as part of the culture of the adult world they are about to enter. Prohibition didn't work for adults, and it won't work for young people. They won't wait until their 21st birthday for that first drink.

When we tell young people they cannot drink, we merely encourage secretive, excessive drinking on their part. Instead of trying to stop teen-age drinking, we must find ways to control its excesses and its results: drunk driving, alcoholism and so on.

When we advocate a no-drinking policy for young people, we adults lose our credibility. They know such a policy is unrealistic. It forces them to sneak around, to drink hard liquor rather than beer because it is concealable, drinking to excess because it is forbidden. It forces them to lie and cheat in order to drink. And they drink out of sight where they can't be found or helped.

We see the results of our failed policies toward teen-age drinking every day.

Our challenge as adults and responsible citizens is to encourage our young people, as they approach adulthood, to be responsible drinkers, to know when to stop, to know how to behave while drinking.

If we don't — if we try to make teen-agers into teetotalers — we risk making them alcoholics.

EXERCISE 9-15

You covered the state press association convention at the conference center on campus today and picked up the text of a speech given this morning by Seymour Topping, director of editorial development for The New York Times. Write something for tomorrow's paper.

Isn't it time for editors and publishers to cease moaning about the tribulations of the newspaper industry? Like all other media, newspapers have been jolted by recession, changes in lifestyles and demographics, technological challenges and fragmentation of the advertising markets. Yet somehow the lamentations of our executives about the erosion of penetration and diminishment of the fat profits of the 1980s have reverberated in the land louder than other media. Less has been heard from our spokesmen and not many dollars have been spent by our industry, in comparison to television and magazines, to promote newspaper journalism.

Our breast-beating has engendered doubts among readers and advertisers as to the viability of newspapers. We take for granted mistakenly that the public at large still recognizes the enduring institutional value of newspapers. Many of the younger generation, told nothing to the contrary, treat newspapers as media dinosaurs shortly to be replaced by computer chips. Most references to media in college textbooks, including those at schools of journalism, center on television. Who is standing up for newspapers?

Self-criticism is healthy. There is nothing wrong in confessing that newspapers have lagged in adjusting to new tastes in our society and must become more competitive. Newspapers have needed spurring. But isn't it time to speak about our strengths? We are not doing enough to remind the rising generations that newspapers are indispensable to a democratic society because they are best suited to provide a full understanding of events and issues.

We should be projecting a more complete picture of the state of our industry. Certainly, the news about the struggle of newspapers to hold and win new readers is not all that bad. Many are enjoying gains in circulation and penetration as they adapt more sensitively to the concerns of their communities. Newspapers generally are becoming more readable, accessible and relevant. The steady growth of Sunday circulation is a success story in itself. We probably must live with the reality that in the next years newspaper readership will continue to be more selective than we like. But there are new strategies in play to win younger readers. A growing number of parents, appalled by the quality of television fare, are being persuaded that the newspaper can serve as a vehicle to literacy. As the lives of the new immigrants and minorities become enhanced through better jobs

continued on next page

and higher education, there will be an opportunity for another surge in circulation. Success will turn on the initiatives taken by the nation's 1,600 dailies to improve product and delivery.

As a business, newspapers can anticipate an upturn with the ebbing of the recession. Revenues will be enhanced by new, effective techniques of customer service to subscribers and advertisers. Advertisers will continue to find the most affluent consumers among newspaper readers. Yes, we have suffered some loss of market share and there may be more slippage, but profit margins of newspapers in general remain larger than those of many other business enterprises.

In sum, newspapers are indispensable, viable and becoming more useful, but the public is not fully aware of where we stand and what we offer. Editors and publishers need to do better in reporting our story in print and on public platforms.

Write a brief sidebar to your speech story to tell your readers a little more about Topping. He's listed in Who's Who. He's been active in the American Society of Newspaper Editors, and you might find more about him in back files of The Bulletin.

EXERCISE 9-16

Using this text, write a three-paragraph lead for a speech story. Follow the format shown in the speech-story blank on page 215. You may write a naming lead or a blind lead. The speaker is Fred Courtwright III, publisher of The Morning Record. You can say he spoke on campus last night. Excerpts from his remarks:

Newspaper publishers who ignore the lessons television can teach them do so at their peril.

At The Morning Record, we are applying many of the same principles and techniques of news coverage that are being applied to television coverage of the news.

We are organizing the content of the newspaper more consistently. We are using more color and graphics. We are writing stories much more concisely.

Our readers — and they are television viewers, too — are easily bored. They are used to the quick pace and the brevity of news on television.

We have to tailor our news presentation to the needs of the reader.

EXERCISE 9-17

While you were at the state press association convention at the conference center on campus today, you sat in on a panel discussion on journalism education. Here's what one speaker, Robert Clark, a retired newspaper editor and former newspaper consultant to Harte-Hanks newspapers, had to say. Write something for tomorrow's paper.

I doubt that any editor would disagree that we want educated, well-rounded people on our staffs. We want people who can go right to work, yes, but we also want them to have backgrounds in economics and history and political science and other things that become more and more important as society generally becomes more educated and more sophisticated. This is especially true, it seems to me, in a society that relies on television for spot news, for generally superficial information about events, but that relies on newspapers to give them depth and understanding.

We need to insist on educated people in the newsrooms. If we are blind to that need, in today's world, again we run the risk of losing credibility and put ourselves in jeopardy.

The public will not accept shoddy journalism for long, in my view. I suppose trash will always sell, but it's not journalism. We all know the basics of our business. We know how to report, how to edit, how to display pictures, how to write convincing editorials. But, we need to remember the things that give us depth, give us quality, that maintain our heritage as public servants dedicated to the public good.

We have no guarantee that the First Amendment will be with us forever and ever. We in journalism hold it sacred, but a huge segment of the public is not even aware of what it is. The press does not have a divine right to exist. We must deserve our place in society and carry it out responsibly. Only then will the public feel that the press is indeed a credible, honorable institution worthy of support.

Only if we take seriously the problems that face us, and address them earnestly, can we be assured that we are playing our rightful and responsible role in a free society.

EXERCISE 9-18

Your city editor has asked you to do a round-up story for AP on the talks you covered at the state press convention. Pull together the Topping speech, Clark's comments and John Chancellor's remarks. Hit the high spots of each speaker's views. You should put a Carolton dateline on the story.

EXERCISE 9-19

You were assigned to cover a public hearing last night at city hall. The hearing concerned a proposal to establish a wildlife refuge along the Indian River near Carolton. You took copious notes and picked up copies of materials discussed at the hearing. Write a detailed story for tomorrow's paper. There has been very little in the paper on this, and there is wide public interest in environmental protection.

Your notes:

```
All council members and mayor present — mayor presided —
about 150 people in audience — meeting lasted until after
10 —

Proposal by US Fish and Wildlife Service —

   3,200 acre wildlife refuge — both sides of river — partly
in Washington county — partly in Franklin and Madison
counties —

   about 1200 acres already protected — conservation
easements or public ownership —

   agency would purchase other lands or accept conservation
easements —

   no funds available for this now — agency will ask Congress
for funds next year —

   proposal explained by Carl Melberg and Mary Varteresian,
US Fish/Wildlife — from Washington/DC —


Comments from various speakers:

   (Melberg) — only 500 refuges in US — quote I think this
is a wonderful thing for Carolton and this part of the state
unquote

   — refuge will bring people to the area —

   (mayor) — city owns land within boundaries of proposed
refuge — holding for future well sites — quote a protected
well site fits in with our plans unquote —

   (Herbie Cooper/state dept. nat resources) — quote a unique
project because so much of land in this area already
protected unquote — refuge only adds to value of state park
on the river —
```

continued on next page

(George Rogers) — county owns lot of land in refuge area — county funds for protecting and managing land are limited — quote will fish/wildlife help out with management costs of county lands unquote

(melberg) — quote we'll work out management plans and help you out in any way we can unquote —

(John Clark) — quote I'm member rod and gun club — what you are proposing and what we've been doing is certainly compatible —

(mayor) — several local groups own land in the refuge area — Rod and Gun Club — Carolton Beagle Club — quote the groups have the same goals as F/W service unquote

(varteresian) — quote our mission is to protect this large area of the river watershed — we'll enter into cooperative management agreements with land owners to manage the area — our goals same as yours — protect the watershed unquote

(melberg) — schedule calls for F/W to draft an environmental assessment by end of year — quote we'll take this to all the people who own land in the area unquote
F/W will hold public hearings as plan is developed — quote hopefully we'll be able to start buying land by end of next year unquote

(varteresian) — quote if someone owns land and they don't want to sell, we won't bother them — we do have right to condemnation — but we won't use it unquote

(rogers) — refuge will take a lot of land off the tax rolls — have an effect on county budget —

(melberg) — F/W will pay county money in lieu of taxes — rate of 3/4 of 1 per cent of property's assessed fair market value —

(Sue Dendramis) — quote I think state will support this plan — state natural resources dept already has land here — and state has new laws to protect watersheds — improve water quality of state rivers unquote

[She is referring to the Indian River State Park.]

(John Gibbs) — owns land on river — quote support this plan — will improve property values — many other benefits to county and city unquote

(Virginia Main) — quote to me it sounds like a great project but public usage is important to people here — what access will public have to the refuge — what about hunting — unquote

236

continued on next page

(melberg) — F/W won't ban hunting on any lands where hunting is permitted now — we certainly want trails and paths through the refuge — quote these points will have to be worked out as the plan progresses unquote

[mayor and rogers both indicated they want some guarantee of public access]

(mayor) — quote public access is very important to us unquote

(mayor asks melberg what city can do to support plan)

(melberg) — write congressmen — certainly enlist support of Sen. Higginbottom —

(varteresian) — F/W does not have a lot of money — will need support in congress — quote F/W is trying to do more with less money and less people so that involves cooperation with others unquote

(main) — quote I recommend that the city be a strong player in this unquote

(mayor) — the city will support this project unquote

No one spoke against the plans for a wildlife refuge, and the mayor told you after the meeting that he's sure council will endorse the plan.

You know those who spoke: Mrs. Main is on the board of county commissioners; Rogers is county auditor; Clark is on city council; Cooper in charge of state Department of Natural Resources office in the county; Miss Dendramis represents Carolton in the legislature; Gibbs lives near the river and is chairman of a neighborhood property owners association.

As you know, public hearings don't always produce concrete results. This one was held to provide information and to get some feedback from the public. As usual, most of those who spoke were either public officials or directly concerned with the impact of the proposed refuge.

Miss Varteresian has a little trouble with grammar — *less and fewer.* Should you clean up her quote? What about Melberg's use of *hopefully?*

[Copy of the F/W proposal you picked up at the meeting has a map showing proposed refuge southwest of Carolton. It will abut the state park on south and west. About one third of the refuge will be in Washington County.]

Write your story.

EXERCISE 9-20

Many editors object to the off-hand creation of verbs from nouns. Although this is a normal and useful way of creating words, sometimes the results are awkward. Objections have been raised to the verbs underlined in these sentences. Revise the sentences to get rid of the underlined verbs.

1. Smith authored the novel "Home in the Islands."

2. He said the college would be glad to host the conference.

3. The members balloted for a new president.

4. Smith, as president, chairmanned the meeting.

5. The theater company repertoried through the state.

6. The strike settled, the company and union inked a revised contract.

7. Smith shared custody, so he parented only on weekends.

8. The bride chose a single color to theme her wedding.

9. The candidates handbilled the entire city.

10. The senior class dance featured the music of Stan Jones.

Number Correct _____

Student _____

EXERCISE 9-21

Eliminate the *redundancies* or wordiness in these items. You may X them out on the typewriter, draw a line through the unnecessary words, or write or type a revision in the space at the right. Some of the items may be acceptable as written.

1. tendered his resignation   _____

2. told her listeners that   _____

3. was able to escape   _____

4. was taken to jail   _____

5. once in a great while   _____

6. on one occasion   _____

7. went on to say   _____

8. in the near future   _____

9. at the present time   _____

10. united in holy matrimony   _____

11. brought to a sudden halt   _____

12. at that time   _____

13. all of a sudden   _____

14. is of the opinion that   _____

15. gave its approval   _____

16. in the event that   _____

17. refer back   _____

18. canceled out   _____

19. another alternative   _____

20. made an investigation of   _____

Number Correct _____

Student _____   241

EXERCISE 9-22

Edit this news story. Correct errors in style. Use standard editing marks and practices. Do *not* rewrite or revise. There may be errors in grammar, spelling, usage or punctuation.

01   Northwest College (NWC) announced Wednesday that they

02   will change to a semester system effective next June.

03   Pres. John R. McKay said the change would benefit

04   faculty and students but not effect taypayers

05   McKay said that in his judgment the change would

06   enhance the college's reputation.

07   "We have considered all aspects of our academic year,

08   he said, "I am sure we are doing the right thing."

09   Faculty members have expressed some reservations.

10   Dr. Henry Huxtable, professor of veterinary medicine,

11   called the move radical.

12   Dr. Granville Holmes, Professor of Journalism, said

13   he welcomed the change.

14   McKay said, however that the change would require

15   additional computer capacity in the registrar's office.

16   Alumni have "mixed feelings" about the semester plan.

17   Mrs. Louise Baxter, president of the Northwest

18   college Alumni Assn. said that many former graduates

19   oppose the plan.

20   "I am an alumni myself, Mrs. Baxter said, "and I don't

21   like the idea."

Number Correct _____

Student _____

EXERCISE 9-23

Edit this news story. Correct errors in style. Use standard editing marks and practices. Do *not* rewrite or revise. There may be errors in grammar, spelling, usage or punctuation.

01   The Chairman of the Washington County Planning and

02   Zoning commission yesterday charged that the commission

03   can't enforce its own regulations.

04   Charles Miller, the commission chairman said that

05   unless the commission increases the size of its staff,

06   there is little chance that the situation will change.

07   "I wonder if all the regulations are really worth it,

08   said Miller.

09   Miller said homeowners object to zoning in any form

10   and pay very little attention to the zoning ordnances.

11   In an interview with "The Morning Record," Miller said

12   he was "astonished" at the violations of zoning

13   regulations coming to his attention.

14   "At least 10% of the violations," Miller said, "are

15   deliberate and willful."

16   "We can't begin to get a handle on the situation."

17   "We're working on redrafting our regulations."

18   Miller said the five member planning commission may

19   come up with new guidelines to improve enforcement.

20   "Its up to the members," he said.

Number Correct _____

Student _____

245

10 Feature Stories

Spelling

kindergarten/kindergartner, impostor, goodbye,* exacerbate, aesthetic, plagiarize/plagiarism, politicking, provocateur, malfeasance, synchronize/synchronous, erudite, separate

Usage

discreet/discrete, complacent/complaisant, capital/capitol, reluctant/reticent, pathos/bathos

Newsroom Vocabulary

feature, featurize, bright, page brightener, human interest, suspended interest, new journalism, pad, slant, stereotype, FYI

247

Features

This topic is treated in detail in George A. Hough 3rd, "News Writing," fifth edition:

Features
Chapter 16, "Feature Stories," pages 339 through 362.

EXERCISE 10-1

Finals week is always an occasion for a news or feature story on students and how they are coping with their examinations. Your editor asked you to work up a feature, so you checked with the news bureau at Northwest College. Bill Morrissey suggested that you talk with Dr. Hirsch in the medical school. He is a nationally known expert on stress. You interview Dr. Hirsch:

You: Dr. Hirsch, what can you tell me about the effect of finals on students?

Hirsch: Well, finals are a little tough on students, but not really more than any other week of the term.

You: No extra stress?

Hirsch: Well, yes, but it's what you might call an escapable stress. If you are studying, you can get up and take a break. You have a feeling of being in control.

You: Has there been any research on this subject?

Hirsch: Yes, a number of animal studies have shown that stress is damaging only if it's inescapable.

You: Do you find more illness during finals than at other times during the term?

Hirsch: Actually, no, though there is a well-known relationship between stress and illness. But it's not true of college students. At least it doesn't show up during finals.

You: Any data on that subject?

Hirsch: Yes, we have reviewed the record of student visits to the health service over the past 10 years, and we found that, oddly enough, students visit the health service less during finals week than during other weeks of the term.

You: I wonder why.

Hirsch: Well, we think it's because students just won't take the time to trek over here to the clinic.

You: But there's sort of a tradition that students tend to get tired and sick a lot during finals.

Hirsch: That's something of a myth. Students talk a lot about how tough they're having it, how late they study and how sick they feel, but that's not the same as being truly ill.

You: Any advice for students about how to cope with finals?

Hirsch: Sure. They ought to start studying before the last minute, and they ought to get a good night's sleep before taking an exam. A good night's rest is a sure cure for stress.

EXERCISE 10-2

Ted Davis, the Record's advertising manager, stopped in the newsroom today to tell you about a classified ad that appeared in this morning's paper.

```
The ad, you learn, was placed by Horace Gilmore, vice
president of a local construction company. He runs the ad
every year on his wife's birthday. The ad asks readers of The
Morning Record to telephone Mrs. Gilmore and wish her a happy
birthday. Mrs. Gilmore always gets lots of calls, Davis tells
you. He suggests you call Mrs. Gilmore and get a few more
details.
```

From Mrs. Gilmore:

```
The calls never stop. I have to take the phone off the hook
long enough to take a bath or have a cup of coffee. I'm
getting a little weary of this kind of birthday. Why, I get
a couple of hundred calls every year. I hope he'll think of
something different next year.

One year he was going to put a birthday message on a
billboard down on Main street, but my daughter talked him out
of it. My god, that would have been up there a month.
```

You thank Mrs. Gilmore and wish her a happy birthday. Then you call her husband.

From Mr. Gilmore:

```
He's run the ad for the past five years. It costs about $50
for the ad. He thinks it's a great idea, but admits that his
wife is getting a bit tired of the gag.

The calls start coming as soon as the paper is out and go on
all day. Most of the people who call are complete strangers.
They are all very nice. Some even sing "happy birthday to
you."
```

This story has feature possibilities. See what you can do.

EXERCISE 10-3

While you were in the office today, the Record's police reporter called in. The city editor was laughing as she asked you to take the story. Make it bright. You could make page one.

```
Police are holding John Jewell, 31, Mobile, Alabama, at
headquarters — charge is attempted theft — he was arrested
by police on West Main a block from headquarters — he had
attempted to grab a purse from a police officer — Sergeant
Gail Ivory — attached to juvenile division — she was just
going up steps of headquarters — Jewell grabbed at her
shoulder bag — she held on to the bag — he tugged, then gave
up and ran —

A couple of police officers who were on their way into the
building ran after him — Ivory yelled at him to stop and
fired two warning shots in air — officers caught him about a
block from headquarters — Ivory works in plain clothes —
Jewell apparently didn't know she was a cop — happened about
7:45 this morning —
```

EXERCISE 10-4

You were at the city desk today when your city editor asked you to take a call from the Record's police reporter. "Here's a good one," you were told. "Write something funny. We need a little humor for page one."

Reporter: This is a funny one. A prisoner tried to escape from Joe Marshall this morning.

You: What happened?

Reporter: Joe was walking the guy from police headquarters over to municipal court when he broke loose and ran.

You: He get away?

Reporter: Nope. Marshall's too fast for him. Heck, when he caught up with him, Joe had hardly hit his stride.

You: How far did the guy get?

Reporter: A block or so. He was winded and just quit running.

You: What happened to him?

Reporter: Oh, Joe just took him on over to court. The poor guy was too winded to say much. Judge Hughes gave him 30 days. He was charged with d and d.

You know that Marshall runs the mile on the police track team and holds a number of records. He also competes in road races. He plans to enter the Peachtree road race in Atlanta next summer. *D and d* means *drunk and disorderly.*

EXERCISE 10-5

While you were in the office today, the Record's police reporter called with a story he thinks is funny. He told you:

```
The robbery squad just nabbed a guy who must be the dumbest
thief in the world. Listen. They had a burglary the other
night at the Copper Kettle restaurant. No big deal. The
burglars got about a hundred bucks from the cash register and
broke open a cigaret machine and took maybe fifty bucks worth
of cigarets. They caught the guy this morning. Found his
fingerprints in the restaurant. He was on file because he'd
been arrested before. He got hungry while he was in the
restaurant and fixed himself a bowl of chili. Left his
fingerprints all over the bowl and the spoon he used. Name
is Pete Rigsby. Arrest last year was for theft. He served 30
days. Detectives just went over to his house, and there he
was.

You can quote Lieutenant Begg if you want to.
```

_____

FYI: Rigsby's prints were on file in the police identification bureau.

EXERCISE 10-6

While you were in the office this morning, the Record's county building reporter called with what he thinks is a funny story. Here are your notes:

```
A clerk in the county clerk's office wrote a letter to a
friend the other day, using a computer terminal in the
clerk's office. She forgot to clear the letter out of the
system when she finished, and somehow it got into the central
computer, and the next day it was printed out with a lot of
official memos and circulated around the entire building.

In the letter she had told her friend that she was finding
Carolton pretty quiet — said her love life was dull. Quote
I'd sure like to meet a good-looking guy unquote.

The county clerk laughed it off. Said it was just a technical
error in the computer system. He doesn't think anyone in his
office will write personal letters at work after this.

The woman has taken a lot of kidding, but she says it has
been worth it. Most of her free evenings and weekends for the
next several weeks have been spoken for.
```

_____

The clerk's name is Joycelene Jackson. She's 22 and has been working at city hall for less than a year. She's a newcomer to Carolton. Before coming here last year, she worked for a computer firm in Wollaston, Mass.

EXERCISE 10-7

While you were in the office today, the Record's police reporter called with a fire story. The city editor asked you to take the call. She tells you that there was a three-alarm fire at 5:45 this morning — church at 911 Grant — pretty serious damage — fire trucks didn't return to station until after 8.

She doesn't have anything else, but suggests you talk to someone from the church. You check the city directory, find the name of the church, call the pastor, John Duttweiler, and ask him about the damage.

From Duttweiler:

```
quote this is a terrible blow to the congregation unquote.

We just last week finished renovation of the sanctuary.
Members of the congregation have been raising money, and we
have taken up special collections for two years to pay for
the renovations. We paid for it ourselves because we didn't
want to mortgage the church.

He has been pastor for five years.

The renovation just completed was the first phase of a
three-year program to renovate the church and parish hall.

The entire interior of the church was burned out in the fire.
Church has some 600 members. Work so far has cost $40,000.
Loss only partly covered by insurance.

Work had included new wiring, refinishing the pews, new
stained-glass windows, wall-to-wall carpeting and a new
baptismal font.

Congregation had been planning to hold special services this
Sunday to mark the 50th anniversary of the founding of the
congregation and to celebrate completion of the first phase
of the renovation project. Services will be held somewhere
else now.

Quote I've been a member of this congregation all my life —
this hurts unquote
```

This is more than a routine fire story. Give it feature treatment. Use the best direct quotes.

EXERCISE 10-8

You were covering the police and fire beat today, and while you were at the downtown fire station, you picked up this story:

From firefighter at the desk:

```
Rescue squad called to 503 East Vermont yesterday afternoon
at 4:15. Child stuck in chimney.

Rescue squad had to get help from firemen. They used hammers
and chisels to get the kid out. He was so far down the
chimney you couldn't see him from the roof.

Finally got him out. Kid's story is that he got home from
school and found the house locked. Figured he could get in
by shinnying down the chimney. He's a little guy. Only 8.

Mother came home about four o'clock and heard him screaming.
When she finally figured out where the kid was, she called
the fire department.
```

Lt. Strauss tells you:

```
Kid looked like a little old chimney sweep when we got him
out. He was scared, but he's a tough little guy. He'll be
all right. Good thing we've got a couple of bricklayers in
the department. They told us how and where to cut and chisel
to get him out.

We started in the fireplace and worked up. All we could see
of him from the fireplace were the bottoms of his feet.

It took us about four hours to get him out.
```

You call the boy's home and get this from his mother:

```
It was Jimmy, James. He's our youngest. He's all right. Just
got a chipped tooth.

I asked him why he tried to go down the chimney, and he said
it was a mistake.
```

EXERCISE 10-9

The Record's stringer on campus called this morning with a story that you might be able to do something with. Here are your notes:

From the stringer:

```
Students managed to put all the plumbing in Hallowell hall —
the new residence hall on campus — out of commission last
night.

College maintenance crews can't fix it and college has had
to call in a plumbing contractor.

Students synchronized their watches last night and at exactly
ten o'clock flushed every toilet in the building. Nothing has
worked since.
```

From Terry Dawson at campus public relations:

```
Students have been agitating for longer break between terms.
The synchronized flush was part of the protest. Students
thought college would give in, postpone final exams and let
them go home early. President McKay has issued a formal
notice that the college's exam and vacation schedule will
remain unchanged.

The college is going to bill residents of the hall for the
damage, too.

About 450 students live in Hallowell hall. It's one of the
co-ed halls — it houses both men and women students.

There are 237 toilets in the building.
```

Write this for tomorrow's paper.

EXERCISE 10-10

When you came into the newsroom today, you found Bill Jones, one of the Record's copy editors, passing out cigars and accepting congratulations on the birth of twins. His wife, Betty, went into Carolton General last night, and the babies were born this morning.

Jones tells you:

```
Betty is pretty upset in some ways, though she is terribly
pleased with the twins — girls — who haven't been named yet.
They were a week or so early, and Betty didn't get to finish
the bar exam.

Betty has been going to the law school at Northwest since
their first child started school three years ago. She got her
```

continued on next page

255

degree last June. She took the first part of the state bar
examination last week. She was supposed to take the second
part today, but instead she's in the hospital.

You call Mrs. Jones at the hospital and chat with her. She tells you:

I don't know whether they'll call me a flunk or a non-taker.
They're beautiful babies, but I wish they had waited another
day or so.

She isn't sure when she can take the exam again. She does
want to practice law, even with three children to look after.
She thinks she can do it but perhaps will have to set up her
law office at home.

She is interested in women's issues and has been a volunteer
at the shelter for women here.

Write the story for tomorrow's paper. Keep it short.

EXERCISE 10-11

The Record's police reporter turned up an odd theft story today. He gave you
what he was told by police. You made a phone call to the complainant. Here's
what you have:

From police report:

Complaint this morning — theft of a tree from residence at
641 North Sherman — sawed down and removed — probably last
night or early this morning — Canadian spruce — valued at
five hundred dollars — complainant is H.C. Anderson.

From Mrs. Anderson:

I cried all morning. That tree meant the world to us. How
could anyone hurt us like that?

We're both 80 years old. We won't live long enough to see
another tree grow up to be so beautiful.

We planted that tree when we bought this house 15 years ago.
It was the most beautiful tree.

The tree was about fifteen feet high and broad at the base.
A perfect Christmas tree. They will have a Christmas tree
indoors, but they have always put lights on this tree at
Christmas time. They were going to get the lights on it
today.

This sort of theft happens occasionally at the Christmas season. There's
feature material here, but this is not a humorous story. Write the story carefully. There's a fine line between sentiment and sentimentality.

EXERCISE 10-12

Your federal beat reporter called this story in this morning. Your city editor liked it. "Give me a bright for the front page," she told you.

One of the stamp machines at a self-service postal unit on campus had to be repaired today because it jammed. The postmaster had a visit this morning from a student who handed him a whole roll of stamps that came out of the machine. She put in enough money for one stamp and got a whole roll. The postmaster said he was glad to get the stamps back. The roll had 250 stamps. The stamps can go back in another machine.

Student is Helen Fraser.

Postmaster didn't offer her any reward. He just said "thanks."

Postmaster wouldn't say which stamp machine was at fault but did say that the malfunction was not likely to recur.

EXERCISE 10-13

While you were in the office today, The Record's reporter at the Federal Building called with a story about a bomb scare. The city editor asked you to take the call and to write the story. Here's what the Federal beat reporter told you:

Federal building was evacuated this morning — bomb scare — clerks in the Internal Revenue Service office called police — said they had a suspicious package in the office — package was leaking an unidentified liquid —

Carolton police bomb squad went to federal building — ordered building evacuated — several hundred persons had to go out to the street while the bomb squad went into the IRS office —

Package was a gym bag — it was leaking — bomb squad took it to city landfill off Territorial road and blew it up —

Package was only someone's lunch — from what was left of it, police identified a bologna sandwich wrapped in aluminum foil, a thermos of coffee and several chocolate chip cookies —

FBI agents learned later lunch belonged to an IRS agent — he had left it in a gym bag under his desk while he went out to do some errands —

Bomb squad officer-in-charge — Sgt. Hal Floyde — says it was quote just a little case of nerves up in IRS unquote —

Practice Exercises in News Writing

EXERCISE 10-14

The Record's staffer at the courthouse called this story in just now. Your city editor wants it for tomorrow's paper.

In municipal court today — before Judge Hughes — attempted theft case — Stanley C. Updyke — age 34 — gave address of city rescue mission — sentenced to 30 days in county jail on plea of guilty —

City cops nabbed him about 2 this morning outside bank at 604 West Main —

Complaint said he was trying to fish night deposits out of the bank's night-deposit chute —

He had a fish line with hooks and a sinker — cops spotted him and made arrest — before he had been able to haul anything out —

Bank says about a dozen deposits were in the night depository, but as far as they know nothing is missing.

EXERCISE 10-15

Everyone in the newsroom has been kidding Jim Sullivan, the news editor, about his wife's allergy. She's allergic to newsprint and news ink. Jim thinks he may have to get another job. Every night he brings home enough ink and newsprint dust to make his wife ill.

Sullivan tells you:

Carolyn didn't know she was allergic to printer's ink and newsprint when we got married last summer. But ever since, she has sneezed constantly. Her doctor didn't know what was wrong, so last week he sent her to an allergist.

She had more than 100 tests before they found out what it was that made her sneeze.

She can't even pick up a newspaper without sneezing.

Worse yet, she sneezes when she gets too near me.

———

Jim isn't amused, but a lot of people in the newsroom think it's funny. There are elements of humor in the situation. See if you can write this as a page brightener in the suspended-interest format.

258

EXERCISE 10-16

The Record's city hall reporter called this in this morning. Write it for tomorrow's paper.

Tax office at city hall is a madhouse. Tax bills went out last week, but lots of people didn't get them and the tax office has been getting phone calls from all over town.

They've been blaming the mail. Joe Thompson even went over and raised cain with the post office.

Then this morning they found that the mail chute in city hall was plugged up. When they finally got it cleared, they had a couple of thousand letters. Some had been in the chute a week. About half of them were tax bills. Tax office is on third floor at city hall, and clerks had been putting the bills in the mail chute.

Joe says he's going to send the tax clerks over to the main post office with mail after this. Postmaster says all the delayed mail is being hand stamped and handled as a priority.

EXERCISE 10-17

The Record's courthouse reporter called this in today. Today is Valentine's Day, so this is a timely story.

Employees at the courthouse got into the spirit of the day. In the county clerk's office, they had red hearts plastered all over the place. Also had a big sign: "Congratulations and Best Wishes for a Long Life Together."

Miss Williams says they thought they ought to do something for couples who apply for a marriage license on Valentine's day.

Employees in clerk of court's office didn't have any signs up, but they kept a tally on the number of divorce actions filed today. There were five.

Miss Williams says only three couples applied for marriage licenses today.

It may be difficult to get in the mood for this story unless you are asked to write it in mid-February. If the season is right, perhaps you can give it a light touch. Be creative.

EXERCISE 10-18

In court this morning, you ran into Don Meyers, Judge Hughes' clerk, who told you about an incident in the judge's court during early morning arraignments.

Meyers: You should have seen the judge's face when he saw that tee-shirt. He was pretty upset.

You: What was on it? A dirty word?

Meyers: You can say that again. It said: "I'm so happy I could . . . er, uh . . . defecate," only it didn't say that.

You: You mean it said . . . ?

Meyers: Yep.

You: What did the judge say?

Meyers: Hughes told the guy — he was in court to be arraigned on a possession charge — marijuana — that there was a dress code in municipal court and that tee-shirts aren't proper dress.

You: That all?

Meyers: No. Then he said that if that was his idea of happiness, he'd accommodate him.

You: What did he mean by that?

Meyers: He accepted the guy's not guilty plea, held him for a preliminary hearing and set bond at a thousand bucks. The guy couldn't post the bond, so he's going to be in the county jail for a while. Hughes told him he'd like the county jail. It's got new plumbing.

You check Judge Hughes' docket and find the man's name: Eric Leonard, no known address, age 22. Pleaded not guilty to a charge of possession of one-quarter ounce of marijuana. Bond set at $1,000. Unable to post bond. Remanded to jail to wait for preliminary hearing.

Write the story for tomorrow's paper. Before you write, however, check the policy section of the Style Guide. What does it say about four-letter words?

EXERCISE 10-19

Write a feature story based on this information. Your city editor wants it for tomorrow's paper.

From the local FBI office:

Robbery last night at the Farmers and Merchants bank downtown. Loss about $15,000 so far.

One or more persons unknown rigged a fake night-deposit box at the bank. Fake box was a standard metal mail drop box of the type the postal service places on streets for deposit of mail. Fake box had been repainted — white with green lettering — that said "Farmers and Merchants Bank" and "Temporary Night Depository."

Box placed in front of opening of regular night depository. Piece of plywood used to seal off regular depository.

Box apparently set in place after dark last night. Removed before daylight this morning.

From Washington county sheriff's office:

A sheriff's road patrol car found the repainted box in a ditch alongside Old Meetinghouse Road about 9 this morning.

From Farmers and Merchants Bank:

Robbery discovered this morning when several customers came into the bank and told bank tellers they had decided not to use the temporary box. So far the bank has identified 7 customers who put deposits in the fake box.

From Carolton postmaster:

Mailbox is one that was reported missing last week from in front of a postal sub-station on the Northwest college campus. He says that he notified campus police and Carolton police about the missing box. He says he thought it had probably been taken by students as a prank.

From the FBI:

No prank. No clues. Special agents are investigating.

EXERCISE 10-20

This morning while you were at work, you got a call from Dalton Arnold at the college public relations office. He wanted to set the record straight on a story that appeared this morning in the Daily Student, the college newspaper. Arnold was upset. He said he'd been getting phone calls all morning. He told you:

Arnold: We've got to straighten this out. President McKay has stopped answering his phone. He's had calls from UPI and AP and the Times.

You: What's this all about?

Arnold: Haven't you seen the Student this morning? The paper carried a front-page story reporting that the college had been sold for $250 million to a consortium of Middle East businessmen who plan to turn the campus into an Islamic studies and research center. The story said the businessmen considered the purchase a tax shelter.

You: Not true?

Arnold: Of course it's not true. The story is a hoax. The college has not been sold. It is not for sale. You can't sell the college, for god's sake, it's a state institution. It belongs to the taxpayers.

You: What's McKay going to do about it?

Arnold: He's issuing a statement saying that the story is a hoax. And he's just got through talking with the editors.

You: Are they in hot water?

Arnold: No, not really. McKay does have a sense of humor, you know.

You don't need McKay's statement. You have the gist of the story here. The college wants a straightforward story explaining the hoax, but your story ought to be more than a correction notice. See what you can do.

EXERCISE 10-21

One of the clerks in the Record's classified department told you about a couple of odd classified ads that ran in the Record during the past few days.

She told you:

A woman came in and placed an ad under "for sale" — for her husband. It ran three days, then she came in and ran a second ad under "notices," canceling her offer.

The woman's name is Tina Lewis, and she lives in Carolton.

You look up the two classified ads:

Husband for sale: cheap. Comes complete with hunting and fishing equipment, one pair jeans, two shirts, boots, black Labrador retriever, and 50 pounds of venison. Pretty good guy, but not home much from October to December and April to October. Will consider trade. Phone 846-3111.

Retraction of husband for sale cheap. Everyone wants the dog, not the husband.

You call Mrs. Lewis. She tells you:

I had no idea I would get any reaction. It was just a joke, though my husband wasn't too pleased about it. I got more than 60 phone calls, and, you know, some of the women who called were real serious.

I think he spends too much time hunting and fishing, but I guess I'll keep him.

___

Mrs. Lewis has an odd sense of humor. The Lewises have been married for 25 years. They celebrated their 25th wedding anniversary last month. Write a page brightener for tomorrow's paper.

EXERCISE 10-22

The Record's police reporter called just now with a story about a mugging. You learn:

From the police reporter:

```
Victim was a woman, age 75, lives in an apartment over on
Arizona — 347 West — she was on her way to a bingo game at
the senior citizen center when a guy grabbed her purse —
right in front of her building — you'll like this — he took
off and she ran after him — nearly caught him, too, but a
cop saw what was going on and went after him — caught him
behind a building going through her purse.

Woman's name is Louisa May Booker.

I just talked to Miss Booker. You'll like this. Listen to
these quotes —

quote that guy took off like a deer, but I was right behind
him — I was so angry I wanted to kill him — chased him to
hell and gone — Then that nice young policeman caught him —

— I didn't give him a chance — he picked on the wrong old
lady unquote

I talked to the cop, too, John Chin, a patrolman. He said he
was on foot patrol when he saw a guy running and an old lady
chasing him. Here's a quote — boy, did she run — I finally
overtook her and went after him unquote

Chin says he caught up to the guy and put the cuffs on him
— man's at police headquarters now — Chin says he's been
booked for unarmed robbery — Name is Sam Walker —

I asked Chin what she had in her purse and he says not much,
about ten bucks and her house keys —
```

For a story like this, you really should talk to the woman herself. You call Miss Booker and learn:

```
Yes, the story is true and the quotes are okay. She adds one
more:

quote — I'm a tough cookie — I don't take any guff from
anybody unquote

She tells you she thinks the Carolton police are great, but
she has one regret. She never got to the bingo game.
```

Write your story. Take advantage of the quotes. Give the story light treatment.

EXERCISE 10-23

You were sent over to Capital City, the state capital, today to do a story on Girls State. A Carolton high school student, Beth Shapiro, is attending and has been elected mayor of one of the Girls State cities.

Beth tells you:

```
I'm so excited about this. This is only the second day and
already I've lost my voice. I'm mayor, so I have to scream
a lot. I had a dead city at first, so I had to encourage
them.

I hadn't intended to run for an office, but you get caught
up in the activities right away.

I'm from a big family — I have five sisters — so you have to
make yourself heard. As mayor, I learned right away to push
for what I need.

First thing, I had to set up a schedule for city council
meetings and draft a budget.

Math is my worst subject, so I appointed somebody to do the
budget.

But you have to make sure everybody does their job. What
isn't done, of course, reflects on me as mayor.

There have been a lot of speeches. The governor spoke
yesterday, and the attorney general is going to speak this
afternoon.

Besides things on the schedule we have time to sit with other
delegates and discuss issues.

Nearly everybody has education on their agenda.

I think everyone agrees that we need parents who can stay
together and who can keep their kids in school. But no one
has any specific ways to go about doing this.

The president's idea of earning money for college by doing
community service is a good one.

What other issues? Well, the death penalty, abortion — and
gun control.

The kids are talking about Social Security, too. When we grow
older, will we be protected?

It has really hit me since I got here that when we get a
little older we will be the ones to change things. We just
```

continued on next page

265

have to be sure we're not too scared to do it. I know I'm going to be able to change things.

Is it fun? Sure. But I'm learning a lot. I could never learn this much in a classroom.

You also learn:

Beth is 16 and a junior at Carolton Central High. She is taking the college prep program and wants to go to Princeton. She thinks now she will major in political science and government.

Her parents are Horace and Naomi Shapiro. The family lives on a farm in rural Washington County.

Beth is tall — 5 feet, 11 inches — and slender. She has red hair and freckles. She wears her hair in a pony tail. She is soft spoken, but very assured. You get the impression that she knows who she is and what she is capable of.

She's active in extracurricular activities at the high school. She is in the band and Drama Club.

She is also active in 4-H work.

The "city" Beth heads is Draper City. She is also a delegate to the Federalist Party convention.

———————————————————

Girls State is held annually on the state university campus in Capital City. It is sponsored by the American Legion Auxiliary. This year's Girls State, the 48th, winds up tomorrow.

The 630 girls at Girls State are divided into 12 cities. They elect city and state officials and hold political conventions as a hands-on way of learning about government.

You know the governor's name (Exercise 5-16), but you have to look up the attorney general in the state government directory: She is Cynthia Royko.

Should you correct Beth's grammar? Discuss this with your editor.

EXERCISE 10-24

Make any changes in these sentences that may be necessary to make them conform to the standards of informal American English.

1. He said he would only talk with the president.

2. None of the boys were hurt in the accident last week.

3. Everyone in the room seems to be happy, the teacher said.

4. The board of county commissioners was dismayed at the vote.

5. The large number of accidents was attributed to the snow.

6. Neither they nor he is going to get away with it.

7. No one in the class is going downtown for the parade.

8. The board of regents reluctantly announced its decision.

9. Each student's classroom work and exam grade was figured in.

10. The speaker of the house only criticized the governor.

11. Board members reported on their spring vacation plans.

12. Everybody on board said his prayers when the engine failed.

13. All the boys and all the girls were going.

14. We'll give everyone credit for his many contributions.

15. Neither of his short stories was published.

Number Correct _____

Student _____

EXERCISE 10-25

Edit these sentences to improve punctuation. Use standard editing marks to insert or delete punctuation. Do *not* rewrite.

1. Perry Jackson, 81, of 231 Oak St., was confined to a nursing home in Monroe, La. where he died on March 11, 1983 without regaining consciousness.

2. Darrel Smith, the Northwest College football coach has signed an agreement with WOOK-TV for a series of post-game programs this fall.

3. The Felch Lecture will be in the LaFollette Auditorium Monday at 8 p.m. the college has announced.

4. John Jones, 18, of 311 Market St. was arrested early Monday.

5. The surgeon excised the liver, spleen, and gall bladder.

6. Classes will be held in Room 203, Mondays, at 4 pm.

7. Jones, a freshman quarterback has a large collection of medals, trophies, and awards.

8. Military service is not all it's cracked up to be the soldier told his mother, an elderly, miserly, but loving matriarch.

9. Jones was inducted at Fort Benning on Jan. 12 at noon.

10. Eating, drinking and sleeping aren't enough, he said.

Number Correct _____

Student _____

EXERCISE 10-26

Edit this news story. Correct errors in style. Use standard editing marks. Do *not* rewrite or revise. There may be errors in spelling, usage or punctuation.

01   A major earthquake jarred the southeastern United

02   States early yesterday.

03   The quake measured 7.5 on the Richter scale, according

04   to the National Oceanic and Atmospheric Administration.

05   Charlotte, North Carolina, was the epicenter, the

06   weather service reported. The tremblor caused extensive

07   damage in Charlotte and the surrounding area.

08   Charlotte Mayor Henry Schulz said he was shocked by

09   the damage.

10   "It's like WW II," he told the AP. "Everything is

11   gone."

12   Shortly after the quake, the North Carolina highway

13   patrol set up road blocks on Interstate 85 South of

14   Charlotte.

15   Hundreds of homes were leveled at Charlotte and the

16   five story Hilton hotel at the Charlotte airport was

17   heavily damaged. Another hotel was totally destroyed.

18   In other parts of the southeast, the weather service

19   said, damages ranged from light to moderate.

20   Heavy rains were an added problem through the south.

21   It's a tragedy," Mayor Schulz said. "Its awfull."

22   Emergency shelters are sheltering hundreds of

23   homeless people the mayor said.

Number Correct _____

Student _____

271

EXERCISE 10-27

Edit this news story. Correct errors in style. Use standard editing marks and practices. Do *not* rewrite or revise. There may be errors in spelling, grammar, usage or punctuation.

01 Hundreds of people whose homes were damaged or

02 destroyed in yesterday's earthquake in the southeast were

03 crowded into undamaged public buildings — high schools,

04 city halls and auditoriums.

05 Red Cross volunteers served the hungry refugees hot

06 dogs, french fries, and coke.

07 "A dietician would be horrified at the things I'm

08 eating," one homeless man said.

09 The hardest hit areas were placed under martial law as

10 a deterent to looting.

11 At Charlotte, bodies of those killed by the quake

12 were taken to improvised morgues in schools, churches,

13 and warehouses.

14 The National Guard and police were keeping badly

15 damaged public buildings under surveillence.

16 Flags in Charlotte flew at half mast in memory

17 of those who lost their lives in the quake.

18 A heat wave swept over the region after the quake,

19 and the temperature rose to 32 degrees celsius.

20 Public health authorities plan to innoculate all

21 residents of Charlotte to avoid any outbreak of disease.

Number Correct _____

Student _____

11 Numbers in the News

Spelling

rhetoric/rhetorical, accede, pejorative, eleemosynary, coroner, subpoena,* wisdom, caricature, fluorescent, rarefied, phenomenon, excerpt

Usage

exotic/erotic/esoteric, because/since, oriented/orientation, averse/adverse, amend/emend, average/mean/median/norm, mill/mill rate

Newsroom Vocabulary

precision journalism, advance, flag, morgue, state of the art, pagination, future book, box

Numbers in the News

This topic is covered in George A. Hough 3rd, "News Writing," fifth edition.

Taxation
Chapter 17, "Numbers in the News," pages 370 through 372.

Percentages
Chapter 17, "Numbers in the News," pages 372 through 374.

EXERCISE 11-1

When you were in your bank this morning, a bank vice president handed you a press release and suggested that it would make a story for the Record business page. He's right. This is news. Write a story. The press release tells you:

```
The bank is the University City National Bank. The bank's
annual meeting of stockholders was held yesterday. Among
other matters that came up at the meeting, Mr. Elmer, the
bank's president, announced that the board of directors had
declared a quarterly dividend on the bank's common stock.

Earnings per share for the year were $4.10.

The dividend will be 66 cents a share for the quarter ending
this month. Because this is the last quarter of the bank's
fiscal year, the 66 cents brings the dividend for the year
to $2.64. The quarterly dividend will be paid to stockholders
of record the first of this month.

This is the 56th quarter in which the bank has paid a
dividend. The bank has assets of more than $150,000,000.

The bank has 5,000 shares of stock outstanding.
```

EXERCISE 11-2

The relationship between the paired items is expressed in *absolute* terms, that is, in concrete terms. Explain the relationship in *relative* terms. For example:

absolute   The distance from A to B is 20 miles.
          The distance from B to C is 40 miles.

relative   The distance from B to C is twice the distance from A to B.

```
1. James J. Jeffries (heavyweight)   220 pounds
   Young Corbett (featherweight)     110 pounds

2. Mary Smith (daughter)      age 15
   Harriet Smith (mother)     age 45

3. Carolton tax rate, 1987    $80
   Carolton tax rate, 1980    $30

4. William is 6 feet 4 inches tall.
   His younger sister is 3 feet 2 inches tall.
```

EXERCISE 11-3

Your city editor wants to break you in on the city hall beat and as an introduction to city finances suggests that you study up on the budget and city taxes.

Carolton assesses real property, land and buildings, at full market value. Value of real property in the city this year:

Residential property	$278,911,500
Commercial property	9,714,500
Industrial property	7,830,070
Total taxable value	$296,456,070

The city council has approved a budget that includes these figures:

Expenditures	$2,994,110.34
Miscellaneous income	$1,274,665.13

How much must be raised by taxation to balance the budget?

_____

If _____ must be raised by levying taxes on a tax base of $296,456,070, what will the tax rate be?

In dollars _____

What will the tax on your home be if it is assessed at $75,000?

_____

EXERCISE 11-4

You talked today with Dr. Shanks at the Health Center. He filled you in on the anonymous HIV testing program and gave you these figures:

Students tested so far this year:	521
Students tested last year:	63
Students tested previous year:	12

_____

Figure the percentage from year to year. Previous year is 100%.

National average is one person found to be infected for every 250 tested. If that average holds good on campus, how many HIV positives would you expect to result from the number tested so far this year?

EXERCISE 11-5

Property tax rates are stated in terms of dollars per thousand — that is, for every thousand dollars of property you own, you will pay so many dollars.

For example, if the tax rate is $6.00 per thousand and you own a home assessed — that is, valued for tax purposes — at $100,000, you will pay a tax of $600.

The tax rate in Carolton:

This year	$7.50
Last year	$7.00
Previous year	$6.50

1. What will your taxes be this year if your home has been assessed at $75,000?

_____

2. What did you pay last year when your home was assessed at $68,000?

_____

3. What did you pay two years ago when your home was assessed at $65,000?

_____

EXERCISE 11-6

You talked today with Henry Koo, chief meteorologist and director of the National Oceanic and Atmospheric Administration — weather bureau — office at the airport. He tells you that the last couple of months have been awfully wet and gives you some figures on precipitation:

Year	This Month	Last Month
5	4.5	4.8
4	4.6	6.1
3	4.1	3.5
2	2.6	3.4
1	6.9	6.7

30-year average for month of _____ is 4.8 inches.

30-year average for month of _____ is 4.0 inches.

_____

Year 1 is the current year, year 2 is the previous year and so on.

What is the average for this month and last month over the past five years? What is the median for each month?

EXERCISE 11-7

Your city editor has handed you these figures that came in today's mail from the state department of labor. The economy is always a good story, your editor reminded you, and she suggested that you write a story for tomorrow's paper.

Last month

County	Labor Force	Employed	Unemployed	Unemployment Rate
Washington	71,051	66,578	4,473	6.3%
Greene	29,127	27,201	1,926	6.6
Franklin	7,104	6,577	527	7.4
Dodge	39,348	36,625	2,723	6.9
Madison	47,858	43,676	4,182	8.7
5-county region	194,488	180,657	13,831	7.1
State	2,874,904	2,708,749	168,155	5.8

Previous Month

County	Labor Force	Employed	Unemployed	Unemployment Rate
Washington	70,948	66,165	4,783	6.7%
Greene	28,797	28,858	1,939	6.7
Franklin	7,032	6,541	491	7.0
Dodge	39,082	36,188	2,894	7.4
Madison	47,993	43,250	4,743	9.9
5-county region	193,852	179,002	14,850	7.6
State	2,864,509	2,685,602	178,907	6.2

You must report changes in the figures for Washington County, for the five-county region in which Washington is located and for the state. You must explain the figures in both absolute and relative terms.

EXERCISE 11-8

Write a story based on these figures just released by the state Department of Revenue. The figures represent state tax revenues for last month and for the same month last year. Insert the current month in the blank in the line beginning *Month of*. To make your story meaningful, you will have to calculate the percentage of the actual change from last year to this year.

```
State Department of Revenue
Capital City

Revenue Division's report of collections:

Month of _____ this year compared to same month last year.
```

Revenue Source	This Year	Last Year	Change
Sales and Use	$142,479,549.23	131,942,217.11	_____
Motor Fuel	26,300,584.97	25,759,593.23	_____
Individual Income	190,165,512.46	108,812,300.22	_____
Corporate Income	8,954,394.99	10,404,849.77	_____
Cigar and Cigarette	7,140,779.39	7,706,805.89	_____
Motor Vehicle	1,374,458.93	1,219,445.35	_____
Liquor	2,640,650.24	4,557,948.81	_____
Malt Beverage	5,500,552.62	5,389,824.83	_____
Estate	1,029,790.73	1,050,198.92	_____
Property	2,159,770.12	1,892,358.80	_____
Wine	1,003,701.07	1,307,750.34	_____
Miscellaneous	800,711.59	804,540.21	_____
TOTAL	390,228,402.94	300,907,851.48	_____

EXERCISE 11-9

We live in an age of high technology. Here's a list of instruments or scales used for measuring. What does each measure or record? What is the etymology of each word?

```
clinometer; hydrometer; tachometer; taffrail log; Snellen
chart; Beaufort scale; theodolite; stadimeter; tonometer;
Richter scale; Mercalli scale; Mercator's projection
```

EXERCISE 11-10

While you were on campus this morning, you talked with the registrar and he gave you some figures on enrollment for the fall semester and discussed the college's game plan for controlling enrollment.

Freshman Applications

Year	Applied	Accepted	Enrolled	Yield	Average SAT Score
5	5,918	3,708	1,554	_____	1048
4	5,294	3,761	1,542	_____	1045
3	5,677	3,542	1,771	_____	1060
2	5,956	3,658	1,494	_____	1078
1	5,824	3,935	1,656	_____	1086

Total enrollment

Freshman	1,656	23.0 %
Sophomore	1,351	20.0 %
Junior	1,950	27.0 %
Senior	2,158	30.0 %
total	7,115	100.0 %
Graduate	1,011	
total	8,126	

Undergraduate enrollment fall term year ago: 6,888
Graduate enrollment fall term year ago: 946

Transfer students:

    Last year fall term: 740
    This year fall term: 873

Undergraduate enrollment fall term:

    Women   58%
    Men   42%

Undergraduate minority students:

    Last year fall term: 227
    This year fall term: 289

continued on next page

Registrar's comments:

```
College must control enrollments. Goal is student body of
8,000. Goal for freshman class is 1550.

Budgetary restraints control enrollment goals. College has
been affected by the economy and by legislative cutbacks.
Northwest is state assisted, not state supported. Can't
afford larger enrollments right now.

Number of regularly admitted African-American and other
minorities is increasing. Minorities account for 18 percent
of freshman class.
```

———————————

Yield, in the table above, is the average of those accepted and those enrolled. You'll have to figure the percentages.

Year 1 in table above is this year, Year 2 is last year, and so on.

The registrar may not have fully explained the figures. Do you note any trends in the figures for the freshman class? Any other trends or changes? How does this year compare to last year? To five years ago?

Write a story for tomorrow's paper. Perhaps you could also turn the figures into some interesting graphics.

EXERCISE 11-11

Tax rates may be stated in terms of dollars per thousand or they may be stated in *mills*. One mill is equal to 1/1000 of a dollar or 1/10th of a cent.

```
If the tax rate is $6 a thousand, what is the mill rate?
```

Dollars	Rate
$1,000	$6.00
100	.60
10	.06
1	____ mills

```
Review the tax rates shown in Exercise 11-5 and figure the
mill rate for Carolton for this year and the previous two
years.
```

Year	Mills
This year	_____
Last year	_____
Previous year	_____

EXERCISE 11-12

You talked with Dr. Jennifer Chin at the health center on campus this morning. She gave you some figures on hepatitis B, an increasingly serious health problem, even among college-age students.

The figures:

Risk Factors Associated with Hepatitis B

Health care employment	1%
Household contact	3%
Drug abuse	14%
Heterosexual activity	27%
Not known	40%
Other	4%

Dr. Chin tells you:

There are between 250,000 and 300,000 new cases of hepatitis B in this country each year. Young adults — college age — account for a third of the new cases.

The American College Health Assn. has urged all college students to be vaccinated against hepatitis B.

Hepatitis B — like AIDS — can be spread through blood and during sexual intercourse. Hepatitis B about 100 times more infectious than AIDS.

Vaccine is available at the health center. Series of three shots required at one and six month intervals. Cost is $135.

You can write a story based on these figures and Dr. Chin's comments. The figures would make a good graphic.

EXERCISE 11-13

When you were on campus today, you talked with the registrar. He gave you some figures for spring semester enrollments:

Total enrollment up 3.4 percent over fall semester.

Undergraduate enrollment up 4.3 percent.

Graduate enrollments up 2.4 percent.

Your story should report actual figures as well as percentages. You wrote about fall semester enrollment in Exercise 11-10.

EXERCISE 11-14

Your city editor hands you a copy of the annual report of Shook Chemical, one of Carolton's largest employers. She wants a story for tomorrow's business page. Here are the highlights:

Continuing Operations

	This Year	Last Year
Sales	$8,134.6	$7,777.8
Costs and Expenses		
Cost of sales	4,297.6	4,123.2
Selling, general and administrative	2,645.2	2,504.5
Depreciation and amortization	274.2	247.4
total	7,290.6	6,933.3
Earnings before taxes	844.0	844.5
Income Taxes	337.9	338.9
Earnings from continuing operations	506.1	505.6
Discontinued operation after taxes	—	(10.0)
Net earnings	$506.1	$495.6

The figures above are in millions.

If the company has 163 million shares of common stock outstanding, what were earnings per share?

Notice that the company wrote off — that is, took a loss of — $10 million last year from discontinued operations.

When you write your story, give percentages when you discuss year to year changes.

EXERCISE 11-15

When you were at city hall today, you talked with Jerry Hershey, head of the city's health and human services department. He has just received a report from the state on children at risk.

The figures for Washington County:

	This Year	10 Years Ago
Children living below poverty level	21.2%	16.2%
Children living in single-parent households	12.7%	7.1%
Children born to single mothers	13.0%	5.2%
Children born to mothers under 18	2.4%	1.2%
Juvenile arrests (per 1,000)	25.2	11.1
Juvenile delinquents in state institutions (per 1,000)	.5	.1
Children in foster or group homes (per 1,000)	3.6	1.5
Child abuse/neglect reports (per 1,000)	4.7	2.3
Child abuse/neglect reports substantiated (per 1,000)	2.0	.9
Number of children under 16	7,027	7,315

Hershey tells you:

Median income for married couples with children in Washington County last year was $28,229.

Median income for single mothers with children in Washington County last year was $12,879.

Median income for single fathers with children in Washington County last year was $19,229.

Washington County ranks 23rd among this state's 46 counties for arrests of juveniles per thousand children.

Only 10 other counties in the state have a higher rate of child poverty.

What are the trends?

EXERCISE 11-16

When you were at city hall today, the chairman of the City Council Finance Committee gave you a copy of the city's proposed capital outlay budget. There is news here. Write a story for tomorrow's paper.

```
                      Capital Improvements Budget

                                 Summary

                Next Fiscal   Year 1    Year 2    Year 3    Year 4    Year 5

High School Roof
     & Addition   $ 21,750   $237,001  $225,708  $214,708  $203,121  $191,278

Davis School Addition
                    10,342   (222,755)        0         0         0         0

Fire Station
     Renovation,
     & Davis School
     Addition Shortfall
     (Combined Borrowing)
                    92,946     88,069    83,641    79,214         0         0

Fire Truck Purchase,
     Library Addition,
     Adult Center
     (Combined Borrowing)
                    80,285     77,278    74,271    71,264    38,984    37,432

Park Land
     Purchase/Adult
     Center Shortfall
                    64,307     62,157    60,007    57,857    55,707    53,557

Elementary School
     Expansion      11,267    271,571   368,604   350,229   331,854   313,478

     total        280,897    513,321   812,231   772,979   629,666   596,295

Effect on Tax Rate $   .56   $   1.03  $   1.63  $   1.55  $   1.26  $   1.19

Average Tax Bill  $112.00    $206.00   $326.00   $310.00   $252.00   $238.00
```

You ask for some explanation of the figures and are told:

The first column shows the capital improvement budget for the next fiscal year, beginning 1 July. Years 1 through 5 are the next five fiscal years.

The capital outlay budget is made up of funds raised through taxation each year and by borrowing.

The high school addition and renovation is financed for 20 years at a 6.5 percent interest rate. The state will reimburse the city for approximately 56 percent of the cost.

The elementary school addition figures reflect state reimbursement of $222,755. This debt is being retired a year early and a year before state reimbursement.

Purchase of parkland on the West Side for $300,000 and an additional $130,000 for the Adult Center required 10-year borrowing at an interest rate of 4.966 percent.

continued on next page

287

The expansion of the Mann Elementary School will be financed over 20 years. The design phase will cost approximately $390,000 and total cost of the project will be $6,615,000. The city expects to finance this at 6.25 percent. Figures reflect an estimated 52 percent reimbursement by the state.

Effect on the tax rate and average tax bill are based on an average assessment of $200,000 and a tax rate of $7.66 per thousand.

All expenditures on this budget have been approved previously by the council. The borrowing for the Davis school, of course, is an old item.

Borrowing for the Mann school was approved by the voters in a referendum last year.

There are just three long-term projects here: the three school projects. Borrowing for other projects is short term and does not require voter approval.

Shortfall in the projects listed indicates costs not covered in previous budgets. Shortfalls are made up by borrowing or additions to current and future appropriations.

The finance chairman, Bill Ott, tells you the proposed capital outlay budget will be presented to the council at its regular meeting Monday.

He also tells you:

Quote — This is the best we can do. We are being careful of taxpayer dollars. We have secured very favorable interest rates on our bonds. — Unquote

EXERCISE 11-17

The state's Bureau of Economic Opportunity has released figures on the state's trade with Canada and Mexico — the country's new trade partners under the North American Free Trade Agreement. Here are the figures:

Year	To Canada	To Mexico	Total Exports
5	$127,964,227	$23,940,827	$559,849,541
4	$136,127,142	$32,107,803	$649,675,471
3	$198,856,404	$41,011,190	$756,212,736
2	$224,660,721	$24,095,681	$783,786,065
Year	$292,809,774	$41,326,330	$1,003,997,781

What are the trends here? How do exports to Mexico compare to exports to Canada in percentages? Can you make any comparisons in *relative* terms?

Write a few paragraphs for tomorrow's paper.

288

EXERCISE 11-18

Eliminate the *redundancies* in the items below. You may X them out on the typewriter, draw a line through the unnecessary words, or write or type a revision in the space at the right. Some of the items may be acceptable as written.

1. at a speed of six knots an hour   _____

2. a cousin of his   _____

3. the exact same   _____

4. is currently working at   _____

5. was positively identified as   _____

6. is already in the process of   _____

7. is required to   _____

8. a new recruit   _____

9. broke a past record   _____

10. along with   _____

11. the sum total is   _____

12. a coroner's inquest   _____

13. in the field of journalism   _____

14. ink pens   _____

15. located at   _____

16. completely destroyed   _____

17. appointed to the position of   _____

18. doomed to failure   _____

19. is currently   _____

20. four different kinds   _____

Number Correct _____

Student _____

EXERCISE 11-19

Make any changes in these sentences that may be necessary to make them conform
to the standards of informal American English.

1. Each of the prisoners took his rations and walked away.

2. "If I was able," he said, "I would be the first to volunteer."

3. John was not absent often. He only missed a couple of lectures.

4. Smith is presently superintendent of schools in Carolton.

5. "I'm not hurt," he said. "I'm perfectly alright."

6. The number of things one shouldn't do is enormous.

7. The money was divided between the three boys.

8. Everybody thought that they played the game well.

9. Neither John, Bill or Henry were accepted by a college.

10. The sound of the bells mingle with the voices of the choir.

11. Two weeks are not long enough for a restful vacation.

12. Sloppy sentences or careless grammar are not acceptable.

13. "Get up!" he said. "You can't lay around all day like this."

14. Smith was awarded for his bravery. He was given a medal.

15. "Thanks alot," the girl said. "Now I only need the notes for the

    history lecture."

Number Correct _____

Student _____

EXERCISE 11-20

Edit this news story. Correct errors in style. Use standard editing marks and practices. Do *not* rewrite or revise. There may be errors in spelling, grammar, usage or punctuation.

01   Two Cleveland, O., residents have filed suit in

02   Washington county circuit court against the Territory

03   and Western Railroad.

04   The suit was filed as a result of an accident last

05   May in which Rev. Edgar D. Callahan was killed at the

06   rail crossing on Territorial Rd. just north of Perimeter

07   Road.

08   The suit seeks $8,000,000 in damages, $7500 for

09   medical expenses and $1000 for pain and suffering.

10   Attorneys for Callahan's daughter, Mrs. Consuela

11   O'Byrne, 40, and her son, Mark, four, filed the suit

12   yesterday.

13   Their suit accuses the railroad of negligence and

14   alleges that crossing signals weren't operating that day.

15   Callahan, Mrs. O'Byrne and Mark were on their way to

16   visit Callahan's mother on Mother's day when the

17   accident occured. Callahan, 70, was the former church

18   editor of The "Morning Record."

19   Mrs. O'Byrne said yesterday that she still is not

20   well.

21   "Every time I think of the accident," she said, "I

22   feel nauseous. Its been weird."

23   The railroad has retained legal council.

Number Correct _____

Student _____

EXERCISE 11-21

Edit this news story. Correct errors in style. Use standard editing marks and practices. Do *not* rewrite or revise. There may be errors in spelling, grammar, usage or punctuation.

01   Bank robbers yesterday blasted open a two foot thick

02   concrete wall at the back of the First National bank and

03   took $2000 from an open safe.

04   The bank, at 16 West Main St., is the oldest bank in

05   the city. The principle stockholder is Mrs. Helen

06   Overkampf, a former resident of Carrolton, who now lives

07   in Portland, Oregon.

08   The bank is usually not open after three in the

09   afternoon. John C. Elmer, the bank's vice president,

10   said 7 customers and fourteen bank employes were in the

11   bank yesterday afternoon.

12   Mr. Elmer said the bank's losses are covered by

13   insurance. The bank is insured for losses up to fifty

14   million dollars.

15   A bank customer, Alice Short, 27, of 604 Washington

16   Rd. was injured by the blast. She was standing by the

17   24 inch thick back wall. She was taken to Holy Cross

18   hospital by ambulance.

19   The Carrolton police bomb squad is investigating.

20   Police Sergeant Alex Cordoba said he believed the robbers

21   used plastic explosive in coke bottles.

22   Police have issued an eight state alarm for the

23   robbers.

Number Correct _____

Student _____

12 Editing, Revising, Rewriting

Spelling

defunct, acknowledgment, catalog,* colloquial, hurricane, straightforward, asphyxiate, egregious, homicide, credible/credibility, athlete/athletic, canvass, penitentiary

Usage

adopt/approve/enact/pass, citizen/resident/native, accuse/charge/indict, comprise/compose/constitute, perquisite/prerequisite

Newsroom Vocabulary

rewrite, trim, boil, cut, electronic carbons, handout, press release, public relations/public information, release date, embargo

Editing, Revising, Rewriting

These topics are treated in detail in George A. Hough 3rd, "News Writing," fifth edition:

Editing, Revising, Rewriting
Chapter 6, "Be Clear, Complete and Accurate," pages 99 through 113.
Chapter 8, "Editing, Revising, Rewriting," pages 137 through 155.

EXERCISE 12-1

You took the call today when the Record's police reporter called in with several stories. You asked the city editor for instructions. "Lead with the Williams shooting," she said, "and shirttail the others."

(williams shooting)

```
Police are holding James Williams, 57, for investigation of
murder — he's an insurance adjuster — lives at 70 W. Utah —
arrested last night — at his home — neighbors called the cops
— they found him in the kitchen with a .45 pistol — he took
a couple of pot shots at the officers — quite a little
shoot-out before he gave up — he has a flesh wound in the
left arm — cops took him to Carolton General emergency then
to headquarters — cops found his wife in bedroom upstairs —
four bullets in her chest — dead on arrival at Carolton
General — detectives said neighbors heard them quarreling and
then heard shots — there was a record of trouble between them
— cops called there once or twice before — Det. Sgt. O'Neil
is in charge — he says Williams will probably be arraigned
tomorrow — wife's name is Marcia — she's an attorney and an
accountant — kept books for a lot of businesses in town —
she's pretty well known — used to be on the city council —
no children.
```

(robbery)

```
shooting at 103 E. Main — liquor store — attempted robbery —
owner winged a guy trying to hold him up — cops looking for
the guy now — about 30, maybe five ten and about 180 —
wearing army jacket — work pants — combat boots — sandy hair
— white — scar on left cheek — may have a bullet wound in
his right arm — guy went into store about closing time last
night — ten or so — and pulled a gun — owner — Clyde Morris
— sixty-eight — ducked behind counter and the guy shot at him
— Morris fired back with a .38 he had under the counter —
police car going by heard the shot and investigated — the guy
ran, but the cops shot at him and they swear he was hit —
cops are Bill Sturdevant and Tom Rickles.
```

(body)

```
cops found a guy in the parking lot behind post office last
night — dead — bullet wound in the head — Robert Turkington
— about 30 — lived at 601 E. Main — had a social security
card on him — and that was about all — cops say he was a wino
— probably rolled for his last buck — no clues —
```

You check the reference library and find that Mrs. Williams served two terms on the City Council, 1980 through 1984, and did not seek re-election. She was admitted to the bar last month.

EXERCISE 12-2

Rewrite this press release. Use as much as you think necessary, but be sure that your story is a news story, not a sales pitch for the candidate.

News Release

From: Ms. Lillian Leamy
211 S. Sherman St.
Carolton

For Immediate Release

A long-time advocate of equal rights for women and minorities, Ms. Lillian Leamy today announced that she will be a candidate for Washington County Clerk.

Active in community affairs, Ms. Leamy is a member of the Executive Board of 11th Congressional District Democrats, the NAACP, the Women's Caucus of the Washington County Democratic Party, the Carolton Democratic Committee, and the Washington County Chapter of the National Organization for Women.

In announcing her candidacy, Ms. Leamy pointed out that she was instrumental in obtaining the first mobile registration unit in Washington County. Ms. Leamy went on to say: "I drove that mobile registration unit countless miles throughout the county, the city of Carolton, and nearby communities in an effort to register voters. And from this experience I found out how hard it is to get people to register. As such, I have decided to run for county clerk. If elected, I will do whatever is necessary to make registering to vote easier."

Turning her attention to Carolton, Ms. Leamy vigorously attacked the existing situation. She said: "Every means possible must be employed to make voting simpler and more convenient."

Ms. Leamy, formerly a lobbyist for the Washington County Education Assn., was a strong supporter of the Equal Rights Amendment. She was also the first woman in the state to be registered as a lobbyist. She is a member of the National Organization for Women and is on the board of the Carolton Women's Shelter.

EXERCISE 12-3

Your city editor handed you this story with instructions to rewrite it. The story originally appeared in yesterday's paper. "Rewrite and cut it," your editor said.

The story, as you can see, has a feature lead and is told chronologically. Rewrite, use a summary lead and organize the story in the inverted-pyramid format.

For a time Branson Potter had the upper hand in a classic game of hide-and-seek.

But about the time he figured he was well hidden, the police guessed just where he was.

As a result, Potter's sitting behind bars at Carolton police headquarters.

It all started about 11:40 a.m. today when Potter was in Municipal Judge Arthur B. Hempstead Jr.'s courtroom to stand trial for aggravated assault and battery.

Taking advantage of a momentary distraction in the courtroom, Potter ran into the hall. Police ran after him, but Potter eluded them.

Two police officers driving along Main Street saw Potter running from the courthouse and recognized him as a recent guest at police headquarters. They followed him as far as the 400 block on North Grant and called for reinforcements.

Four police cars and two teams of detectives converged on the 400 block. Diligent search failed to locate Potter.

Either it wasn't Potter they had been chasing, or he had found a secure hiding place.

Later in the afternoon, Potter was apprehended at his home at 508 South Sherman by Detective Sgt. Emil Crow. Potter was sitting in his kitchen reading a newspaper and eating a sandwich when Crow knocked at the back door.

He surrendered quietly.

EXERCISE 12-4

Your city editor handed you this story, from the first edition of today's paper. "Sharpen this up," she said. "I want it for the second edition."

    Richard Higgins of Madison, a representative of the state Human Rights Commission, will speak at Sunday's meeting of the Huxley Institute for Biosocial Research.

    The meeting will be from 3-5:30 p.m. in Room 112 of the Holiday Inn in Carolton.

    He will discuss "Protecting Human Rights of Mental Patients."

    The institute is a non-profit voluntary organization dedicated to educating persons about prevention and elimination of schizophrenia and hypoglycemia.

EXERCISE 12-5

You found a memo from the city editor on your desk this morning. The memo — about a program coming up on campus —didn't seem to be complete, so you call Don Harmon and get a few more details.

The memo:

Colloquium Monday — faculty lounge Mark Twain Hall — 4:00 pm. — speaker Luisa Flores — she will discuss the work of a Spanish novelist — Ana Maria Matute — colloquium is one held each term by the romance language department — Flores will speak in Spanish — you can get more from Don Harmon in the romance language department —

From Harmon:

Matute is a distinguished novelist — lives in Madrid — won a number of literary prizes — she writes novels and short stories — also children's books — many have been translated into English — and other languages, including French, German, Italian and Portuguese —

Her manuscripts are at Boston University in the Ana Maria Matute Collection — she is a member of the Hispanic Society of America —

Flores wrote her doctoral dissertation on Matute —

Write this for tomorrow's paper.

EXERCISE 12-6

While you were in the office this morning, the Record's police reporter called in with a shooting story. It has a couple of good angles. Your notes:

```
Gardner Green — age 14 — condition critical — Carolton
General — brought in from home — 714 North Jackson — gunshot
— bullet in right chest — removed last night — police say
accidental shooting — father shot him with 22 caliber target
pistol —

Father cleaning pistol — didn't realize it was loaded —
father is Virgil, age 35 — security guard — Farmers Bank —
says he and son were going to go target shooting yesterday
afternoon — he is pretty shaken up —

Green says quote — I didn't know it was loaded — I was
cleaning the pistol and turned around to put it back in the
rack — it just went off — Gardner was standing a few feet
away — I heard a kind of "pow" and he said, "Dad, you shot
me" — I didn't believe it until I saw the blood — unquote
```

EXERCISE 12-7

You took the call when the Jenkins Funeral Home called in the Clark obit. Write it for tomorrow's paper. Be sure you include background on the accident (Exercise 7-14) in your story.

```
Kim Clark, age 18, 608 East Ohio — parents: John and Wilma.

Services Friday at 4 p.m. at Liberty Baptist church.
Duttweiler to officiate. Burial — Evergreen cemetery —

Family:   parents
          grandparents — m/m Harry Clark, Charlotte, N.C.
          brother — Arthur, student at U of Texas
          sister — Marilyn, student at Johns Hopkins
          sister — Anne (Mrs. John L. Natwick, Pittsfield,
          Mass.)

Kim a senior at Carolton Central — honor student — had been
accepted at Bowdoin for fall — born in Carolton — on high
school swim team — member National Honor Society — French
club, Drama club and Science club — members of her high
school class will be honorary pall bearers — parents want
memorial gifts to go to scholarship fund at high school.
```

EXERCISE 12-8

This story was handed to you by the Record's state editor. He wants a rewrite. Give the story a strong summary lead and include an itemized list of the victims.

Special to the Morning Record

BREWSTER — He was trapped upstairs with his wife and four children as flames engulfed the first floor of their home, said Elmer Vernor, so he broke a window and jumped to safety. He told his wife to have the rest of the family follow.

But, Vernor told neighbors, his wife apparently was overcome by fumes and smoke. She and the couple's four small children perished in the flames early Monday.

Authorities identified the victims as Mrs. Renee Vernor, 26, her three daughters, Mary, 7, Margaret, 5, Marion, 3, and a son, Michael, 1. Vernor, age 28, and his brother, Edward, age 25, who leaped to safety from another upstairs window of the two-story frame home, drove a pickup truck to the Warren Freitag home about a mile away to get help. Both were scantily dressed in the below-freezing weather.

Firefighters from Brewster found the flames out of control when they arrived. The house was destroyed.

Vernor told the Freitags that he, his wife and their four children made their way to a stairway landing but were unable to get through the smoke and fumes.

Vernor said he broke a window on the landing and told his wife he would jump to the ground, then she should toss the children to him, then jump. The rest of the family did not make it.

Vernor and his brother are self-employed loggers. The family moved to the Brewster area last summer from near Carolton.

EXERCISE 12-9

Your city editor handed you a memo with notes for a story. "Here," she said. "Fix this up." (See Exercise 7-14.)

New scholarship fund at high school — memorial to Kim Clark — started with ten thousand dollar gift from grandparents — Mr. and Mrs. Harry Clark — school also has about $2600 that came in after the funeral — memorials — to add to the fund — fund will be called the Kim Clark scholarship —

EXERCISE 12-10

This story was brought in by the engineers' publicity chairman. Your city editor thinks it should be rewritten.

How Northwest college is using computers in research and teaching will be discussed by Dr. Richard Verway, chairman of the college's computer science department and director of the college's computer laboratory, before a dinner meeting tomorrow night at 6:30 p.m.

Dr. Verway is responsible for all computer systems at Northwest college, including the system that has just been installed in the college library. Northwest will take delivery on a new computer system next month that will link all college departments and residence halls to the computer lab and the main library. Details concerning these computers will be presented by Dr. Verway. A discussion will follow.

The Washington County Society of Professional Engineers will meet at the Lenox Hotel in the Centennial Room.

EXERCISE 12-11

This story was written for the Record's first edition. Your city editor thinks it could be improved if it had a better lead. Rewrite the story and give it an itemizing lead.

Two employees of the Shook Chemical Corp., 950 N. Meade St., were burned seriously and another was overcome by smoke yesterday in an explosion and fire in the plant's mixing room.

Fire Chief John Wiggins described the explosion as a "blowback" and said it apparently occurred because chemicals were not mixed in the proper order.

Edward Dean, 25, of 408 S. Meade, suffered burns over 60 percent of his body and Mark Diaz, 30, of 520 E. New York Ave., was burned over 70 percent of his body. Both are in critical condition at Carolton General Hospital.

Another employee, James Abrams, 31, of 422 E. Wisconsin Ave., and James Nixon, 32, of 217 S. Grant, a Carolton fireman, were overcome by smoke. Both are being treated at Holy Cross Hospital.

Fire Lt. Jacob Strauss said it could not be determined immediately what chemicals the employees were mixing or what went wrong. The mixing room, in a small building near the chemical company's main building, was badly damaged by the explosion and the fire that followed.

EXERCISE 12-12

Rewrite this story. Your editor wants something other than a direct quote lead. The story is a little long, too.

"This was just one of those things," June Price said Monday as she walked back from the firing line at the 80th annual Grand American Trapshooting Tournament.

The slim, blonde 40-year-old Carolton secretary had shattered 200 straight targets to become the first woman ever to record a perfect score in Grand American shooting.

"I've never even had 100 straight before," she said. "Everything just seemed to fall into place."

Mrs. Price, the state women's champion, is a novice at the game. Her husband, Flynn, taught her to shoot just four years ago.

As state champion, she also competed Monday in the 100-target extra event for state champions only.

In that competition, she broke 97 of 100. She also had to pick her clay targets from among a flock of birds that picked a poor place to feed as the nation's best trapshooters were going about their sport.

"The birds didn't bother me," the attractive Mrs. Price said. "I'd just had it for the day."

EXERCISE 12-13

While you were in the office this morning, the Record police reporter called in with a story. Police have arrested a suspect in the campus rape (Exercise 7-4), and she tells you:

Man arrested last night — police will charge him with rape — and breaking and entering in the night time — and assault with intent to do great bodily harm —

Dwight Germain — age 28 — unemployed — says he's a bus driver — lives on south Airport road —

Police found his fingerprints in girl's apartment — matched prints taken when Germain applied for job with city bus system —

Denies he did it — says he was out of the state that day —

Girl has been released from hospital — parents have taken her home —

———————————

Write this for tomorrow's paper. Fill in the background.

EXERCISE 12-14

Your city editor handed you this story, a clipping from this morning's Daily Student. She wanted a quick rewrite for tomorrow's paper. "Boil it down," she said.

Although most of the dozen lectures scheduled at the Conference Center on campus during the term are open to the public without charge, the great majority of them are too technically oriented for most people. However, tomorrow evening's lecture by Sheldon Simms of the Population Council and the special lecture next Thursday by George Green of Harvard University will be of interest to the general public.

Tomorrow night Dr. Simms, one of the world's experts on population control, will speak on "Population Issues: A Timely Report." Dr. Simms plans to stress the societal rather than the scientific aspects of his subject. His lecture is scheduled for 8:00 in the Auditorium.

George Green's lecture, scheduled for 8:00 next Thursday night, will treat a subject that has become quite controversial. Prof. Green will lecture on "The Efficacy of Acupuncture." He has seen acupuncture practiced in China and will describe his observations of the technique and discuss recent evidence as well as his own views.

EXERCISE 12-15

Your editor handed you a story written earlier by another reporter. "Rewrite this," she said, "and sharpen it up." She needs your copy for the state/region section of tomorrow's paper.

In Dodge county about three miles east of Homer on interstate highway 210, 18-year-old John Eisenbrod of Route 1, Greeenville, lost control of his 1990 Ford pickup on a curve about 2 a.m. yesterday.

The truck skidded over 80 feet on the pavement, travelled for some distance on the shoulder, hit a highway sign, and turned over three times, said Dodge county sheriff's officers.

A passenger in the pickup, 21-year-old Roscoe Ernest, of Route 1, Greenville, was killed in the accident.

Eisenbrod and a passenger, 17-year-old Tracy Thomas, Homer, were listed in serious condition at Greenville's Dodge Medical Center last night.

You check the state highway map on the newsroom wall to verify the location of the accident. Dodge County is an adjacent county. Greenville is the county seat, and Homer is a rural town nearby. Highway 210 runs south of Carolton and east through Dodge County. Slug the story *fatal*.

307

EXERCISE 12-16

You were in court yesterday when Snodgrass was sentenced for the drive-by shooting you wrote about earlier (Exercises 7-25 and 8-6). Your editor will want a complete story for tomorrow's paper.

```
Judge gave Snodgrass 10 years in state penitentiary —

5 years for each count of reckless endangerment — to run
consecutively — 10 years on attempted murder — to run
concurrently —
```

Judge Gordon's remarks:

```
I can't think of a case where I have seen less remorse. You
continue with the absurd belief that you didn't shoot through
the window of the car.

[S. had claimed at trial that he shot over the top of Kirby's
car.]

You may not have intended to hit the driver, but you didn't
care if you caused an accident that killed the other driver.

It's apparent that you have an abnormal interest in firearms.
That odyssey out west to shoot prairie dogs and rattlesnakes
with the weapons in your truck — that troubles me.

Any bad driving on the part of someone else is no reason to
do what you did. Even a deplorable action like cutting in is
no reason.

We're lucky we're not here for sentencing for homicide.

You're an emotionally damaged time-bomb. You're disconnected
from society and your family. This case reminds me of people
who go into McDonald's or the post office and start randomly
shooting.

I hope in the future someone can get to the bottom of your
problems, deal with your demons.

But I have to protect the public.
```

—————————————

```
Snodgrass attorney — public defender — Greg Kelley — argued
— before sentencing — for leniency —

Said S. has no previous record — except one arrest for DUI
— veteran — 4 years in Marines — honorable discharge — good
employment history —

Quote — you can't ignore a life-time of good behavior — he's
already paid — will never hunt again — felon can't own a
firearm — and he will lose his truck — unquote
```

—————————————

At the trial, which was concluded last week, the jury didn't believe the self-defense argument and found Snodgrass guilty on all counts.

EXERCISE 12-17

Who said it? Identify the author, the approximate date and, where possible, the circumstances that prompted the remark.

1. Here I stand, I cannot do otherwise.

2. I shall return.

3. Ich bin ein Berliner.

4. This generation of Americans has a rendezvous with destiny.

5. War is hell.

6. I have not yet begun to fight.

7. The public be damned.

8. I have nothing to offer but blood, toil, tears and sweat.

9. History is more or less bunk.

10. Th' supreme coort follows th' illiction returns.

Student _____

EXERCISE 12-18

Make any changes in these sentences that may be necessary to make them conform to the standards of informal American English.

1. During the exam, everyone must sit in their seat.

2. The instructor said that hopefully the exam would be easy.

3. "That's the most unique thing I ever saw," he said.

4. He will likely be elected president next year.

5. He's the type person no one really likes.

6. There were only a handful of people who attended the meeting.

7. He can only sing when he is inebriated.

8. The man was accused of allegedly embezzling bank funds.

9. Smith had a quiet day. He just laid around the house and read.

10. The City Council scheduled it's meeting for Tuesday night.

11. Ethics, he said, are an important part of the course.

12. "Try and be good," the mother said to the child.

13. "Of course I'll be there," Smith assured hurriedly.

14. The train derailed when it reached the open switch.

15. Two hours are not long enough for a difficult final exam.

16. "Just give me a couple minutes," he said, "and I'll be ready."

17. The mayor convinced the council to vote yes on the measure.

18. He said the likely outcome would be an increase in taxes.

19. "I never saw such a nauseous mess," he said after he had inspected the town dump.

20. The grand jury handed down the indictment Monday.

Number Correct _____

Student _____

EXERCISE 12-19

Edit these sentences to improve punctuation. Use standard editing marks to insert or delete punctuation. Do *not* rewrite or revise.

1. The new officers are: John Foster, president; William Cook, vice president; Henry James, secretary, and Helen Moody, treasurer. Warren Hobbs will be president elect.

2. Smith, a native of Washington, D.C. has enrolled at Northwest College.

3. District Attorney John Doe, a Democratic candidate for governor has failed to file his federal tax returns.

4. According to the almanac the sun will rise at 7 a.m.

5. John Doe, the president's deputy press secretary said he hoped consultations would come early next month.

6. Jones lost his way in the storm police said Monday.

7. He married a graduate of Smith College, a native of Albany, N.Y. and they moved to Athens, Ga. where she worked for the Daily News weekdays, Saturday, and Sunday.

8. Darrel Smith, the Northwest College football coach has signed with a publisher to write a novel, a play, and a history of college football the Daily News reported Thursday.

9. City Council will meet at City Hall, Monday, at 7 p.m.

10. Its too bad you can't come with me, she said.

Number Correct _____

Student _____

EXERCISE 12-20

Rewrite the following sentences so that the numbers are changed as they are in the following example:

Ten inches of snow fell overnight and paralyzed the city.

A 10-inch snowfall paralyzed the city overnight.

1. Firemen responded to two alarms and extinguished the fire.

2. Carolton police cars carry two officers at all times.

3. A Carolton boy, age 7, was injured in the accident.

4. The union approved a contract that will expire in two years.

5. The fire that destroyed the Barnes Hotel started on the first floor and spread through the other five floors.

6. Two Carolton residents were injured last night when their cars collided on Main Street.

7. Economists think the state must wait two more years before business conditions improve.

8. The injured man was struck twice with a pipe three feet long.

9. They hadn't expected to wait for two hours.

10. Her ancestry was both Irish and American.

Number Correct _____

Student _____

315

EXERCISE 12-21

Eliminate the *redundancies* or wordiness in these items. You may X them out on the typewriter, draw a line through the unnecessary words or write or type a revision in the space at the right. Some of the items may be acceptable as written.

1. dead body   _____

2. brown colored cloth   _____

3. new innovation   _____

4. first of all   _____

5. announced his future plans   _____

6. completely decapitated   _____

7. high school education   _____

8. started off   _____

9. on Easter Sunday   _____

10. perhaps it may happen   _____

11. in the year 1986   _____

12. at a meeting held here   _____

13. equilateral triangle   _____

14. past experience has shown   _____

15. old adage   _____

16. consensus of opinion   _____

17. book of poetry   _____

18. uniformed chauffeur   _____

19. an invited guest   _____

20. small in size   _____

Number Correct _____

Student _____

317

EXERCISE 12-22

Edit this news story. Correct errors in style. Use standard editing marks and practices. Do *not* rewrite or revise. There may be errors in spelling, grammar, usage or punctuation.

01   Senator Ernest F. Higginbottom formally entered the

02   democratic presidential race yesterday.

03   Higginbottom, who lives in Carrolton, has been in the

04   United States Senate since 1978.

05   In a press briefing at the National Press club in

06   Washington, D.C. he told his staff, friends, and members

07   of the working press about his political aspirations.

08   He then flew from Washington National airport last

09   night to Carrolton where he is scheduled to speak at a

10   Law day convocation at the School of Law at Northwest

11   College. Higginbottom earned an M.A. and a J.D. at

12   Northwest College.

13   He will tell the Law day audience that he expects to

14   win in primaries in New Hampshire, Wis., and Minn.

15   Higginbottom, a spry 61 year old believes his party

16   can win the next election if they develop programs

17   for the '90's and the next century.

18   Higginbottom was governor from 1970 to 1976. He was

19   the first governor to serve a four year term. Rumors

20   of his candidacy have been published in "The Morning

21   Record." He is the 3rd Democrat to enter the race.

Number Correct _____

Student _____

EXERCISE 12-23

Edit this news story. Correct errors in style. Use standard editing marks and practices. Do *not* rewrite or revise. There may be errors in spelling, grammar, usage or punctuation.

01   Services for Alexander G. Bell, 72, a Professor

02   Emeritus at Northwest college, will be held at 12 p.m.

03   tomorrow at the First Baptist church, 602 West Florida

04   Avenue, Carolton.

05   The Rev. John Q. Lewis will officiate. Burial will be

06   in the church cemetery.

07   Bell was a native of Bangor, Me., and was educated in

08   the schools there and in Boston. He was a graduate of

09   Boston university and earned a Master of Arts degree

10   in history at Olivet College, Olivet, Michigan.

11   He is survived by his wife, Jane; two sons, John and

12   Alexander, Jr.; a brother, William, a well-known writer

13   who has authored a book on satellites; a sister, Anne,

14   Pasadena, Calif.; and a cousin, Arthur, Dallas, Tex.

15   He was a member of the Sons of the American

16   Revolution, the Carolton Rotary Club, the Ohio Valley

17   Historical Assn., and Veterans of Foreign Wars.

18   He was a veteran of WWII. He served in the Air Force

19   in the Pacific Theater. He remained in the reserve and

20   retired as a United States Air Force colonel.

21   Bell joined the faculty at Northwest college in 1957.

Number Correct _____

Student _____

EXERCISE 12-24

Edit this news story. Correct errors in style. Use standard editing marks and practices. Revise, but do *not* rewrite. There may be errors in spelling, usage, grammar or punctuation.

01   The Chairman of the Washington County zoning

02   commission said in an interview yesterday that the

03   commission is so tied up in red tape it can't get it's

04   work done.

05   "People tell us "You people have too many regulations"

06   -- and their correct," Charles Miller said.

07   Miller said the commissioners have been accused of

08   acting like "dictators" when they do try to enforce

09   zoning ordnances.

10   "We're just enforcing zoning requirements," Miller

11   said, "We are not policemen."

12   Miller said he agrees with critics that there may be

13   "too many" regulations.

14   "But the fact is, we have to enforce them (zoning

15   regulations) if we are to do it (the job) right," Miller

16   said.

17   Miller said the commission does not have the manpower

18   it needs.

19   "We need more people or less regulations," he said.

20   Even when violations are found, said Miller, there is

21   no guarantee of punishment.

Number Correct _____

Student _____

323

EXERCISE 12-25

Edit this news story. Correct errors in style. Use standard editing marks and practices. Revise, but do *not* rewrite. There may be errors in spelling, usage, grammar or punctuation.

01   A statewide alarm has been issued for the men who held

02   up O'Flynn's yesterday, took two hostages and fled.

03   The trio shoved their hostages out the door and into a

04   car with Ga. license plates. The car left the club

05   parking lot in the general direction of Columbia,

06   South Carolina.

07   Detectives are interviewing witnesses in an attempt to

08   get descriptions of the holdup men.

09   "One resembled the six-foot-two-inch tailback on the

10   Northwest team," detective Lieut. Jacob Bernstein said.

11   "The similarity just occured to me," he said. "I hope

12   that is not an unfortunate inuendo."

13   O'Flynn's may lose their liquor license because of the

14   holdup. Bernstein said the nightclub was supposed to

15   close at 12 p.m. It was still open when the holdup men

16   entered the building at 1 A.M.

17   Mrs. Helen Shonsky, whose husband was wounded during

18   the holdup, screamed nonstop after he was shot. A

19   bartender had to hit her on the head with a coke bottle

20   to quiet her.

21   Sheriff Abel Look was at the nightclub yesterday

22   seeking any evidence that might be admissable if the

23   bandits are tried.

Number Correct _____

Student _____

1 Reference Library

Newspaper Reference Library

The Morning Record's reference library has the following reference works available for use by the newsroom staff:

The Associated Press Stylebook and Libel Manual

Webster's New World Dictionary of the American Language

Webster's Third New International Dictionary

The New Columbia Encyclopedia

Who's Who in America

Black's Law Dictionary

The World Almanac

Editor & Publisher International Yearbook

State Press Association Directory

Statistical Abstract of the United States

State Statistical Abstract

Rand McNally New Cosmopolitan World Atlas

United States Government Organization Manual

Bulfinch's Mythology

The Careful Writer by Theodore Bernstein

Practical English Handbook by Watkins and Dillingham

The Baseball Encyclopedia

Maps
> State Highways
> City of Carolton and Washington County
> Northwest College Campus

The Record's library has computer terminals that can be used to access the Northwest College Library, the state university library and state library in Capital City, and, through Internet, many other useful sources of information.

2 Directories: City of Carolton and Northwest College

Carolton Residents

A

Abrams, James   *foreman*   434 E. Wisconsin
Anderson, H.C.   *retired*   641 N. Sherman
Anderson, Hattie (Mrs. H.C.)
Applegate, Charles O.   *book dealer*   714 N. Sheridan
Arnold, Dalton   *state employee*   84 Beech
Ashford, John   *bank teller*   157 S. Houston

B

Baker, Howard L.   *landscaper*   247 S. Jackson
Baker, William   *lawyer*   84 Oak
Baker, Harold   *student*
Baker, Mary (Mrs. William)   *accountant*
Banks, Charles   *book dealer*   510 E. New York
Barke, Willis   *detective*   602 W. Florida
Barth, Julius E.   *florist*   278 W. Ohio
Bates, Alpha E.   *physician*   311 Sycamore
Begg, John   *police officer*   570 W. California
Bell, Alexander Graham   *retired*   308 Beech
Bell, Jane (Mrs. Alexander G.)
Bell, Alexander Jr.   *ornithologist*   308 Beech
Bell, John A.   *electrician*   108 W. California
Berg, Lanny Marie   *police officer*   552 W. Newton
Bernstein, Jacob C.   *detective*   715 N. Lee
Bettencourt, Walter Jr.   *retired*   87 Indian River Place
Bettencourt, Elizabeth (Mrs. Walter Jr.)
Blaine, Harold E.   *teacher*   708 W. California
Blaine, Marilyn (Mrs. Harold)
Blake, John   *bookkeeper*   104 E. Perimeter
Blake, Vivian (Mrs. John)
Block, Bert   *police officer*   335 Walnut
Boise, Hardy C.   *minister*   215 Beech
Booker, John   *florist*   726 N. Sheridan
Booker, Jody (Mrs. John)
Booker, Roger   *student*
Booker, Louisa Mae   *retired*   347 W. Arizona
Boomershine, John E.   *veterinarian*   386 W. Nevada
Boomershine, Madeline M. (Mrs. John E.)
Boomershine, Brian
Boomershine, John Jr.
Boylan, Harold S.   *attorney*   587 E. Utah
Brackett, Marlene   *publicist*   782 N. Scott
Brewster, Alex   *salesman*   258 W. Oregon
Brewster, Helene (Mrs. Alex)
Brewster, David   *student*
Brown, Deborah   *reporter*   180 E. Arizona
Brown, Robert   *teacher*   301 Beech
Brown, Myla (Mrs. Robert)
Brown, Robert E.   *student*
Buchanan, H.L.   *contractor*   503 E. Vermont
Buchanan, Rose (Mrs. H.L.)
Buchanan, James
Buchanan, Robert
Burt, Henry   *social worker*   210 W. Virginia
Butler, Ray   *computer specialist*   280 River Road

C

Callendar, Herbert A.   *police chief*   810 N. Lee
Carew, Alfred   *administrator*   146 Walnut
Carew, Luther   *painter*   210 W. California
Carew, Melanie (Mrs. Luther)
Carew, Lawrence   student
Carter, Alison   *minister*   533 S. Meade
Carter, Dawson   *salesman*   212 E. Florida
Carter, Maura (Mrs. Dawson)
Carter, Anthony   *student*
Carter, Marilyn   *editor*   227 S. Calhoun
Chin, John   *police officer*   S. Western Avenue
Chin, Nancy   *police officer*   S. Western Avenue
Chin, Jennifer   *physician*   502 E. Utah
Choate, Stephen P.   304 S. Jackson
Choate, N.L. (Mrs. Stephen P.)   *office worker*
Clark, John   *grocer*   608 E. Ohio
Clark, Wilma (Mrs. John)
Clark, Kim   *student*
Cleveland, William R.   *truck driver*   539 S. Grant
Cook, Gerald A.   *administrator*   604 N. Houston
Coolidge, Calvin R.   *building manager*   510 W. Lexington
Coolidge, Ethel (Mrs. Calvin R.)
Coolidge, John   *student*
Cooper, Herbert W.   *conservation officer*   304 W. Nevada
Cordoba, Alexis   *police sergeant*   512 S. Grant
Cordoba, Luz   *social worker*   512 S. Grant
Courtwright, Fred III   *publisher*   212 E. New York
Courtwright, Anne (Mrs. Fred)
Cristo, S.   *teacher*   109 S. Lee
Crow, Emil   *police sergeant*   412 Sycamore
Curtis, Raymond   *county employee*   618 Washington
Curtis, Eileen (Mrs. Raymond)   *beautician*
Curtis, Eileen   *student*

D

Daggett, Richard   *civil engineer*   380 E. Arizona
Daggett, Emma (Mrs. Richard)   *cartographer*

Davis, Theodore   *advertising manager*   875 N. Stuart
Dawson, Ronald   *printer*   308 S. Houston
Dawson, Gilda (Mrs. Ronald)
Dawson, Stephen   *student*
Dean, Edward S.   *chemist*   408 S. Meade
Delaney, John R.   *service station owner*   202 Maple
Dendramis, Sue Ellen   *attorney*   942 N. Grant
Diaz, Mark L.   *factory worker*   520 E. New York
Dickens, Henry   *county manager*   27 Maple
Dickens, Anne (Mrs. Henry)   *writer*
Dobbins, J. Vernon   *meteorologist*   286 E. Virginia
Donnelly, William T.   *college administrator*   307 E. California
Door, W.T.   *physician*   327 S. Houston
Duglay, Heather   *nurse practitioner*   216 N. Scott
Duttweiler, John R., Rev.   *minister*   210 Walnut
Dwight, Marion   *registered nurse*   810 N. Grant
Dwight, Robert   *contractor*   350 W. Arizona
Dwight, Carolyn (Mrs. Robert)

E

Ellenberg, Kellie   *editor*   216 N. Scott
Elmer, John C.   *banker*   408 W. Utah
Evans, Clayton   *fire marshal*   308 S. Calhoun
Evers, Edward E., Rev.   *minister*   683 N. Jackson

F

Feldpausch, J.   *teacher*   347 W. Arizona
Ferguson, Gerald S.   *bookkeeper*   Airport
Ferreira, Richard Sr.   *security guard*   127 Maple
Ferreira, Frances (Mrs. Richard)
Ferreira, Elwyn   *mechanic*
Ferreira, Richard Jr.   *student*
Fine, Elias   *rabbi*   560 E. Newton
Fiore, Emil Jr.   *restaurant owner*   581 N. Lee
Fiore, Carlotta (Mrs. Emil Jr.)
Fiore, Eleanor   *student*
Floyde, Halbert O.   *police officer*   622 S. Jackson
Flynn, George A., Rev.   *priest*   478 W. Maryland
Franklin, Ben   *printer*   18 Beech
Franklin, Charity (Mrs. Ben)
Franklin, Robert   *student*
Frogge, Kermit L.   *retired*   347 W. Arizona
Funderburke, James L.   *stockbroker*   418 S. Lee

G

Galina, Caroline   *teacher*   408 E. Oregon
Garcia, Jose   *union agent*   201 W. Virginia

Germain, Dwight   *chauffer*   S. Airport
Gibbs, Beverly   *teacher*   505 W. Florida
Gibbs, John   120 Indian River Place
Gibbs, Kathrine (Mrs. John)
Gillette, Ralph   *electrician*   437 S. Lee
Gillette, Helen (Mrs. Ralph)
Gilmore, Horace A.   *contractor*   335 W. Oregon
Gilmore, Sarah (Mrs. Horace A.)
Gilmore, Horace N.   *artist*   583 S. Grant
Gold, Harold S.   *accountant*   180 N. Calhoun
Gold, Morris   *jeweler*   408 W. Arizona
Gold, Esther (Mrs. Morris)
Gomes, Octavio   *personnel director*   347 W. Arizona
Gomez, Delores   *secretary*   184 Maple
Gomez, Luis   *student*
Gordon, Sybil   *circuit judge*   642 E. Nevada
Green, Virgil   *security guard*   714 N. Jackson
Green, Rachel (Mrs. Virgil)   *clerk*
Green, Debra   *student*
Green, Gardner   *student*

H

Hale, Edward Everett   *teacher*   111 W. Wisconsin
Hall, Henry   *chauffeur*   301 S. Sherman
Hall, Myra (Mrs. Henry)
Handy, W.H. III   *banker*   306 E. Oregon
Hardy, James   *teacher*   97 River
Harmon, Donald   *teacher*   518 W. Lexington
Harris, Charles   *pharmacist*   216 N. Grant
Harris, Christine   *pharmacist*
Hawkins, Emma   *antique dealer*   411 N. Grant
Hazelton, William M.   *police officer*   704 W. Perimeter
Hazelton, Margaret (Mrs. William M.)
Hempstead, Arthur B. Jr.   *municipal judge*   657 N. Sheridan
Hempstead, Jane (Mrs. Arthur B.)
Hempstead, Michael   *student*
Henderson, Maurice   *medical technician*   462 W. Florida
Hershey, Gerald R.   *physician*   401 W. Oregon
Hickock, Bruce B.   *banker*   371 E. Nevada
Hickock, Walter   *state police officer*   350 Sycamore
Higginbottom, Ernest F.   *U.S. Senator*   590 E. Nevada
Hill, Harold O.   *restaurateur*   92 S. Meade
Hillman, Walter   *sales representative*   240 W. Wisconsin
Hirsch, Dr. H.L.   *physician*   850 N. Stuart
Hoffman, Rita   *banker*   224 E. Florida
Holmes, Granville   *teacher*   15 Sycamore
Hope, Jonathan   *fire captain*   409 E. New York
Howe, George A.   *printer*   616 E. Wisconsin
Howe, Harriet (Mrs. George A.)

Huang, Charles O.   *state employee*   327 E. Florida

Hughes, Charles E.   *jurist*   540 E. Nevada

I

Irving, William H.   *editor*   710 W. Florida

Ivory, G.R.   *police officer*   550 W. Newton

J

Jackson, Terry   *teacher*   97 Oak

Jackson, Ella (Mrs. Terry)

Johnson, Harry O.   *insurance*   260 Washington

Johnson, Mary (Mrs. Harry O.)   *teacher*

Johnson, Nancy   *hardware dealer*   111 E. Oregon

Jones, Myron   *computer programmer*   141 N. Meade

Jones, Ellen (Mrs. Myron)

Jones, Mary   *student*

Jones, William F.   *editor*   115 Sheridan

Jones, Elizabeth (Mrs. William F.)

Jones, Lydia

K

Kane, Wadsworth   *insurance*   599 W. Maryland

Kane, Hilda (Mrs. Wadsworth)

Kane, Brian   *student*

Kelley, Gregory E.   *attorney*   216 N. Scott

Kelley, Greg   *editor*   301 Walnut

Kelly, James   *contractor*   S. Western Avenue

Kelly, Maureen   *registered nurse*   S. Western Avenue

Kershaw, Sally   *college student*   412 S. Grant

Kirby, Helen   *librarian*   211 Sycamore

Kirby, Jason   *sales representative*   213 Sycamore

Koo, Henry   *meteorologist*   109 W. Virginia

Korth, Frank   *laborer*   Old Meetinghouse

Krug, Herbert   *state employee*   560 W. Newton

Krug, Jessie W.   *state employee*   215 River

L

LaFrance, Genevieve   *professor*   340 E. New York

Latham, Eric   *editor*   212 N. Calhoun

Leamy, Lillian   *attorney*   27 W. Ohio

Leavitt, Rollin R.   *teacher*   221 Maple

Lewis, Elwyn   *IRS agent*   345 W. Ohio

Lewis, Tina (Mrs. Elwyn)

Lewis, Edward   *student*

Lewis, John Q.   *minister*   550 N. Sheridan

Lodge, John A.   *county auditor*   197 River

Look, Abel   *sheriff*   861 Battle

Look, James   *reporter*   552 W. Newton

Look, Stanley   *county employee*   301 W. Oregon

Look, Helen (Mrs. Stanley)

Look, Ann   *student*

Love, Henry   *art teacher*   17 W. Ohio

Lund, Aaron O.   *clerk*   48 S. Meade

Lutz, Helen   *artist*   477 E. Main

Lyons, Eugene R.   *taxidermist*   277 E. Arizona

Lyons, Evelyn (Mrs. Eugene R.)

Lyons, Suzanne   *student*

M

MacClure, Lawrence   *banker*   580 N. Sheridan

MacComber, Rufus   *city employee*   465 W. Perimeter

MacComber, Mahalia (Mrs. Rufus)

MacDonald, Stewart   *hotel manager*   345 N. Sherman

Maher, Thomas O.   *detective*   104 N. Battle

Main, Roger   *accountant*   804 N. Sherman

Main, Virginia (Mrs. Roger)

Malcolm, William T.   *police officer*   581 W. California

Marks, Ellen   *registered nurse*   347 W. Arizona

Marks, Mary   *teacher*   120 W. Ohio

Marks, Patricia   *county employee*   125 Scott

Marks, Peter   *teacher*   305 N. Houston

Marks, Mary (Mrs. Peter)

Marshall, Joseph R.   *police officer*   234 E. Ohio

May, Earl   *county employee*   86 Beech

McGregor, James L.   *musician*   927 N. Stuart

McGregor, Vangie (Mrs. James L.)

McGuire, Edwin (Micky)   *trainman*   385 W. Wisconsin

McGuire, Harold   *retired*   85 River

McGuire, John   *insurance*   158 S. Stuart

McLaren, Joyce Ann   *publicist*   780 N. Grant

McLeod, Mary Margaret   *physician*   610 W. Oregon

Meade, Horace W.   *physician*   414 W. Ohio

Meade, June (Mrs. Horace)

Medford, John E.   *deputy sheriff*   35 W. Nevada

Medford, Stephanie (Mrs. John E.)

Medford, John Jr.   *student*

Meyers, Don   *court clerk*   150 E. Arizona

Miller, Kenneth L.   *school employee*   442 E. Wisconsin

Miller, L.L.   *editor*   216 N. Scott

Miller, Robert L.   *plumber*   807 S. Jackson

Miller, Warren E.   *Realtor*   201 E. Florida

Miskell, William   *surveyor*   415 E. Maryland

Miskell, Sybil (Mrs. William)

Miskell, Raymond L.   *student*

Mitchell, Johnston,   *city employee*   439 E. Nevada
Moore, James L.   *federal employee*   210 S. Stuart
Morris, Clyde   *package store manager*   560 S. Grant
Morrissey, William A.   *state employee*   27 Oak
Murphy, Wanda   *dressmaker*   980 N. Houston

N

Nelson, Fred W.   *city editor*   900 N. Sheridan
Nesbitt, Wallace   *attorney*   275 W. Virginia
Newhouse, Harold H.   *postal worker*   682 N. Scott
Newhouse, Mildred (Mrs. Harold H.)
Ng, Joseph   *computer specialist*   408 E. Florida
Ng, Cynthia (Mrs. Joseph)
Ng, Anna   *student*
Nguyen, Arnold   *college employee*   200 S. Stuart
Nguyen, Mary Ann (Mrs. Arnold)
Nightingale, H.L., Rev.   *pastor*   715 N. Scott
Nixon, James   *firefighter*   217 S. Grant
North, Henry L.   *teacher*   311 N. Grant
Norton, Homer H.   *clerk*   271 Washington
Norton, Frances (Mrs. Homer H.)

O

Oberdorfer, Harry   *police officer*   604 W. Nevada
O'Byrne, John L.   *SBA assistant administrator*   187 Sycamore
O'Kelly, Sean   *police officer*   270 W. Vermont
Olds, Gerald   *hotel manager*   49 Beech
Olejnik, H.   *social worker*   109 S. Lee
O'Neil, James   *detective sergeant*   75 Oak
Ormsby, Zelig   *retired*   347 W. Arizona
Ormsby, Harriet (Mrs. Zelig)
Orr, Marion   *city attorney*   811 E. Wisconsin
Ott, Wilhelm V.   *sales representative*   270 W. Wisconsin

P

Page, Christine   *attorney*   418 E. Florida
Page, John   *retired*   375 E. California
Page, Ethel (Mrs. John)
Page, Walter E.   *interior decorator*   311 N. Grant
Palmer, Bernard E.   *retired*   350 River
Parks, Marshall   *SBA administrator*   408 N. Jackson
Peters, Don   *production manager*   79 W. Utah
Peters, Paul   *security guard*   87 Oak
Potter, Branson   *laborer*   506 S. Sherman
Powers, Hubert   *oil dealer*   108 E. California
Powers, Gladys (Mrs. Hubert)
Price, Flynn   *state police*   3 S. Meade
Price, June (Mrs. Flynn)

Q

Quill, Henry   *retired*   218 N. Lee
Quill, Martha (Mrs. Henry)

R

Reeves, Marshall   *dry cleaner*   487 N. Grant
Reimenschneider, Russell   *paramedic*   847 N. Battle
Rickles, Arturo   *salesman*   450 E. Ohio
Rickles, Thomasina (Mrs. Arturo)   *police officer*
Rickles, Arturo Jr.   *student*
Ricketts, John   *pharmacist*   622 W. Lexington
Rigsby, Peter   *painter*   922 S. Territorial
Rivera, Carlos J.   *auditor*   87 S. Meade
Rivera, Marie (Mrs. Carlos)
Rivera, Diane   *student*
Rivera, Helen E.   *student*
Robbins, Benjamin   *retired*   336 S. Sherman
Robbins, Diana (Mrs. Benjamin)
Roberts, Fred H.   *accountant*   401 E. California
Robinson, George T.   *designer*   321 S. Scott
Rogers, George A.   *city treasurer*   627 N. Jackson
Rogers, Hazel (Mrs. George A.)
Rowland, John J.   *jurist*   211 Beech

S

Sawyer, Albert H. Jr.   *teacher*   640 E. Nevada
Sawyer, Martha (Mrs. Albert H. Jr.)
Scissors, Floyd R.   *restaurateur*   104 ½ N. Calhoun
Shanker, Albert L.   *teacher*   637 W. Lexington
Shanks, Hubert L.   *physician*   321 W. Newton
Shaw, Harlan   *computer specialist*   317 E. Oregon
Shaw, Roberta (Mrs. Harlan)   *teacher*
Shonsky, John T.   *retired*   408 N. Houston
Shonsky, Helene (Mrs. John)
Short, Alice   *teacher*   604 Washington
Smith, Henry Clay   *teacher*   280 E. Wisconsin
Smith, Nancy (Mrs. H.C.)
Snell, Jacob (Jake)   *service station operator*   252 W. New York
Snook, Ivan   *long-distance hauling*   540 W. Lexington
Snook, Ellen (Mrs. Ivan)
Snook, Christian
Snook, Mitchell
Souza, Albert T.   *banker*   461 W. California
Souza, Donald   *civil engineer*   333 River
Souza, John   *retired*   458 S. Scott
Souza, Mary (Mrs. John)
Souza, Joseph   *plumber*   401 W. Arizona

Souza, Lewis   *dentist*   27 Beech
Spaulding, Ernest   *actuary*   273 W. Wisconsin
Spaulding, Evelyn (Mrs. Ernest)
Speizman, Harold E.   *public relations*   761 N. Lee
Spinoza, Arturo   *builder*   211 E. Perimeter
Spinoza, Mary   *sales representative*   211 E. Perimeter
Spooner, Randolph M.   *insurance*   910 N. Sheridan
Spooner, Janet (Mrs. Randolph M.)
Spooner, Jane   *student*
Spooner, Joseph   *student*
Spooner, Randolph Jr.   *student*
Stahl, John   *county agent*   650 W. Florida
Stahl, Virginia (Mrs. John)   *teacher*
Stahl, Mark H.   *student*
Stephenson, William A.   *musician*   125 Indian River Place
Stephenson, Deborah (Mrs. William A.)
Stephenson, Mitchell   *student*
Stieber, Kenneth   *insurance*   822 E. Nevada
Strauss, Jacob O.   *firefighter*   280 S. Scott
Stroh, Walter   *railroad engineer*   250 N. Sherman
Sturdevant, Willis   *police officer*   201 E. Nevada
Sullivan, James J.   *editor*   35 Maple
Sullivan, Caroline (Mrs. James J.)
Swift, Franklin T.   *hotel clerk*   216 N. Scott
Sylvester, Rebecca   *heavy-equipment operator*   304 E. Maryland

T

Talcott, John A.   *police officer*   210 W. State
Tate, Lawrence D.   *deputy sheriff*   409 S. Sheridan
Teacher, Walker E.   *salesman*   603 W. Utah
Timulty, John O.   *photographer*   410 W. Newton
Toefel, Mary Jane   *bank teller*   216 N. Scott
Tombs, Catherine   *court clerk*   216 N. Scott
Toy, Jack E.   *state police*   85 W. Utah
Trask, John   *court clerk*   212 S. Jackson
Trosko, Julia A.   *teacher*   347 W. Arizona
Tsui, Charles E.   *teacher*   212 N. Houston
Tsui, Lynn (Mrs. Charles)
Tsui, Betsy   *student*
Turnbull, Anna   *bookkeeper*   310 E. Virginia
Turner, Ralph   *chemist*   207 S. Calhoun
Twardzynski, Otto   *teacher*   104 E. Florida
Twardzynski, Maryann (Mrs. Otto)   *teacher*
Twardzynski, Lorie   *student*

V

Vanderpol, Ray E.   *rail superintendent*   805 N. Lee
Verway, Richard L.   *teacher*   111 W. Oregon
Vogel, Ralph E. Jr.   *foreman*   504 W. Vermont
Vogel, Helen (Mrs. Ralph E. Jr.)

W

Wagner, S.E.   *teacher* 510 W. Lexington
Waldron, Donald E. (Duke)   *service station manager*   115 E. Main
Wang, James   *teacher*   504 E. Utah
Wang, Helen (Mrs. James)
Wang, James Jr.   *student*
Wang, Mary Sue   *bank teller*   410 S. Houston
Warren, Richard   *stockbroker*   407 W. Virginia
Warren, Evie (Mrs. Richard)
Warren, Richard   *student*
Watson, Charles   *hotel clerk*   107 S. Meade
Watson, Myrtle   *cashier*   107 S. Meade
Wells, Roger   *steelworker*   105 E. Newton
West, Henry A.   *welder*   915 N. Meade
West, Thelma (Mrs. Henry A.)
West, Ellis   *student*
Wetherbee, Beatrice   *college employee*   216 N. Scott
White, Elmer   *public relations*   235 Maple
White, Betty (Mrs. Elmer)
White, Mark   *student*
Wiggins, John F.X.   *city employee*   75 W. Utah
Williams, Anne   *county clerk*   216 N. Scott
Williams, Deborah   *public relations*   450 S. Meade
Williams, Donna   *city clerk*   108 E. Oregon
Williams, Henry   *business agent*   710 E. Main
Williams, Samantha (Mrs. Henry)   *lawyer*
Williams, Nancy   *student*
Williams, James   *insurance adjuster*   70 W. Utah
Williams, Marcia (Mrs. James)   *accountant*
Willoughby, Roger   *mechanic*   234 River
Wilson, James L.   *state employee*   508 N. Scott
Wilson, Lamar   *county employee*   250 N. Sheridan
Wood, Helen   *college employee*   571 E. Maryland
Woods, Donald   *police sergeant*   S. Western Avenue
Worthington, Lorraine M.   *Realtor*   450 E. Nevada

Y

Yaffee, Bette   *architect*   317 S. Scott

337

Practice Exercises in News Writing

Carolton Business Directory

Acme Fire and Accident Insurance Co.	Airport Road
Applegate Books	604 W. New York
Barth Flowers	411 E. Vermont
Belk's	245 E. Main
Belle View Apartments	216 N. Scott
Bi-Low Supermarket	400 Washington Road
Booker Floral	102 N. Jackson
Bulldog Wine and Beer Store	103 E. Main
Carolton Construction Co.	245 Washington Road
Carolton, City of	
Carolton-Washington Adult Center	412 E. Main
Civic Center	312 W. Newton Road
Community Development Agency	128 N. Meade
James L. Polk, director	
Community Mental Health Clinic	550 W. Maryland
Fire Department	
Fire Chief John F.X. Wiggins	
Fire Capt. Jonathan Hope	
Fire Lieut. Jacob Strauss	
Fire Marshall Clayton Evans	
Central Station	381 E. Main
Rescue Squad	
East Side Station	808 S. Territorial
West Side Station	Airport Road
Franklin Library	400 E. Vermont
Jail	616 W. Vermont
Municipal Building	210 E. Main
Mayor Henry Clay Smith	Room 112
Johnston Mitchell, administrative assistant	Room 113
City Clerk Donna Williams	Room 104
City Treasurer George A. Rogers	Room 12
Tax Collector Joseph E. Thompson	Room 318
City Auditor	Room 15
Human Rights Commission	Room 328
Planning Commission	Room 330
Vocational Rehabilitation	Room 211
Municipal Court	100 E. Virginia
Judge Carol Brown	
Judge Arthur B. Hempstead Jr.	
Judge Charles E. Hughes	
Special Master Enrique Martinez	
Police	612 W. Vermont
Accident Prevention	Room 211
Administration	Room 100
Herbert A. Callendar, chief	
Crime Lab	Room 310
Detective Bureau	Room 215
Drug Enforcement	Room 128
Uniform Division	Room 101
Public Housing Authority	412 E. Main
Receiving Hospital	700 W. Vermont
Recreation Department	608 W. Florida
Rescue Squad	381 E. Main
Carolton Public Schools	
Central High	608 W. Florida
Harvey O'Higgins Junior High	350 E. California

338

Copyright © by George A. Hough 3rd. All rights reserved.

Carolton, City of (*cont.*)	
Carolton Public Schools (*cont.*)	
Horace Mann Elementary	480 W. Oregon
Richard Harding Davis Elementary	612 E. Maryland
Board of Education	608 W. Florida
Alfred Carew, superintendent	
Carolton Country Club	158 River Road
Carolton Hardware Co.	12 N. Jackson
Carolton-Washington County Chamber of	
Commerce	304 W. Vermont
Cedar Village Apartments	550 E. Newton
Churches	
All Saints Episcopal	680 N. Jackson
Carolton Jewish Congregation	318 E. Newton Road
Congregational	301 W. Arizona
First Baptist	604 W. Florida
First Methodist	522 S. Meade
Liberty Baptist	911 N. Grant
St. Thomas Roman Catholic	480 W. Maryland
Trinity A.M.E.	234 N. Stuart
City Rescue Mission	601 E. Main
College Standard Service	1182 S. Territorial
Colonial Village Apartments	510 W. Lexington
Commerce Club	427 W. Lexington
Copper Kettle Restaurant	450 W. Lexington
Curious Book Store	340 W. New York
Daily Student	357 E. Lexington
Delta Mall	Airport Road
Door Brothers Funeral Home	250 N. Scott
Duke's Shell Service	511 S. Territorial
Evergreen Cemetery	Airport Road
Farmers and Merchants Bank	250 E. Main
First National Bank	16 W. Main
First National Food Stores	Airport Road
Graham Associates, public relations	100 W. Main
Great Atlantic and Pacific Tea Co.	106 W. Vermont
Hawkins Antiques	515 W. New York
Higginbottom Sons Co., real estate	316 E. Main
Holiday Inn	350 E. Main
Hospitals	
Carolton General Hospital	250 S. Calhoun
Holy Cross Hospital	E. State Road
Receiving Hospital	700 W. Vermont
Hotel Lenox	450 W. Lexington
Hudson, J.L. Co.	Delta Mall
Jefferson Village Apartments	347 W. Arizona
Jenkins Funeral Home	217 N. Scott
Jollity Building	Airport Road
Kelly Construction Co.	Airport Road
Kroger	Delta Mall
Leamy, Goldstick and Gray, attorneys	211 S. Sherman
McKay Funeral Home	550 E. Virginia
McKim, Oglethorpe and Dodge, architects	100 E. Main
Medical Arts Building	317 E. Main
Meijer's Thrifty Acres	Airport Road
Mercy Ambulance Service	213 W. Main
Modern Decor, interior decorating	101 E. Main
Montgomery Ward	Delta Mall
Morning Record Publishing Co.	312 E. Main
O'Flynn's	104 River Road
O'Malley's Restaurant and Bar	104 N. Calhoun

Piggly Wiggly Food Stores	Western Avenue
Presbyterian Home	E. State Road
Quick Coin Laundry	210 W. Main
Reuther Building	106 River Road
Riley Brothers Funeral Chapel	426 W. Arizona
Sears, Roebuck and Co.	Delta Mall
Shook Chemical Corp.	950 N. Meade
Smith and Jones Funeral Chapel	Airport Road
Snell's Texaco	585 S. Grant
State Government	
National Guard Armory	Airport Road
State Police	Airport Road
Vocational Rehabilitation Services	211 City Hall
Territory and Western Railroad	T&W Depot
Tri-State Education Assn.	255 Washington Road
University City National Bank	604 W. Main
U.S. Government	
Federal Building	106 S. Lee
Internal Revenue Service	Federal Building
National Oceanic and Atmospheric	
Administration	Airport
Postal Service	306 W. Main
Harold E. Rogers, Postmaster	
Postal Inspectors	
Small Business Administration	Federal Building
Utilities	
General Telephone Co.	211 W. Main
Midstate Gas and Electric Co.	417 E. Main
Washington County	
County Auditor	John A. Lodge
County Clerk	Anne Williams
Coroner	W.T. Door
Sheriff	Abel Look
Carolton-Washington Adult Center	412 E. Main
Carolton-Washington County Airport	Airport Road
Extended Care Facility	512 Washington Road
Highway Department	700 Washington Road
Lamar Wilson, superintendent	
Health and Human Relations Commission	300 W. Main
Department of Public Health	516 Washington Road
Department of Public Safety	600 Washington Road
House of Correction	612 Washington Road
Sheriff	612 Washington Road
Welfare Department	300 W. Main
Women's Clinic	516 Washington Road
Washington County Courthouse	300 W. Main
Circuit Court	Room 104
Judge Sybil Gordon	
Clerk of Court	Room 103
Clerk of Court John Trask	
County Clerk	Room 115
District Court	Room 204
Family Court	Room 110
Council on Aging	Room 120
Human Relations	Room 208
Jury Commission	Room 212
Mental Health Department	Room 234
Prosecutor	Room 308
Harold S. Boylan	
Welfare Department	Room 310
Wirtz Building	128 N. Meade

Carolton Organizations and Associations

Alianza Hispana	106 River Road
American Association of Retired Persons	
American Civil Liberties Union	
American Federation of State, County and Municipal Employees	106 River Road
American Legion, John Hennessey Post No. 12	Airport Road
American Legion Auxiliary	
Boy Scouts of America, Troop 43	
Carolton Association of Police	128 N. Meade
Carolton Community Relations Association	128 N. Meade
Carolton Council of Churches	
Carolton Day Care Council, Inc.	419 N. Battle Road
Carolton HIV-AIDS Community Partnership	
Carolton Hospice	250 E. California
Carolton Labor Council	106 River Road
Carolton Professional Women's Club	501 E. Main
Carolton Senior Citizens Organization	100 N. Stuart
Carolton-Washington County Chamber of Commerce	304 W. Vermont
Carolton-Washington County Council on Alcoholism	County Building
Citizens for the Arts	
City Art Club	310 W. Newton Road
Daughters of the American Revolution	
Forest Lawn Neighborhood Association	
Friends of the Museum	
Gay/AIDS Support Group	
Habitat for Humanity	106 River Road
Mothers Against Drunk Driving	
National Association for the Advancement of Colored People	
National Organization for Women	
Northwest College Alumni Club	
Parent-Teachers Association	
Planned Parenthood Association	704 W. Vermont
Service Clubs	
Challenge	
Civitan	
Rotary	
Society of the Holy Ghost	
Society of Professional Journalists, Central State Professional Chapter	
State AFL-CIO Council	106 River Road
Veterans of Foreign Wars Post 182	600 W. Newton Road
Veterans of Foreign Wars Ladies Auxiliary	
Visiting Nurses Association	306 E. Vermont
Washington County Assn. for the Blind	128 N. Meade
Washington County Council on Aging	
Washington County Democratic Committee	128 N. Meade
Washington County Democratic Women's Organization	
Washington County Education Association	
Washington County Foundation	
Washington County Heritage Assn.	
Washington County Historical Society	
Washington County Human Relations Association	
Washington County Mental Health Association	317 E. Main
Washington County Public Relations Club	
Washington County Society of Professional Engineers	
Women's Crisis Center	704 W. Vermont

Northwest College Faculty and Staff

Arnold, Dalton	director, news bureau
Blaine, Harold E.	professor, history
Brown, Robert	professor, physics
Butler, Ray	computer specialist, journalism
Chin, Jennifer	physician/research, health services
Cook, Gerald A.	chairman, business
Dawson, Terry	news bureau
Donnelly, William T.	chairman, agriculture
Feldpausch, Julia	professor, physics; chairman, department of physics
Flores, Luisa	associate professor, Romance languages
Gibbs, Beverly	professor, business; assistant chairman, business
Harmon, Donald	professor, Romance languages
Hirsch, H.L.	professor, medicine
Holmes, Granville	professor, journalism
Huang, Charles O.	professor, physics; director, physics research lab
Lafferty, Charles E.	professor, economics
LaFrance, Genevieve	distinguished professor, entomology
Leavitt, Rollin R.	professor, family science
McKay, John R.	president; professor, economics
Morrissey, William A.	editor, news bureau
Ng, Joseph	director, computer services
Nguyen, Arnold	director, placement services
Nichols, Robert	professor and chairman, environmental design
Sawyer, Albert H. Jr.	professor, history
Shanks, Hubert L.	director, health service
Shaw, Roberta	assistant professor, natural science
Sherman, Amasa	registrar
Smith, Henry Clay	professor, psychology
Trosko, Julia A.	professor, agronomy
Tsui, Charles E.	research professor, agronomy
Verway, Richard L.	director, computer laboratory
Wagner, Shirley	assistant professor, education
Wetherbee, Beatrice	assistant dean, student affairs
Wood, Helen	general manager, college press

Northwest College Students

Allen, Richard S.	freshman, journalism, Cleveland, Ohio 504 S. Meade
Arp, William	senior, computer science, Columbus, Ga. Hallowell Hall
Bakatsas, Sarah	junior, Petoskey, Mich. Shaw Hall
Devartanian, Hugo	graduate student, Paterson, N.J. Wells Hall
Fraser, Helene	senior, computer science, Atlanta, Ga. Lawrence Hall
Gould, Gregory	freshman, biology, San Francisco, Calif. Hallowell Hall
Haag, Robert J.	senior, journalism, Marietta, Ga. Chartwell Hall
Haugabook, Cheryl	sophomore, home economics, Chicago, Ill. Lawrence Hall
Henderson, William	freshman, Romance languages, Boston, Mass. 540 S. Meade

Herrera, Renato	graduate student, Brownsville, Texas Shaw Hall
Kershaw, Sally	freshman, women's studies, Aiken, S.C. 412 S. Grant
Keskonis, David	sophomore, history, Kalispell, Mont. Shaw Hall
Lawrence, Joan	senior, journalism, Austin, Texas 240 Lawrence
Lawrence, Quimby	freshman, English, Dallas, Texas Hallowell Hall
Matthews, Harold	junior, speech, Dubuque, Iowa Hallowell Hall
McClanahan, John King	senior, chemistry, Pittsfield, Mass. Chartwell Hall
Ney, Marshall	junior, political science, Toledo, Ohio Shaw Hall
Oberhansly, Bennie Jr.	freshman, humanities, Lincoln, Neb. Chartwell Hall
Ong, James E.	junior, journalism, Wilmington, Del. Hallowell Hall
O'Quinn, Rick	senior, journalism, Memphis, Tenn. Hallowell Hall
Osorio, Jorge	graduate student, Cali, Colombia Wells Hall
Pirkle, Jerald	freshman, mathematics, Lawrence, Kans. Chartwell Hall
Putterbaugh, Henry	freshman, computer science, Troy, N.Y. Shaw Hall
Quattlebaum, Jennifer	junior, women's studies, Dayton, Ohio Lawrence Hall
Rzsa, Sandra N.	senior, biochemistry, Smithtown, L.I., N.Y. Lawrence Hall
Roberts, Daniel B.	senior, computer science, Portland, Ore. 540 S. Meade
Salcido, Ashley	junior, family and child sciences, Hendersonville, N.C. Lawrence Hall
Simpson, Paul	senior, history, Memphis, Tenn. Hallowell Hall
Sims, Maryanne	senior, history, Lenox, Mass. Lawrence Hall
Tilton, Joshua	senior, business, West Tisbury, Mass. Chartwell Hall
Torres, Lamar	sophomore, Romance languages, New Iberia, La. Shaw Hall
Trosko, John William	senior, physics, Carolton Shaw Hall
Uribe, Troy R.	sophomore, communications, Bismark, N.D. Lawrence Hall
Ward, Sheldon	junior, business, Anderson, S.C. Chartwell Hall
Weaver, Christy	sophomore, telecommunications, Havre de Grace, Md. Lawrence Hall
Yu, Cong	graduate student, Hong Kong Wells Hall
Zollars, Penny Anne	senior, music, South Bend, Ind. Lawrence Hall

Northwest College Buildings

Administration Building	N. Campus Drive
Alumni Association	Administration Building
Alumni Chapel	E. Campus Drive
Bloomfield Library	E. Campus Drive
Bookstore	Student Center
Cameron Meyers Graduate Center	Circle Drive
Center for Continuing Education	
(Conference Center)	Circle Drive
Chartwell Residence Hall	Old Brick Road
Cordell Hull Center for International Programs	Circle Drive
Dykstra House	N. Campus Drive
John R. McKay, president	
Forestry School	Circle Drive
Hallowell Residence Hall	E. Campus Drive
Information Services (public relations)	N. Campus Drive
John Marshall School of Law	Marshall Drive
John H. Watson School of Criminal Justice	S. Campus Drive
LaFollette Auditorium	W. Campus Drive
Lawrence Residence Hall	S. Campus Drive
Mark Twain Hall	Washington Entrance
Married Student Housing	
Lexington Village	W. Campus Drive
University Village	E. Campus Drive
Medical College	S. Campus Drive
Memorial Hall (student center)	N. Campus Drive
Military Science	Western Avenue
Air Force Reserve Officers Training Corps	Room 110
Army Reserve Officers Training Corps	Room 210
Placement Services	Administration Building
Public Safety Department	Service Road
School of Agriculture	S. Campus Drive
School of Education	S. Campus Drive
School of Journalism	Greeley Road
School of Veterinary Medicine	Research Road
Shaw Residence Hall	S. Campus Drive
State Arts Center	N. Campus Drive
Wells Graduate Residence Hall	Wells Road
Women's Studies Center	W. Circle Drive

Northwest College Organizations and Associations

African-American Student Center		Memorial Hall
Alpha Phi Sorority		210 E. Newton Road
Alpha Zeta Omega Fraternity		540 S. Meade
Angel Flight	military honorary	
Arnold Air Society	military honorary	
Asian Student Organization		Memorial Hall
Daily Student	student daily newspaper	
Delta Mu Delta	business honorary	
Democratic Students Association		
Faculty Women's Organization	women faculty	
Friends of the Library		106 Bloomfield
Gay and Lesbian Alliance		Memorial Hall
James Madison Debating Society		
Maison Francaise		575 W. Newton Road
Native American Cultural Society		
Society of Professional Journalists		journalism students
Young Republicans		

Reverse Directory

Airport Road, North

Acme Fire and Accident Insurance Co.
Delta Mall
   J.L. Hudson Co.
   Kroger
   Montgomery Ward
   Sears, Roebuck and Co.
Ferguson, Gerald S.
Jollity Building
Kelly Construction Co.
Meijer's Thrifty Acres
National Guard Armory
Smith and Jones Funeral Chapel
State Police
West Side Fire Station

Airport Road, South

American Legion Post No. 12
Carolton-Washington County Airport
Evergreen Cemetery
First National Food Stores
Germain, Dwight E.
Weather Service, Airport

Arizona, East

150	Meyers, Don
180	Brown, D.
277	Lyons, Eugene R.
380	Daggett, Richard

Arizona, West

301	Congregational Church
347	Jefferson Village Apartments
	Marks, Ellen
	Booker, Louisa Mae
	Feldpausch, J.
	Frogge, Kermit L.
	Gomes, Octavio
	Ormsby, Zelig
	Trosko, Julia A.
350	Dwight, Robert
401	Sousa, Joseph
408	Gold, Morris
426	Riley Brothers Funeral Chapel

Battle Road, North

104	Maher, Thomas O.
419	Carolton Day Care Council, Inc.
847	Reimenschneider, Russell
861	Look, Abel

Beech

18	Franklin, Ben
27	Sousa, Lewis
49	Olds, Gerald
84	Arnold, Dalton
86	May, Earl
211	Rowland, John J.
215	Boise, Hardy C.
301	Brown, Robert
308	Bell, Alexander G.
	Bell, Alexander G. Jr.

Calhoun, North

104	O'Malley's Restaurant and Bar
104 ½	Scissors, Floyd R.
180	Gold, Harold S.
212	Latham, Eric

Calhoun, South

207	Turner, Ralph
227	Carter, Marilyn
250	Carolton General Hospital
308	Evans, Clayton

California, East

108	Powers, Hubert
250	Carolton Hospice
307	Donnelly, W.T.
350	O'Higgins Junior High
375	Page, John
401	Roberts, Fred H.

California, West

108	Bell, John A.
210	Carew, Luther
461	Souza, Albert
570	Begg, John
581	Malcolm, William T.
708	Blaine, Harold E.

Florida, East

104	Twardzynski, Otto
201	Miller, Warren
212	Carter, Dawson
224	Hoffman, Rita
327	Huang, C.O.
408	Ng, Joseph
418	Page, Christine

345

Practice Exercises in News Writing

Florida, West

462 Henderson, Maurice
505 Gibbs, Beverly
602 Barke, Willis
604 First Baptist Church
608 Central High School
     School District Headquarters
650 Stahl, John
710 Irving, William H.

Grant, North

216 Harris, Charles
311 Page, Walter E.
     North, Henry L.
411 Hawkins, Emma
487 Reeves, Marshall
780 McLaren, Joyce Ann
810 Dwight, Marion
911 Liberty Baptist Church
942 Dendramis, Sue Ellen

Grant, South

217 Nixon, James
412 Kershaw, S.
512 Cordoba, Alexis
539 Cleveland, William R.
560 Morris, Clyde
583 Gilmore, Horace N.
585 Snell's Texaco

Houston, North

212 Tsui, Charles E.
305 Marks, Peter
408 Shonsky, J.T.
604 Cook, Gerald A.
980 Murphy, Wanda

Houston, South

157 Ashford, John
308 Dawson, Ronald
327 Door, W.T.
410 Wang, M.

Indian River Place

87   Bettencourt, Walter Jr.
120 Gibbs, John
125 Stephenson, W.A.

Jackson, North

12   Carolton Hardware
408 Parks, Marshall

627 Rogers, George A.
680 All Saints Episcopal Church
683 Evers, E.E.
714 Green, Virgil

Jackson, South

247 Baker, Howard L.
304 Choate, Stephen P.
212 Trask, John
622 Floyde, Halbert O.
807 Miller, Robert L.

Lee, North

218 Quill, Henry C.
581 Fiore, Emil Jr.
761 Speizman, Harold E.
805 Vanderpol, R.E.

Lee, South

106 Federal Building
109 Cristo, S.
     Olejnik, H.
418 Funderburke, James L.
437 Gillette, Ralph

Lexington Road, East

357 Daily Student

Lexington Road, West

427 Commerce Club
450 Hotel Lenox
     Copper Kettle Restaurant
510 Colonial Village Apartments
     Coolidge, Calvin R.
     Flores, Luisa
     Wagner, S.E.
518 Harmon, Donald
540 Snook, Ivan
622 Ricketts, John
637 Shanker, Albert L.

Main, East

100 McKim, Oglethorpe and Dodge
101 Modern Decor
103 Bulldog Wine and Beer Store
115 Waldron, D.E.
210 Municipal Building
245 Belk's
250 Farmers and Merchants Bank
312 Morning Record Publishing Co.
316 Higginbottom Sons Co.

346

Main, East (*cont.*)

317 Medical Arts Building
    Washington County Mental Health
      Association
350 Holiday Inn
381 Central Fire Station
    Rescue Squad
412 Carolton-Washington Adult Center
    Public Housing Authority
417 Midstate Gas and Electric Co.
477 Lutz, Helen
501 Carolton Professional Women's Club
601 City Rescue Mission
710 Williams, Henry

Main, West

16 First National Bank
100 Graham Associates
210 Quick Coin Laundry
211 General Telephone Co.
213 Mercy Ambulance Service
300 Washington County Courthouse
604 University City National Bank

Maple

27 Dickens, Henry
35 Sullivan, James J.
127 Ferreira, Richard Sr.
184 Gomez, Delores
202 Delaney, John R.
221 Leavitt, Rollin R.
235 White, Elmer

Maryland, East

304 Sylvester, Rebecca
    Thors, Ernestina
415 Miskell, William
571 Wood, H.
612 Davis Elementary School

Maryland, West

478 Flynn, George A.
480 St. Thomas Church
550 Community Mental Health Clinic
599 Kane, Wadsworth

Meade, North

128 Wirtz Building
    106 Community Development Agency
    112 Carolton Community Relations
           Association
    204 Carolton Association of Police
    311 Washington County Association
           for the Blind

141 Jones, Myron
915 West, H.A.
950 Shook Chemical Corp.

Meade, South

3   Price, Flynn
48 Lund, Aaron O.
87 Rivera, Carlos J.
92 Hill, Harold O.
107 Watson, Charles
408 Dean, E.S.
450 Williams, D.
522 First Methodist Church
533 Carter, Alison
540 Alpha Zeta Omega Fraternity

Nevada, East

201 Sturdevant, Willis
371 Hickock, Bruce B.
642 Gordon, Sybil
439 Mitchell, Johnston
450 Worthington, Lorraine M.
540 Hughes, Charles E.
590 Higginbottom, Ernest F.
640 Sawyer, Albert H. Jr.
822 Stieber, Kenneth

Nevada, West

35 Medford, John E.
304 Cooper, Herbert W.
386 Boomershine, J.E. DVM
604 Oberdorfer, Harry

Newton Road, East

105 Wells, Roger
210 Alpha Phi Sorority
540 Fine, Elias
550 Cedar Village Apartments
    Charvat, Joe

Newton Road, West

310 City Art Club
312 Civic Center
321 Shanks, H.L.
410 Timulty, John O.
550 Ivory, G.R.
552 Look, James
560 Krug, Herbert
575 Maison Francaise
600 Veterans of Foreign Wars

New York, East

212 Courtwright, Fred III
340 LaFrance, Genevieve

347

New York, East (*cont.*)

409	Hope, Jonathan
510	Banks, Charles
520	Diaz, Mark L.
640	Sawyer, Albert J. Jr.

New York, West

252	Snell, Jacob
340	Curious Book Store
515	. Hawkins Antiques
604	Applegate Books

Oak

27	Morrissey, W.A.
75	O'Neil, James
84	Baker, William
87	Peters, Paul
97	Jackson, Terry

Ohio, East

234	Marshall, Joseph R.
450	Rickles, Arturo
608	Clark, John

Ohio, West

17	Love, Henry
27	Leamy, Lillian
120	Marks, Mary
278	Barth, Julius E.
345	Lewis, Elwyn
414	Meade, Horace W.

Old Meetinghouse Road, South

Korth, Frank

Oregon, East

108	Williams, Donna
111	Johnson, Nancy
306	Handy, W.H. III
317	Shaw, Harlan
408	Galina, C.C.

Oregon, West

111	Verway, Richard L.
258	Brewster, Alex
301	Look, Stanley
335	Gilmore, Horace A.
401	Hershey, Gerald R.
480	Mann Elementary School
610	McLeod, M.M.

Perimeter Road, East

104	Blake, John
211	Spinoza, Arturo

Perimeter Road, West

465	MacComber, Rufus
704	Hazelton, William M.

River Road

85	McGuire, Harold
97	Hardy, James
104	O'Flynn's
106	Reuther Building
	Alianza Hispana
	AFSCME, AFL-CIO
	Habitat for Humanity
	State AFL-CIO Council
	Carolton Labor Council
158	Carolton Country Club
197	Lodge, John A.
215	Krug, Jessie W.
234	Willoughby, Roger
280	Butler, Ray
333	Souza, Donald
350	Palmer, Bernard E.

Scott, North

216	Belle View Apartments
	Duglay, H.
	Ellenberg, Kellie
	Miller, L.L.
	Swift, Franklin
	Toefel, M.J.
	Tombs, Catherine
	Wetherbee, B.
	Williams, A.
217	Jenkins Funeral Home
250	Door Brothers Funeral Home
508	Wilson, James L.
682	Newhouse, Harold H.
715	Nightingale, H.L.
782	Brackett, Marlene

Scott, South

12	Marks, Patricia
280	Strauss, Jacob O.
317	Yaffee, Bette
321	Robinson, George T.
458	Souza, John

Sheridan, North

250	Wilson, Lamar
550	Lewis, John Q.
580	MacClure, Lawrence

Sheridan, North (*cont.*)

657	Hempstead, A.B. Jr.
714	Applegate, Charles O.
900	Nelson, Fred W.
910	Spooner, Randolph M.

Sheridan, South

115	Jones, William F.
409	Tate, L.D.

Sherman, North

250	Stroh, Walter
345	MacDonald, Stewart
641	Anderson, N.C.
726	Booker, John
804	Main, Roger

Sherman, South

211	Leamy, Goldstick and Gray, attorneys
301	Hall, Henry
336	Robbins, Benjamin
506	Potter, Branson

State Road, East

Holy Cross Hospital
Presbyterian Home

State Road, West

210	Talcott, John

Stuart, North

100	Carolton Senior Citizens Organization
234	Trinity A.M.E. Church
850	Hirsch, H.L.
875	Davis, Theodore
927	McGregor, James L.

Stuart, South

158	McGuire, John
200	Nguyen, Arnold
210	Moore, James L.

Sycamore

15	Holmes, Granville
187	O'Byrne, John L.
211	Kirby, Helen
213	Kirby, Jason
311	Bates, Alpha E.
350	Hickock, Walter
412	Crow, Emil

Territorial Road, South

511	Duke's Shell Service
808	East Side Fire Station
922	Rigsby, Peter
1182	College Standard Service

Utah, East

502	Chin, Jennifer
504	Wang, James
587	Boyland, Harold S.

Utah, West

70	Williams, James
75	Wiggins, John
79	Peters, Don
85	Toy, Jack E.
408	Elmer, John C.
603	Teacher, Walker E.

Vermont, East

400	Franklin Library
411	Barth Flowers
503	Buchanan, H.L.

Vermont, West

106	A&P
270	O'Kelly, Sean
304	Chamber of Commerce
504	Vogel, Ralph Jr.
612	Carolton Police Department
614	City Jail
700	Receiving Hospital
704	Planned Parenthood

Virginia, East

100	Municipal Court
286	Dobbins, John V.
310	Turnbull, Anna
550	McKay Funeral Home

Virginia, West

109	Koo, Henry
201	Garcia, Jose
210	Burt, Henry
275	Nesbitt, Wallace
407	Warren, Richard

Walnut

146	Carew, Alfred
210	Duttweiler, John R.
301	Kelley, Greg
335	Block, Bert

Washington Road

245	Carolton Construction Co.
255	Tri-State Education Association
260	Johnson, Harry O.
271	Norton, Homer
400	Bi-Low Supermarket
512	Washington County Extended Care
516	Washington County Health Department Women's Clinic
600	Washington County Department of Public Safety
604	Short, A.
612	Washington County House of Correction
618	Curtis, Raymond

Western Avenue, North

Piggly Wiggly Food Stores
Territory and Western Railroad Depot

Western Avenue, South

Chin, John
Kelly, James
Woods, Donald

Wisconsin, East

280	Smith, N.C.
434	Abrams, James
442	Miller, Kenneth L.
616	Howe, George A.
811	Orr, Marion

Wisconsin, West

240	Hillman, Walter
270	Ott, Wilhelm V.
273	Spaulding, Ernest
385	McGuire, Edwin

Appendix

3 Maps

City of Carolton and Washington County

N

Territory and Western Railroad

Perimeter Road

Industrial Park

City of Carolton

West State Road   Main Street   East State Road

Airport Road

Lexington Road

Northwest College

Washington Road

U.S. 210   Newton Road

Western Avenue

Territorial Road

Old Meetinghouse Road

U.S. 210

County Airport

Lancaster Road

River Road

South Street

Battle Road

Boiling Springs Road

Indian River
State Park

Indian River Place

Indian River

Boat Landing

City of Carolton and Northwest College Campus

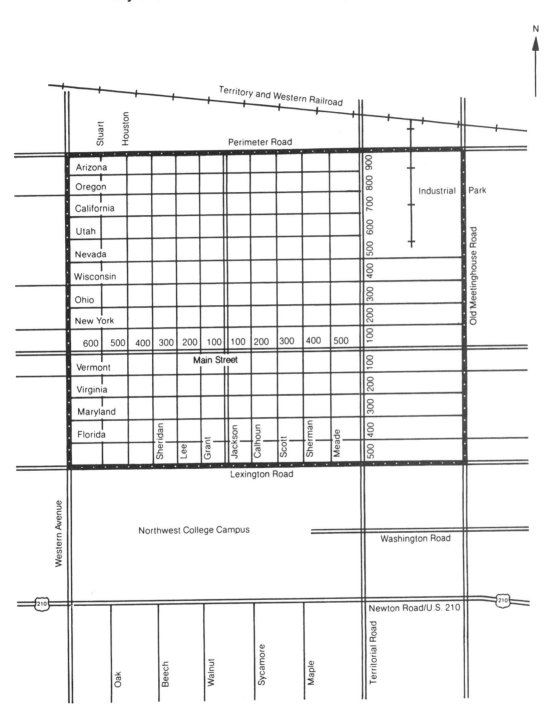

Note: East-west streets are avenues unless otherwise identified. North-south streets are streets unless otherwise identified.